Henry Tattam

A Compendious Grammar of the Egyptian Language

As contained in the Coptic, Sahidic, and Bashmuric dialects;

Henry Tattam

A Compendious Grammar of the Egyptian Language
As contained in the Coptic, Sahidic, and Bashmuric dialects;

ISBN/EAN: 9783337227555

Printed in Europe, USA, Canada, Australia, Japan

Cover: Foto ©Andreas Hilbeck / pixelio.de

More available books at **www.hansebooks.com**

A COMPENDIOUS GRAMMAR

OF THE

EGYPTIAN LANGUAGE

AS CONTAINED IN THE

COPTIC, SAHIDIC, AND BASHMURIC DIALECTS;

TOGETHER WITH

ALPHABETS AND NUMERALS IN THE HIEROGLYPHIC AND ENCHORIAL CHARACTERS.

BY THE

REV. HENRY TATTAM. LL. D., D. D., F. R. S.

Rector of Stanford Rivers.

SECOND EDITION

REVISED AND IMPROVED

WILLIAMS & NORGATE:

14, HENRIETTA STREET, COVENT GARDEN, LONDON,

AND

20, SOUTH FREDERICK STREET, EDINBURGH.

1863.

TO

JOHN LEE ESQ^R.

LL. D., F. R. S., P. A. S., &. &.

IN GRATEFUL REMEMBRANCE OF

THE MANY FACILITIES AFFORDED

IN THE PROSECUTION OF

HIS EGYPTIAN STUDIES

THIS VOLUME IS RESPECTFULLY DEDICATED

BY THE AUTHOR.

PREFACE.

Egyptian Literature has of late years attracted particular attention. All that has come down to us of the Language and Literature of ancient Egypt is contained in the Coptic, Sahidic, and Bashmuric Dialects; and in the Enchorial, Hieratic, and Hieroglyphic Inscriptions, and Manuscripts.

Without attempting to trace the origin of the Egyptian Language, we may just remark that the learned Rossius in his "Etymologiæ Ægyptiacæ," has shown the affinity of a number of Coptic and Sahidic words to the Oriental Languages; which affinity to a certain extent, it must be admitted, does exist.*)

*) In Rawlinson's Herodotus are the following observations. "The Egyptian Language might, from its grammar, appear to claim a Semitic origin, but it is not really one of that family, like the Arabic, Hebrew,

Nor need we be surprised at this, when we consider the intercourse of the Jews, Syrians, Persians,
Chaldeans, and Arabians with the Egyptians: but whether these words were originally Egyptian, or whether
they were adopted from other languages, it is impossible
for *us* to determine. M. Klaproth, a Gentleman well
acquainted with Asiatic Languages, has also pointed out
the resemblance of a considerable number of Egyptian

---

and others; nor is it one of the Sanscrit family, though it shows a
primitive affinity to the Sanscrit in certain points; and this has been
accounted for by the Egyptians being an offset from the early "undi-
vided Asiatic stock;" — a conclusion consistent with the fact of their
language being "much less developed than the Semitic and Sanscrit,
and yet admitting the principle of those inflictions and radical forma-
tions which we find developed, sometimes in one, sometimes in the other,
of those great families." Besides certain affinities with the Sanscrit,
it has others with the Celtic, and the languages of Africa; and Dr.
Ch. Meyer thinks that Celtic "in all its non-Semitic features most
strikingly corresponds with the old Egyptian." It is also the opinion
of M. Müller that the Egyptian bears an affinity both to the Arian and
Semitic dialects, from its having been an offset of the original Asiatic
tongue, which was their common parent before this was broken up into
the Turanian, Arian and Semitic.

In its grammatical construction, Egyptian has the greatest resemblance to the Semitic; and if it has less of this character than the
Hebrew, and other purely Semitic dialects, this is explained by the
latter having been developed after the separation of the original tongue
into the Arian and Semitic, and by the Egyptian having retained a
portion of both elements. There is, however, a possibility that the
Egyptian may have been a compound language, formed from two or
more *after* the first migration of the race, and foreign elements may
have been then added to it, as in the case of some other languages.
Rawlinson's Herodotus vol. II. p. 279.

words to some of the dialects of the north of Asia, and
the north of Europe: this discovery appears to have
raised a doubt in his mind of the African origin of the
Egyptians. The fact is, the remains we possess of the
Egyptian Language, when separated from the Greek,
with which it is in some measure mixed up, have no near
resemblance to any one of the ancient or modern languages.*   ·

The importance of the Ancient Egyptian Language to
the Antiquary, will at once appear, when we consider that
the knowledge of it is necessary before the inscriptions
on the Monuments of Egypt can be properly understood,
and the Enchorial and Hieratic Manuscripts can be fully
deciphered.

Nor is it of less importance to the Biblical Stu-
dent. The Egyptian Versions are supposed to have been
made about the second century;** and if they were not

---

* Dr. Murray says, "The Coptic is an original tongue, for it de-
rives all its indeclinable words and particles from radicals pertaining
to itself. Its verbs are derived from its own resources. There is no
mixture of any foreign language in its composition, except Greek."
Bruce's Travels, vol. II. p. 473.

** Zosimus, as quoted by Fabricius, says, that the old Testament
was translated into Egyptian, when the Septuagint Translation was
made. "Biblia tunc non in Graecam tantum, sed etiam Aegyptiis in
vernaculam linguam fuisse translata." p. 196.

The Talmudists say, "It is lawful for the Copts to read the Law
in Coptic." *Tychsensius.* See also *Buxtorf's Talmudic Lex.* p. 1571.
Also. "It is permitted to write the Law in Egyptian." *Babyl. Talmud,*
**

the first, they certainly were among the most early
Translations of the Scriptures into the Languages of the
East: and perhaps the Egyptian New Testament is of
equal or even of greater authority than any of the ancient Versions. The Coptic or Memphitic, and the Sahidic or Thebaic, are distinct versions. The Translations
of the old Testament, as will be readily supposed, were
made from the Septuagint, and not from the Hebrew
Scriptures. These versions will be found of great use
in assisting to determine the reading of many passages
of the Septuagint, and in fixing the meaning of many
expressions. We may also observe that the quotation
from Jeremy the Prophet, Matthew XXVII, 9. is found
in fragments of Jeremiah in these versions: it is different from the parallel passage in Zachariah XI, 12, 13.
and agrees with the quotation in St. Matthew. The Sahidic
New Testament contains many important readings, and
merits the closest attention of the Scholar and Divine.

The terms C o p t i c and S a h i d i c were adopted in
the first edition of the grammar, instead of M e m p h i t i c
and T h e b a i c, lest confusion should be created; as the

Seder Med. Schul. f. 115. These expressions seem to imply the existence of the Law in Coptic.

For the arguments in support of the Translation of the New Testament into Egyptian in the second century, see *Wilkinson's Introduction
to the Coptic New Testament*, and *The Introduction to the Sahidic Fragments*.

former terms are used in those Egyptian Publications which have issued from the Oxford University Press.

The defects and mistakes of the former edition the Author trusts have been corrected in this, and he has endeavoured to render this edition worthy of the confidence and patronage of the Students of Egyptian Literature.

Stanford Rivers Rectory.

May, 1862.

Observations

on the

Hieroglyphic and Enchorial Alphabets,

with a few remarks relative to their use.

The glory of Egypt has long since passed away, but enough of its learning remains in the Sculptured Monuments of Ancient Egypt, and in existing Papyri to excite the most intense interest. These stores had long engaged the attention of the Learned who had in vain endeavoured to decipher them till our indefatigable and learned countryman Dr. Young, and a little later in point of time M. Champollion, turned their energies to the subject with considerable success. And since their day the subject has not been permitted to slumber, for other learned men have entered the field, and put before the world all that these monuments have preserved, which had been hid from the researches of the wise for so many ages.

In the year 1814 Dr. Young commenced a laborious examination of the triple Inscription on the Rosetta Stone. This stone, which is much mutilated, was discovered by the French at Rosetta, and was shortly afterwards brought to this country. The Inscription is written in Greek, in Hieroglyphic, and in the Enchorial (εγχωρια)* or native character. Dr. Young entered upon the investigation after the Baron De Sacy and Mr. Akerblad had given up the attempt. By writing the Greek above the Enchorial, which reads from right to left, and comparing one part with another, Dr. Young succeeded in deciphering it, being aided by the words *King, Country, and,* &c. which had been discovered. Dr. Young next turned his attention to the Hieroglyphic Inscription, which was much mutilated: this he also deciphered by the aid of the two other Inscriptions. Having satisfactorily ascertained the name of *Ptolemy*, which was enclosed in a ring or oval, he justly conceived that the characters composing the name might be used otherwise than symbolically; he therefore proceeded to apply these characters *Phonetically,* or *Alphabetically,* as well as those contained in the name of *Berenice,* which he had ascertained, which was found with that of Ptolemy at Karnak: and by the aid of these characters he succeeded in de-

---

* This word is used in the Rosetta inscription and elsewhere.

ciphering other groups. Mr. Banks, who had received a communication from Dr. Young while he was in Egypt, discovered the names of *Ptolemy* and *Cleopatra* on a Temple and Obelisk at Philæ, which corresponded with the Greek dedicatory Inscriptions found upon the buildings, thus confirming Dr. Young's discoveries.

The letters in these names being thus ascertained and established, the system was taken up and extended by M. Champollion, and afterwards by Mr. Salt, our then consul general in Egypt. Since then, many eminent individuals, too numerous to name, have successfully pursued. this branch of the Literature of Ancient Egypt, and the world is in possession of their labours.

From the researches of Dr. Young, M. Champollion, and others, the accompanying Alphabets are constructed.

The names of Kings, and of other distinguished individuals, are generally enclosed in ovals.

The characters are sometimes read from right to left, and at others from left to right, or from the top downwards; nor is the order in placing the characters always strictly observed, for in many instances it could not conveniently be done. We however state as a rule that the characters are always read from the side towards which the animals look.

The gender of nouns is expressed by Articles as in Coptic; the Hieroglyph ⊟ or ▢, corresponding with п or ф, masculine singular, and ▲, with т, ө or † sing. fem. in Coptic, as in the names of Cleopatra, Arsinoe, and Berenice. The character ⌐ʄ has the power of q in the Rosetta Inscription. If we may be allowed to reason from analogy I should be induced to say that the plural is formed by ⏦⏦⏦ — or ✹ agreeing with ΝΙ Coptic, or by these characters doubled; as ⏦⏦⏦⏦, ═ or ✹, ΝϜΝ, or ΝΙ, Coptic. The plural is also formed by ΙΙΙ, and the dual by ΙΙ, in the Rosetta Inscription. I am also inclined to think that the genitive is formed by ⏦⏦⏦, and the Prefixes, Pronouns, &c. by the grouping of several of the Phonetic characters: as ⌐⏦⏦, ΝΚ, or ΝΑΚ, ⌐⏦⏦ʄ, Νq, or ΝΑq; ⊟⊟ ΝϹ, or ΝΑϹ &c.

   The Alphabetic or Phonetic,* was one of the

---

* Clemens Alexandrinus, who flourished about the second century is supposed to mention with correctness the kinds of writing used by the Egyptians. His words are these:

Αυτικα οἱ παρ᾽ Αἰγυπτιοις παιδενομενοι, πρωτον μεν παντων των Αἰγυπτιων γραμματων μεθοδον εκμανθανουσι, την επιστολογραφικην καλουμενην δευτεραν δε, την ἱερατικην, ἡ χρωνται οἱ ἱερογραμματεις· ὑστατην δε και τελευταιαν την ἱερογλυφικην, ἡς ἡ μεν εστι δια των πρωτων στοιχειων κυριολογικη· ἡ δε συμβολικη· της δε συμβολικης ἡ μεν κυριολογειται κατα μιμησιν ἡ δ᾽ ὡσπερ τροπικως γραφεται, ἡ δε αντικρυς αλληγορειται κατα τινας αινιγμους· ἡλιον γουν γραψαι βουλομενοι κυκλον ποιουσι σεληνην δε σχημα μηνοειδες, κατα το κυριολογουμενον ειδος· τροπικως δε κατ᾽ οἰκειοτητα μεταγοντες και μετατιθεντες, τα δ᾽ εξαλλαττοντες, τα δε πολλαχως μετασχηματιζοντες χαραττουσιν. Strom. 1. 4. c. 4.

„Jam vero qui docentur ab Aegyptiis, primum quidem discunt Aegy-

modes of Hieroglyphic writing; but besides this the Egyptians had another called Symbolic, which is sub-divided into various kinds. One kind of Symbolic writ-ing was by direct imitation, or pictorial representations of the things intended to be expressed; as a bullock or a ram was represented by a figure of the animal; and a bow and arrow by a graphic imitation of them. Another kind of Symbolic writing was the Tropical or Figurative; that is by metaphors and similitudes. The third kind of Symbolic writing was called Enigmatical. For instance,

ptiarum litterarum viam ac rationem quae vocatur Epistolographica: se-cundo autem hieraticam, qua utuntur Hierogrammates: ultimam autem Hieroglyphicam: cujus una quidem species est per prima elementa, Cyriologica dicta: altera vero Symbolica. Symbolicae autem una qui-dem proprie loquitur per imitationem: alia vero scribitur velut Tropice: alia vero fere significat per quaedam Aenigmata. Qui solem itaque volunt scribere, faciunt circulum: lunam autem figuram lunae, cor-nuum formam prae se ferentem, convenienter ei formae quae proprie loquitur. Tropice autem per convenientiam traducentes et transferentes, et alia quidem immutantes, alia vero multis figuris imprimunt."

Porphyry has communicated much the same information on the subject.

Εν Αιγυπτω μεν τοις ιερευσι συνην ὁ Πυθαγορας, και την σοφιαν εξεμαθε, και την Αιγυπτιων φωνην· γραμματων δε τρισσας διαφορας, επιστολογραφικων τε και ιερογλυφικων και συμβολικων· των μεν κοινολογουμενων κατα μιμησιν, των δε αλληγορουμενων κατα τινας αινιγμους.

De Vit. Pythag. CII, 12.

„In Aegypto cum sacerdotibus vixit Pythagoras, et sapientiam didicit, ac linguam Aegyptiorum: literarum autem tria genera, Episto-lographicas, Hieroglyphicas, et Symbolicas, quarum illae (Hierogly-phicae) quidem res exponunt imitatione. Hae (Symbolicae) vero sub Aenigmatis quibusdam latenter ostendunt."

***

to express the sun they formed a circle, and for the moon they traced the figure of a crescent.

At what period Hieroglyphic writing was first used in Egypt it is impossible to say; but the inscriptions on the monuments carry us back to a very ancient date. The name of Tirhakah king of Ethiopia, (2. Kings XIX, 9.) who flourished about 700 years before Christ, was discovered by Mr. Salt at Medinet Haboo, and at Birkel in Ethiopia in Phonetic Characters. M. Champollion also found at Karnak the name of Shishak king of Egypt, (1. Kings XIV, 25, 26.) Phonetically written, who lived about 970 years before Christ. "He is represented as dragging the chiefs of thirty conquered Nations to the feet of the Theban Trinity." Among these he found written in letters at full length, Joudaha Melek, "The king of the Jews." This may be considered as a commentary on the above named chapter. We may probably conclude in the words of the Poet:

„Nondum flumineas Memphis contexere biblos
Noverat: et saxis tantum volucresque feraeque
Sculptaque servabant magicas animalia linguas."
                    Lucan. Phars. lib. III. 221.

The Hieratic or Sacerdotal characters are immediately derived from the Hieroglyphic, which will at once appear evident on comparing them. "These characters appear to have been intended for simple imita-

tions of the Hieroglyphics: and from these the Enchorial or Popular characters seem to have been derived."

"The manuscripts, which belong to the time of
Psammetichus, appear to be decidedly Hieratic, and to
follow closely the traces of the distinct characters, while
those of Darius approach in some degree to the Enchorial form, which probably came into common use as the
"epistolographic" character, while the Hieratic was so called
as being more employed by the Priests for the purposes
of their religion."

I am indebted to the kindness of C. W. Goodwin
Esqr. for the Hieroglyphic and Enchorial Alphabets, and
for the following observations on those Alphabets.

"The Hieroglyphic writing comprises between 60
and 70 signs which are alphabetic, that is, which represent simple vowel and consonantial sounds. There
are also nearly 200 more which are syllabic, that is they
represent combinations of simple sounds. Some of these
latter signs are appropriated to particular words, others
are in common use, and occur in the spelling of words
of all kinds.

As an example of the Alphabetic signs we may take
the owl, which represents the letter *m*. It often however stands alone, like ꝳ in Coptic, in which case we
must suppose that a vowel sound *a* or *e* was either prefixed or postfixed in pronunciation. An example of the

syllabic signs is ⊹ which represents the combination *am*. Signs of this kind are often com ined with one or more of the alphabetic signs. Thus for the simple ⊹ we have sometimes ⊹ ▲, sometimes ❙ ▯ ▲ both of which combinations are sounded simply *am*. Many characters which are really syllabic were inserted in the earlier lists which were formed, as alphabetic. It is probable that all the Hieroglyphic characters were originally syllabic, and that those which subsequently became pure consonants, had at first a complementary vowel.

The Hieroglyphic list includes only those characters which are purely alphabetic. Those which are found in late inscriptions are marked with an asterisk. * A few of which the sound may be considered still open to doubt are marked with a query ?" —

"The Hieratic writing was formed from the Hieroglyphic, by a gradual modification of the original forms, many of which became so altered as to be capable of identification only by comparison of identical texts written in both kinds of characters, of which the Rituals furnish abundant examples. Many varieties of Hieratic exist, just as there are many kinds of handwriting amongst ourselves, all reducible to the old square Roman character.

About 600 B. C. the Demotic or Enchorial was ormed, being only an abbreviated or degenerated form of the Hieratic, trough which its letters may be traced

up to the original Hieroglyphics. — The Demotic or Enchorial writing comprises, like the Hieroglyphic and Hieratic, a limited number of purely alphabetical characters,
and also a good many syllabic ones. The list here given
is taken from the Demotic Grammar of Dr. Brugsch, and
comprises only those characters which may be considered
as purely alphabetic. The reading is from right to left."

Enchorial or Demotic Alphabet.

A	⊥ (II) 〈I 3 ⊃ ↵ I |
I	Ϥ ⁄ ⌣⌣ ///
OU	Io ('ϟ) ? ∫
B	⅃ 4
F, V	⅄
K	⌐ 𝟥𝄃 ⅄ ⅃ ∠ ⌐ ⅃
R	ろ ∞ ⌒ ◯ ⁄
L	✗
M	⊃ 𝟑
N	⌐ ⌐ ⌐ ⌐ ⌐
P	Ζ 2 ⌐ μ ⌣
S	⊥ ⅄ ✛ 〈II Ꮙ
SH	λ Ꮿ 3
T	𝟑 ⅃ ﹨ ∠ ∠ ∠
x, σ	I+ ⅃ ⌐
KH, Ƅ	Ɛ σ Ɔ
H	⌒ 9 ⌒ 3⌒

Hieroglyphic Alphabet.

A

I, E

U, OU,

B

F, V

K

R, L

M

N

P

S

Sh

T

T (x)

KH

H

All these figures admit of being turned the other way and read from left to right.

Enchorial or Demotic Numbers.

1	၇ ʇ ׀		60	⊻ =
2	५		70	?
3	þ þ ℿ		80	?
4	⩔ ⩔ ⩒ ⋂ ℿℿ		90	Ƕ
5	٦ ٦		100	⟋
6	⟨ ⟨ ⟨		200	⟋
7	ʓ ׳ʓ		300	ℿ⟋
8	⟫ ⟫		400	ℿℿ⟋
9	⟨ ʓ׀		500	⟵ʓ
10	⋏		600	⟶ℿ
20	⟩		700	⟶?
30	℥		800	⟶ℿℿ
40	⟋		900	⟵ʓ
50	ʓ		1000	Ⴑ

Hieroglyphic Numbers.

1. I.	21. ∩∩I.
2. II.	22. ∩∩II.
3. III.	30. ∩∩∩.
4. IIII.	40. ∩∩∩∩.
5. IIIII. ᵘᵘ	50. ∩∩∩∩∩.
6. III III.	60. ∩∩∩/∩∩∩.
7. IIII III. ᵘᵘ.	70. ∩∩∩∩/∩∩∩.
8. IIII IIII. ⁞⁞⁞⁞	80. ∩∩∩∩/∩∩∩∩.
9. IIIII IIII. ᵘᵘ.	90. ∩∩∩∩∩/∩∩∩∩.
10. ∩. ⊓.	100. ⟩.
11. ∩I.	200. ⟩⟩.
12. ∩II.	300. ⟩⟩⟩.
13. ∩III.	400. ⟩⟩⟩⟩.
16. ∩IIIIII.	500. ⟩⟩⟩⟩⟩.
20. ∩∩.	1000. ⊥. ⚲.

Index to the Subjects.

Chap. VII.

Chap. VIII.

CHAP. I.

The Coptic, or Egyptian Alphabet.

Egypt. Alphabet.		Names of Letters.	English sounds.		Numb.
Ⲁ	ⲁ	ⲀⲖⲪⲀ	alpha	*a*	1
Ⲃ	ⲃ	ⲂⲎⲦⲀ	beta	*b*	2
Ⲅ	ⲅ	ⲄⲀⲘⲘⲀ	gamma	*g*	3
Ⲇ	ⲇ	ⲆⲈⲖⲦⲀ	delta	*d*	4
Ⲉ	ⲉ	ⲈⲒ	ei	*e* short	5
Ⲍ	ⲍ	ⲌⲎⲦⲀ	zeta	*z*	7
Ⲏ	ⲏ	ⲠⲎⲦⲀ	heta	*e* long	8
Ⲑ	ⲑ	ⲐⲎⲦⲀ	theta	*th*	9
Ⲓ	ⲓ	ⲒⲰⲦⲀ	iota	*i*	10
Ⲕ	ⲕ	ⲔⲀⲠⲠⲀ	kappa	*k*	20
Ⲗ	ⲗ	ⲖⲀⲨⲆⲀ	lauda	*l*	30
Ⲙ	ⲙ	ⲘⲒ	mi	*m*	40
Ⲛ	ⲛ	ⲚⲒ	ni	*n*	50
Ⲝ	ⲝ	ⲌⲒ	xi	*x*	60
Ⲟ	ⲟ	ⲞⲨ	ou	*o* short	70
Ⲡ	ⲡ	ⲠⲒ	pi	*p*	80

1

Egypt. Alphabet.		Names of Letters.	English sounds.		Numb.
Ⲣ	ⲣ	ⲣⲟ	ro	r	100
Ⲥ	ⲥ	ⲥⲓⲙⲁ	sima	s	200
Ⲧ	ⲧ	ⲧⲁⲩ	tau	t	300
Ⲩ	ⲩ	ⲉⲩ	hu	u	400
Ⲫ	ⲫ	ⲫⲓ	phi	ph	500
Ⲭ	ⲭ	ⲭⲓ	chi	ch	600
Ⲯ	ⲯ	ⲯⲓ	psi	ps	700
Ⲱ	ⲱ	ⲱⲩ	ou	o long	800
Ⲿ	ⲿ	ⲧⲉⲓ	shei	sh	900
Ϥ	ϥ	ϥⲉⲓ	fei	f	90
Ⳉ	ⳉ	ⳉⲉⲓ	khei	kh	
Ϩ	ϩ	ϩⲟⲣⲓ	hori	h	
Ϫ	ϫ	ϫⲁⲛϫⲓⲁ	gangia	gi	
Ϭ	ϭ	ϭⲓⲙⲁ	shima	sh	
Ϯ	ϯ	ⲧⲉⲓ	dei	ti	

It will be seen from the foregoing Alphabet that the Egyptians adopted the Greek Letters with the addition of seven other characters. Anciently the Hieroglyphic, Hieratic, and Demotic characters were only used in Egypt: but when Christianity prevailed in that country those characters were discontinued, and the Alphabet here given was generally, if not altogether adopted in their stead. It may be here observed that the five following letters, viz. г, ᴅ, ᴢ, ᴣ and ѱ were not used by the Egyptians in their own language, but only in words adopted from the Greek.

CHAP. II.

The pronunciation of the Letters.

The following is the pronunciation of the letters which now prevails among the Copts of Egypt.

ⲁ. is pronounced as *a* in *man* with us, and is often used in Bash. instead of ⲉ, ⲟ and ⲱ: as ⲁⲛⲅ for ⲟⲛⲃ, ⲛⲁⲃⲉ for ⲛⲟⲃⲉ, ⲁⲛⲉⲅ for ⲉⲛⲉⲅ, and ⲡⲉϥⲃⲁⲧⲉⲃ for ⲡⲉϥⲃⲱⲧⲉⲃ.

ⲃ. is sounded as *b* in ⲃⲁⲃⲩⲗⲱⲛ, and as *v* in ⲃⲕⲧⲱⲣ, ⲓⲱⲃⲁⲛ. It is also used instead of ϥ and ⲫ, as ⲃⲓ for ϥⲓ, and ϣⲃⲏⲣ for ϣⲫⲏⲣ, and it sometimes interchanges with ⲡ, as ⲁⲡⲁ for ⲁⲃⲃⲁ.

ⲅ. never occurs in Egyptian words, except when it is used instead of other Letters, or is found in Greek words. It is used instead of ⲕ and ⲝ, as ⲁⲛⲅ for ⲁⲛⲕ̄, ⲛⲅ̄ for ⲛⲕ̄, ⲧⲱⲛⲅ for ⲧⲱⲛⲕ, ⲙⲁⲁⲅⲉ for ⲙⲁⲁⲝⲉ; and in Greek words as ⲁⲛⲁⲅⲕⲏ.

ⲇ. was never used by the ancient Egyptians, and occurs only in foreign words, in which it is sometimes substituted for ⲧ, as ⲇⲁⲍⲓⲥ for ⲧⲁⲍⲓⲥ, ⲑⲉⲁⲇⲣⲟⲛ for ⲑⲉⲁⲧⲣⲟⲛ.

ⲉ. is pronounced as ε in Greek. It is used in Sahidic at the end of words instead of ⲓ in Coptic. It is also used instead of ⲁ in Bashmuric, as ⲅⲉⲡ for ⲅⲁⲡ. It is sometimes written instead of ⲏ.

ⲍ. is only used in words of foreign origin. It is sometimes written for ⲥ, as ⲍⲱⲛⲧ for ⲥⲱⲛⲧ. It is also written for ⲧ, as ⲧⲱⲡⲁⲍⲓⲟⲛ for ⲧⲱⲡⲁⲧⲓⲟⲛ.

1*

ʜ.   is sounded like the Greek letter η, as ⲙⲏⲡⲟⲧⲉ: it was formerly pronounced with a sharp breathing, as ⲌⲎⲅⲉⲙⲱⲛ, ἡγεμών. It is sometimes used for ⲉ and ⲓ, as ⲌⲎⲃⲥ for Ⲍⲉⲃⲥ, ⲧⲏⲙⲓ for ⲧⲓⲙⲓ.

ⲑ.   This letter is pronounced as *th* in ⲑⲁⲁⲁⲉⲟⲥ. It is also pronounced as ⲁ. ⲑ is used instead of ⲧⲌ for expedition in writing. In Sahidic and Bashmuric ⲧ is used instead of ⲑ, as ⲉⲧⲃⲉ for ⲉⲑⲃⲉ. ⲑ is sometimes used in Sahidic for ϭ, as ⲉⲑⲁⲩⲱ for ⲉϭⲟⲩⲱ.

ⲓ.   answers to ⲓ in Greek, or *ee* in English. It often changes with ⲉⲓ, as ⲓⲣⲉ, ⲉⲓⲣⲉ: ⲡⲓⲛⲉ, ⲡⲉⲓⲛⲉ.

ⲕ.   is sounded as $\varkappa$ in Greek. It is used in Sahidic instead of ⲭ, as ⲕⲁⲙⲉ for ⲭⲁⲙⲉ; ⲕⲣⲟⲩⲣ for ⲭⲣⲟⲩⲣ. In Sahidic it is often exchanged for ⲅ, as ⲧⲱⲛⲅ for ⲧⲱⲛⲕ.

ⲗ.   in Bashmuric answers to ⲣ in Coptic, as ⲗⲁⲙⲡⲓ for ⲣⲟⲙⲡⲓ; ⲗⲓⲙⲓ for ⲣⲓⲙⲓ.

ⲙ.   is pronounced as *m* in English.

ⲛ.   also answers to *n* in English.

Ξ.   this letter is seldom found in Egyptian words, but principally occurs in words derived from other languages. It is sometimes used instead of ⲕⲥ, as ⲑⲟⲩⲝ for ⲑⲟⲩⲕⲥ; ⲝⲟⲩⲣ for ⲕⲥⲟⲩⲣ.

ⲟ.   is pronounced as *o* in ⲢⲞⲂⲞⲀⲘ. It is often exchanged for ⲱ long, as ϥⲱⲣⲝ for ϥⲟⲣⲝ.

ⲡ.   is sounded as *b* by the modern Egyptians. ⲡ is used in Sahidic for ϥ in Coptic, as ⲡⲁⲱ Sah. for ϥⲁⲱ Coptic. It is sometimes used for ⲃ, as ⲁⲡⲁ for ⲀⲂⲂⲀ.

ρ. is pronounced as *r* in Ⲁⲣⲁⲙ. It is changed in Bashmuric for ⲗ, as ⲗⲉⲛ for ⲣⲁⲛ Coptic.

ⲥ. is enunciated as s in Ⲉⲥⲣⲱⲙ.

ⲧ. is pronounced as ⲇ; and it is occasionally used for
ⲇ, as Ⲧⲁⲛⲓⲉⲗ for Ⲇⲁⲛⲓⲉⲗ.

ⲩ. is sounded like *u*. It occurs in words of Greek origin instead of ⲓ, ⲏ and ⲉⲓ; as ⲕⲩⲃⲱⲧⲟⲥ, for κιβωτός:
ⲥⲩⲙⲉⲛⲓⲛ, for σημαίνων; and ⲇⲩⲛⲁ for δεῖνα.

ⲫ. is pronounced as *f;* and in the beginning of words
as *b;* as ⲫⲁⲓ *bai*. In Sahidic and Bashmuric ⲡ is
always used instead of ⲫ.

ⲭ. has the sound of *z*, or *χ* of the Greeks. It is exchanged with ⲱ, and ⲉ, as Ⲛⲱⲓⲣ for ⲙⲉⲭⲓⲣ; and
ⲭⲱⲡ ⲉⲱⲡ. In Sahidic ⲕ is used instead of ⲭ.

ⲯ. is pronounced as *ps* in Greek. It is rarely used in
Coptic, but sometimes it is found for ⲡⲥ in the expedition of writing, as ⲯⲓⲧ for ⲡⲥⲓⲧ; ⲯⲟⲗⲥⲉⲗ for
ⲡⲥⲟⲗⲥⲉⲗ.

ⲱ. is sounded like *ω* of the Greeks. It is frequently
exchanged with ο; and in Sahidic oo is often used
for ⲱ; and ⲁ in Bashmuric instead of ⲱ, as ⲁⲓⲕ for
ⲱⲓⲕ.

ⲱ. possesses the same power as *v* in Hebrew. It is
changed with ⲥ, ⲭ, ⲝ, ⲋ, and sometimes with ⲉ.

ϥ. is pronounced as *f;* and it is changed with ⲃ, and
sometimes with ⲫ, as ⲧⲏⲣⲫ for ⲧⲏⲣϥ.

ⲃ. This letter answers to the ⲡ of the Hebrews. Wilkinson says it has the sound of *kh*. It changes with
ⲭ and ⲕⲉ, as ⲭⲉⲣ, ⲃⲉⲣ; and ⲃⲱⲕⲉ, ⲃⲱⲃ. It never

occurs in Sahidic, ⳅ being always used in its stead.

ⳅ. is pronounced as *h* or ⳏ, and is used for the sharp breathing of the Greeks, as ⳅⲟⲡⲗⲟⲛ ὅπλον, ⳅⲩⲥⲱⲡⲟⲥ ὕσσωπος.

ⲝ. Sir Gardner Wilkinson says: "This letter is pronounced hard as *g* in go, and not as *dj*." It appears to answer to the Arabic ح. It changes with ⲅ, ⲭ, ⳝ, and ⳓ; as ⲙⲁⲣⲭⲁⲣⲓⲧⲏⲥ, μαργαριτης, ⲅⲉⲛⲉⲫⲱⲣ for ⲝⲉⲛⲉⲫⲱⲣ, ⲝⲣⲱⲙ for ⲭⲣⲱⲙ, ⳝⲟⲩⳝⲧ for ⲝⲟⲩⳝⲧ, and ⳓⲟⳅ, ⲝⲟⳅ.

ⳓ. This letter is pronounced as *s* or *sh* by the present Copts; as ⲡⲥⲟⳓⲛⲓ, *epsoshni;* ⲡⲉⲛⳓⲟⲓⲥ, *pensuais.* It is exchanged with ⲥ and ⳝ, as ⳓⲱⲛⳅ for ⲥⲱⲛⳅ, and ⳝⲱⲗ for ⳓⲱⲗ. But it is chiefly exchanged with ⲝ in Sahidic and Bashmuric, as ⳓⲓⲛ for ⲝⲓⲛ: It occurs in some words of Greek origin instead of ⲭ.

ϯ. The Copts of the present day pronounce this double letter as *di;* but there are some words in which we should evidently pronounce it as ti, as ⲃⲁⲡϯⲥⲙⲁ, ⲡⲗⲁϯⲁ etc. In Sahidic it is exchanged for ⲧⲉ, as ⳝⲟⲙϯ, Sah. ⳝⲟⲙⲧⲉ.

The following are examples of pronunciation as given by Sir G. Wilkinson while in Egypt. ⲉⲑⲃⲉ, pronounced as *átwa;* ⲥⲱⲧⲉⲙ, *sódam;* ⳓⲟⲙ, *shōm;* ⲝⲟⲙ, *gōm;* ⲛⲓⳝⲧ, *nishdee;* ⲡⲁⲛⲟⲩϯ, *banóode;* ⲡⲓⲟⲩⲱⲓⲛⲓ, *becooóynee;* ⲉ̀ⲃⲟⲗⳃⲉⲛ, *ávelkhán;* ⲉⲑⲃⲏⲧϥ, *atwátf;* ⲧⲡⲉ, *édbe;* ⲙⲉⲑⲙⲏⲓ, *metmái.*

CHAP. III.

Of Points and Abbreviations.

1. When the line in Coptic (`) or the horizontal line in Sah. (-) occurs over consonants, it generally expresses the vowel ε, as ṁ or ᴍ̄, ϥᴍ: ṅ or ᴎ̄, ϥᴎ. The vowel is sometimes written, and at other times it is expressed by the line above the consonant, as ϥᴍκλϩ or ᴍ̇κλϩ, *af-fliction:* Sah. ᴍ̄ᴎ for ᴍϥᴎ, ᴎᴍ̄ for ᴎϥᴍ, ϣᴍ̄ᴍο for ϣϥᴍᴍο.

It appears from some words derived from the Greek, that the line (`) has been used in Coptic to express the vowels λ, ϥ and ο: as ᴎλθωθ, *Ἀναθώθ:* ᴎογϥι, *ὄνουφι;* and ϩϥϲτιᴎ for *ἐξέστην.*

It is equally evident from the Sahidic, that the line (–) is used for λ, ϥ and ο; as λᴎκ̄ for λᴎοκ. *I;* ᴎ̄τκ̄ for ᴎ̄τοκ, *thou:* ογᴎ̄τϥ for ογοᴎτλϥ. *he hath;* ϣᴍ̄τϥ for ϣοᴍτϥ. *three* f.; ᴎᴍ̄ for ᴎϥᴍ *and;* ϩᴎ̄ for ϩϥᴎ.

3. When the line (`) occurs above a vowel in words derived from the Greek, we find it expresses the soft or hard breathing of the Greeks; as ᴎ̇ϲλγ. *Ἡσαῦ;* ωϲλᴎᴎλ. *ὡσαννά;* λ̇ϥιλ, *Ἀβιά:* or it denotes that the letter should be pronounced separately, and agrees with the diæresis of the Greeks, as ϲτοϊϲοϲ, *Στωϊκός.*

4. The line (`) is put over a letter in some words to distinguish them from others; as ᴨϥ̇ᴎϥϩ, *ever*, from ᴨϥᴎϥϩ,` *thy oil* f.

5. A line above ᴍ̇ ᴍ̄. or ᴎ̇ ᴎ̄, distinguishes it from ᴍ or ᴎ radical, and from ᴎ, the definite article plural

before the infix; (see def. art. plur.) as ⲛ̅ⲱⲟⲩ is *glory;*
but ⲛⲱⲟⲩ, without the point above the ⲛ. is *to them.*

6. Two points in Sahidic (··) are sometimes put
over the letter ï. as a contraction of ⲉⲓ. as ⲟⲩⲟïⲛ for
ⲟⲩⲟⲉⲓⲛ, *light;* ⲡⲭⲟïⲥ for ⲡⲭⲟⲉⲓⲥ, *Lord.*

7. Two points are also put over the ï. when joined
with another vowel in Sahidic, in the prefixes and suffixes to verbs, and in nouns and pronouns, thus: ⲧⲁⲭⲣⲟï,
ⲉⲣⲟï, ⲛⲁï, ⲉⲧⲏï, ⲉⲅⲣⲁï, ⲡⲁï, ⲧⲁï, ⲛⲁï, ⲙⲉï, ⲛⲟï, ⲏï &c.

8. The further use of the line (ˋ) and of the points
(··) will be pointed out as we proceed; but it may be
here observed, that hardly two Manuscripts of the same
work, agree in the lines above the letters; and we are
still ignorant of a portion of them.

The Circumflex.

9. The circumflex (ˆ) is found in Sahidic Manuscripts over the vowels ⲁ̂, ⲉ̂, ⲏ̂, ⲓ̂, ⲟ̂ and ⲱ̂; and also
over the ⲉⲓ and ⲟⲩ; as ⲟⲩⲁ̂, *one;* ⲛⲁ̂, *mercy;* ⲡⲏⲟⲩⲉ,
the heavens; ⲛⲏ̂, *they;* ⲱⲧⲉⲕⲟ̂, *a prison;* ϭⲱ̂, *to remain;*
ⲟⲩⲉⲓ, *one;* ⲟⲩ, *what?* In some cases the circumflex appears to be used instead of doubling the vowels, as ⲁ̂,
ⲱ̂, for ⲁⲁ and ⲱⲱ. The circumflex is not always found
in Sahidic Manuscripts.

The Apostrophe.

10. The apostrophe (ʼ) is generally found over the
last letter of a word in Sahidic, but not always. Its use
does not appear to be very apparent. I will not therefore add to the conjectures which have been put forth

concerning it. It is found thus: ⲡⲟⲣⲛⲓⲁ̅, ⲙⲁ̅, ⲛⲟⲩⲃ̅, Ⲗⲁⲅⲉⲓⲁ̅, ϣⲁⲝⲉ̅, ⲥⲅⲓⲙⲉ̅, ⲉⲓⲉⲭⲓ̅, ⲃⲱⲕ̅, ⲭⲱⲕ̅, ⲉⲍⲉⲕⲓⲏⲗ̅, ϣⲏⲣⲉϣⲏⲙ̅, ⲛⲏⲙⲁⲛ̅, ⲣⲏⲙⲁⲟ̅, ⲅⲁⲧ̅, ϣⲃⲏⲣ̅, ⲥⲱⲧⲏⲣ̅. ⲡⲟⲛⲏⲣⲟⲥ̅, ⲅⲁⲡ̅, ⲏⲡϥⲟⲩⲱϣ̅, ⲏⲙⲟϥ̅.

11. It sometimes occurs in the middle of a word, as ⲥⲟⲗ̅ⲥⲗ, ⲣ̅ⲅⲱⲃ, ϣⲧ̅ⲣ̅ⲧⲱⲣ, ⲡⲉⲕ̅ⲕⲁⲅ.

The Abbreviations.

12. Some words in Coptic and Sahidic are abbreviated in the following manner, with a line or lines above the words.

ⲁ̅ⲗ̅ⲁ̅,	ⲁⲁⲅⲓⲁ,
ⲉ̅ⲑ, ⲉ̅ⲑⲩ̅,	ⲉⲑⲟⲩⲁⲃ,
ⲉⲣ⳺,	ⲉⲣⲟⲥ,
ⲑ̅ⲥ̅, ⲑ̅ⲩ̅,	ⲑⲉⲟⲥ, ⲑⲉⲟⲩ,
ⲑ̅ⲓ̅ⲗ̅ⲏ̅ⲙ̅,	ⲧⲅⲓⲉⲣⲟⲩⲥⲁⲗⲏⲙ,
ⲓ̅ⲏ̅ⲗ̅,	ⲓⲥⲣⲁⲏⲗ,
ⲓ̅ⲏ̅ⲥ̅,	ⲓⲏⲥⲟⲩⲥ,
ⲓ̅ⲗ̅ⲏ̅ⲙ̅,	ⲓⲉⲣⲟⲩⲥⲁⲗⲏⲙ,
ⲓ̅ⲏ̅ⲥ̅,	ⲓⲏⲥⲟⲩⲥ ⲛⲁⲍⲁⲣⲉⲟⲥ ⲥⲱⲧⲏⲣ,
ⲓ̅ⲥ̅ⲗ̅,	ⲓⲥⲣⲁⲏⲗ,
ⲓ ⲱ ⲁ, ⲓ̅ⲱ̅ⲛ̅,	ⲓⲱⲁⲛⲛⲏⲥ,
ⲕ̅ⲉ̅, ⲕ̅ⲥ̅, ⲕ̅ⲛ̅,	ⲕⲩⲣⲓⲉ, ⲕⲩⲣⲓⲟⲥ, ⲕⲩⲣⲓⲟⲛ,
ⲕ̅ⲗ̅,	ⲕⲉⲫⲁⲗⲉⲟⲛ,
ⲙ̅ⲛ̅,	ⲙⲙⲁⲣⲧⲩⲣⲓⲁ,
ⲙⲟ̅ⲩ,	ⲙⲥⲟⲩ,
ⲙⲉⲧⲭ̅ⲣ̅ⲥ̅,	ⲙⲉⲧⲭⲣⲏⲥⲧⲟⲥ,
ⲟ̅,	ⲟⲛ, as ⲙⲩⲥⲧⲏⲣⲓⲟ̅,
ⲟ̆,	ⲟⲩ, as ⲟ̆ⲟⲅ,

2

ΟΥ͞,   ΟΥΟϩ,

Πⲁⲣ,   ΠⲀⲣⲐⲈⲚⲞⲤ,

Π̅Ⲛ̅Ⲁ,   ΠⲚⲈΥⲘⲀ.

Π̅Ⲛ̅Ⲉ̅,   ΠⲚⲞΥⲦⲈ,

Ⲥ̅ⲣ̅, Ⲥⲱ̅ⲣ̅, ⲤⲰⲦⲎⲣ.   ☦, ⲪⲚⲞΥϯ,

ⲋ Ⲧ,

ΥΥ, ⳡⲎⲣⲈ,   ⲥ̅ⲧ̅, ⲤⲦⲀΥⲣⲞⲤ,

Ⲫϯ, ⲪⲚⲞΥϯ.   ⲙ̅, ⲘⲀⲣⲦΥⲣⲞⲤ,

Ⲭ̅ⲣ̅, ⲬⲣⲞⲚⲞⲤ.   Ⲡ̅, ⲠⲣⲞⲤ,

Ⲭ̅Ⲥ̅, Ⲭ̅ⲣ̅Ⲥ̅, ⲬⲣⲒⲤⲦⲞⲤ, ⲞⲤ, ϬⲞⲈⲒⲤ. ϬⲞⲒⲤ.

13. Coptic Manuscripts generally begin with Ⲥⲩⲛᶿ اللّٰه, بسم, in the name of God: or with Ⲥⲩⲛᶿ ⲒⲤⲬΥⲣⲞⲤω, in the name of the powerful God.

14. The stops used in Manuscripts, are one or two points, as ⲜⲈ ϩⲚⲀⲎ Ⲁ٩ⲘⲞΥ. ΟΥΟϩ &c. Mark XV, 44. or as ⲈⲖⲰⲒ: ⲈⲖⲰⲒ: ⲈⲖⲈⲘⲀ ⲤⲀⲂⲀⲬⲐⲀⲚⲒ: Mark XV, 24.

Part II. Etymology.

The Articles.

1. The Egyptian Language has the definite and indefinite articles, and also the possessive.

The Definite Article.

Coptic.

Masc. Sing.	Fem. Sing.	Plur. Com.
ΠⲒ. Π. Ⲫ..	Ⲧ. Ⲑ. ϯ.	ⲚⲒ. ⲚⲈⲚ.

Sahidic.

ⲠⲈ. Ⲡ.   ⲦⲈ. Ⲧ.   ⲚⲈ. Ⲛ̄. ⲚⲚ̄.

Bashmuric.

ⲠⲒ. ⲠⲈ. Ⲡ.   ϯ. ⲦⲈ. Ⲧ.   ⲚⲒ. ⲚⲈ. Ⲛ̄.

2. The Coptic uses the article ⲠⲒ and ⲡ promiscu-
ously; either before double consonants or vowels, as ⲠⲒ-
ⲕⲁϩⲓ and ⲡ-ⲕⲁϩⲓ; ⲠⲒ-ⲎⲒ and ⲡ-ⲎⲒ: ⲠⲒ-ⲟⲩⲣⲟ and ⲡ-ⲟⲩⲣⲟ:
ϯ-ⲥⲙⲏ and ⲧ-ⲥⲙⲏ. The Coptic has ⲠⲒ and ϯ also before vowels, even before ⲓ. as ⲠⲒⲁϩ, ϯⲓⲟⲩⲇⲉⲁ. But in
the plural ⲚⲒ is generally used, but sometimes ⲚⲈⲚ, except before ⲈⲦ *who*, and the prefix, as we shall here-
after show. The articles ⲫ and ⲑ, are used instead of
ⲡ and Ⲧ. before the letters ⲃ, ⲓ, ⲙ, ⲛ, ⲟⲩ, ⲣ, as ⲫⲃⲁⲗ,
ⲫⲙⲱⲓⲧ, ⲫⲟⲩⲁⲓ, ⲑⲃⲁⲕⲓ, ⲑⲙⲏⲥⲓ, ⲑⲛⲟⲩⲛⲓ: but we sometimes find these words written ⲠⲒⲃⲁⲗ, ⲠⲒⲙⲱⲓⲧ, ⲠⲒⲟⲩⲁⲓ,
ϯⲃⲁⲕⲓ, ϯⲙⲏⲥⲓ, ϯⲛⲟⲩⲛⲓ.

3. The Sahidic has ⲠⲈ and ⲦⲈ singular, and ⲚⲈ
plural before nouns, beginning with two consonants, as
ⲦⲘⲀⲈⲒⲞ, ⲝⲣⲟ, ⲝⲡⲓⲟ, ϭⲗⲟⲟⲦⲈ, Ⲡⲣⲱ &c. The Articles
ⲡ and Ⲧ singular, and Ⲛ plural, are used not only before vowels, or before one consonant, as before ⲟⲩⲱⲱ,
ⲥⲛϭ, ⲚⲞⲨⲦⲈ, and ⲘⲀ; but even before consonants, when
marked with the line or vowel above, as Ⲡ̄ⲠⲈ, Ⲧ̄ⲂⲂⲞ,
Ⲛ̄ⲚⲦⲣⲈ etc. But either ⲠⲈ, ⲦⲈ. ⲚⲈ are used before ϩ,
as ⲦⲈϩⲓⲎ, ⲚⲈϩⲒⲞⲞⲨⲈ; or Ⲡϩ is contracted into ⲫ, and
Ⲧϩ into ⲑ, as ⲫⲎⲨ, from ⲠϩⲎⲨ. ⲫⲀⲠ, from ⲠϩⲀⲠ: ⲫⲎⲕⲈ
from ⲠϩⲎⲕⲈ: ⲫⲟⲟⲩ from Ⲡϩⲟⲟⲩ: and ⲑⲈ from ⲦϩⲈ, ⲑⲎ from
ⲦϩⲎ, ⲑⲒⲘⲈ from ⲦϩⲒⲘⲈ. ⲑⲀⲓⲂⲈⲥ from ⲦϩⲀⲒⲂⲈⲥ, ⲑ̄Ⲃⲥⲱ from

ⲧⲍ̄ⲃⲥⲱ, ⲑⲗⲗⲱ from ⲧⲍ̄ⲗⲗⲱ. Sometimes ⲡⲍ is found without the contraction, as ⲡⲍⲏⲧ, ⲡⲍⲓⲣ. The vowel ⲉ is admitted before ⲟⲩ, and ⲉⲟⲩ is contracted into ⲉⲩ, as ⲡⲉⲩⲟⲉⲓ︤ⲱ︥ for ⲡⲉⲟⲩⲟⲉⲓ︤ⲱ︥, ⲧⲉⲩ︤ⲱ︥ⲏ for ⲧⲉⲟⲩ︤ⲱ︥ⲏ, and ⲧⲉⲩⲛⲟⲩ for ⲧⲉⲟⲩⲛⲟⲩ. Often ⲛ̄ is prefixed to vowels, as ⲛ̄ⲁⲥⲉⲃⲏⲥ. ⲛ̄ is changed into ⲙ̄, before the letters ⲙ and ⲡ, as ⲙ̄ⲙⲁⲉⲓⲛ, *the signs;* ⲙ̄ⲡⲏⲩⲉ, *the heavens;* ⲛ̄ⲛ̄ sometimes occurs, as ⲛ̄ⲛⲟ̄ⲗⲟ̄ⲟ̄, *the beds.* The ⲛ̄ plur. is very rarely changed into ⲃ, ⲗ, ⲣ, before the same letters, as ⲃ̄ⲃⲣ̄ⲣⲉ, for ⲛ̄ⲃⲣ̄ⲣⲉ, plur. *new;* ⲗ̄ⲗⲁⲟⲥ for ⲛ̄ⲗⲁⲟⲥ, *the peoples;* ⲣ̄ⲣⲱⲙⲉ for ⲛ̄ⲣⲱⲙⲉ, *the men.* The Sahidic very rarely has the Coptic articles ⲡⲓ. ⲧ̄ and ⲛⲓ. but they are sometimes met with; and occasionally ⲧⲉⲓ and ⲛⲉⲓ are used instead of the articles.

The Indefinite Articles.

4. The indefinite article has no distinction of gender.

Coptic.
Sing.	Plur.
ⲟⲩ.	ⲍⲁⲛ.

Sahidic.
| ⲟⲩ. | ⲍⲉⲛ. ⲍⲛ̄. |

Bashmuric.
| ⲟⲩ. | ⲍⲁⲛ. ⲍⲉⲛ. ⲍⲛ̄. |

5. Thus the indefinite article is used, as ⲟⲩⲥⲁⳉⲓ. *a word;* ⲍⲁⲛⲥⲁⳉⲓ, *words;* ⲟⲩⲃⲁⲕⲓ. *a city;* ⲍⲁⲛⲃⲁⲕⲓ. *cities.* When ⲟⲩ the indefinite article precedes the preposition ⲉ̀, as ⲉ̀ⲟⲩ, it is contracted into ⲉ̀ⲩ, as ⲉ̀ⲩ︤ⲱ︥ⲁⲩⲉ

to a desert for **ⲉⲟⲩϣⲁϥⲉ.** The Sahidic uses **ⲋⲉⲛ** and **ⲋⲛ** in the plural, and the Bashmuric the Coptic and Sahidic plurals.

The Possessive Articles.

C o p t i c.

-. Sing. m.	Sing. f.	Plur. com.
ⲫⲁ.	**ⲑⲁ.**	**ⲛⲁ.**

S a h i d i c.

ⲡⲁ.	**ⲧⲁ.**	**ⲛⲁ.**

6. These articles point out persons or things which belong to any one, as **ⲡⲓⲁⲙⲁⲋⲓ ⲫⲁ ⲫ† ⲡⲉ,** *the power is of God.* Ps. LXI, 11. **ⲑⲁ ⲛⲓⲙ ⲧⲉ ⲧⲁⲓ ⲋⲓⲕⲱⲛ,** *of whom is this image.* Mark XII, 16. **ⲛⲁ ⲧⲕⲟⲩⲓ ⲡⲓⲥⲧⲓⲥ,** *of little faith.* Luke XII, 28. **ⲡⲁ ⲡⲉϥⲓⲱⲧ,** *of his father.* Luke IX, 26. ·When used with the name of a person, **ⲫⲁ** signifies *the son of,* as **ⲫⲁ ⲏⲗⲓ,** *the son of Eli.* Luke III, 23.

CHAP. IV.

Of Nouns.

1. An Egyptian noun generally takes an article before it, or other particle, as **ⲟⲩⲣⲱⲙⲓ,** *a man;* **ⲋⲁⲛⲙⲟⲩⲙⲓ,** *lions;* **ⲡⲓⲣⲁⲛ,** *the name;* **ⲛⲓ6ⲏⲡⲓ,** *the clouds;* but when the article is prefixed to the adjective or the substantive, the other takes the prefix **ⲛ,** as **ⲟⲩⲛⲓϣ† ⲛⲋⲟ†,** Copt. **ⲟⲩⲛⲟ6**

ⲚϨⲞⲦⲈ, Sah. *a great fear.* Act. V, 2. ⲞⲨⲔⲀϨⲒ ⲚϢⲈⲘⲘⲞ, *a strange land,* Copt. ⲦϢⲞⲢⲠ ⲚⲚⲦⲞⲖⲎ. *the first commandment.* Sah. ⲞⲨⲚⲒϢϮ ⲚⲚⲈϨⲠⲒ ⲠⲈ⳿ϨⲀⲒ, *this is a great lamentation.* Copt. The Ⲛ̀ is also prefixed to the noun substantive or adjective after the verbs ⲞⲒ, and ϢⲰⲠⲈ. as ⲈϤⲞⲒ ⲚⲞⲨⲰⲒⲚⲒ, *it is light;* ⲀⲔϢⲰⲠⲈ Ⲛ̀ⲂⲞⲎⲐⲞⲤ, *thou hast been a helper.*

2. Adjectives sometimes take the articles, as ⲠⲒⲚⲒϢϮ, *great,* m.; ϮⲚⲒϢϮ, *great,* f.; but when they are united with the particles ⲈⲦ, ⲈϤ, ⲈⲤ and ⲈⲨ, they do not take the article. Adjectives are also distinguished by their prefixes and suffixes.

Of the Gender of Nouns.

3. Every noun of the three Dialects is either of the masculine or feminine gender, and is known by the masculine or feminine article being prefixed, or by the prefix or suffix, or it is known by its agreeing with the verb, or some other word in the sentence which has the sign of the gender; as ϮⲂⲀⲔⲒ, *the city,* f.; ⲠⲒⲈⲭⲰⲢϨ, *the night,* m.; ⲈϤⲞϢ, *much,* m.; ⲈⲤⲞϢ, *much,* f.; ⲈⲐⲚⲀⲚⲈϤ. Copt. ⲚⲀⲚⲞⲨϤ. *good,* m.; Sah. ⲈⲐⲚⲀⲚⲈⲤ Copt. ⲚⲀⲚⲞⲨⲤ, Sah. *good,* f. The Plural has no distinction of gender, nor is there any neuter in the language, but instead of it the feminine is used. Nouns composed with the particle ⲘⲈⲦ Copt. or ⲘⲚⲦ Sah. are all feminine. Those composed with ϬⲒⲚ, Sah. are also feminine, but those compounded with ⲬⲒⲚ, Coptic, are for the most part masculine.

4. There are some masculine nouns which become feminine by adding ι to them in the Coptic and Bashmuric, and ε in the Sahidic; as ⲃⲱⲕ, *a servant*, m.; ⲃⲱⲕⲓ, *a servant*, f. Copt. ⲥⲟⲛ, *a brother;* ⲥⲱⲛⲓ, *a sister*, Copt. ϣⲟⲙ, *a father in law.* ϣⲱⲙⲓ. Copt. ϣⲱⲙⲉ, Sah. *a mother in law.* ϣⲫⲏⲣ, *a friend,* m. ϣⲫⲏⲣⲓ, *a friend,* f. Copt. ϣⲃⲉⲉⲣ, *a friend,* m. ϣⲃⲉⲉⲣⲉ, *a friend,* f. Sah. ϭⲁⲙⲁⲩⲗ, *a camel,* m. ϭⲁⲙⲁⲩⲗⲉ, *a camel,* f. Sah. ⲉⲓⲏⲃ, *a lamb,* m. ⲉⲓⲏⲃⲓ, *a lamb,* f. Copt. ⲉⲓⲉⲓⲃ, *a lamb,* m. ⲉⲓⲉⲓⲃⲉ, *a lamb,* f. Sahidic.

5. Others form the feminine by changing the last short vowel of the masculine into a long one, as ⲃⲉⲗⲗⲉ, *blind,* m. ⲃⲉⲗⲗⲏ, Copt. ⲃⲗ̄ⲗⲏ, Sah. *blind,* f. ⲙⲟⲩⲓ, *a lion,* m. ⲙⲟⲩⲏ, *a lioness,* Copt. ⲟⲩⲣⲟ, *a king,* ⲟⲩⲣⲱ, *a queen,* Copt. ⲣ̄ⲣⲟ, *a king.* ⲣ̄ⲣⲱ, *a queen,* Sah. ⲃⲉⲗⲗⲟ. *an old man.* ⲃⲉⲗⲗⲱ. *an old woman,* Copt. ⲅⲗ̄ⲗⲟ, *an old man.* ⲅⲗ̄ⲗⲱ, *an old woman,* Sah. ϣⲙ̄ⲙⲟ, *a stranger,* m. ϣⲙ̄ⲙⲱ, *a stranger,* f. Sah. ⲥⲁⲃⲉ, *wise.* m. ⲥⲁⲃⲏ, *wise,* f. Copt. ⲃⲁⲉ̀, *the end,* m. ⲃⲁⲏ, *the end,* f. Copt.

6. Likewise by changing the vowel of the penultimate syllable of the masculine, as ϣⲏⲣⲓ, *a son.* ϣⲉⲣⲓ, *a daughter,* Copt. ϣⲏⲣⲉ, *a son.* ϣⲉⲉⲣⲉ, *a daughter,* Sah.

Of the Number of Nouns.

7. The number of nouns is two, the singular and the plural. These can only be distinguished from each other in general, by the singular or plural article being prefixed, as:

ⲟⲩⲝⲱⲙ, *a book;* ⲡⲓⲝⲱⲙ, *the book:* ⲅⲁⲛⲝⲱⲙ, *books;* ⲛⲓⲝⲱⲙ, *the books;* ⲟⲩⲛⲟⲃⲉ, *a sin;* ⲡⲛⲟⲩⲃⲉ, *the sin;* ⲅⲉⲛⲛⲟⲃⲉ, *sins;* ⲛⲉⲛⲟⲃⲉ, *the sins,* Sah.

When nouns occur, without the article being prefixed, the singular or plural can only be known by its connection with other words of the sentence.

8. Some adjectives take the prefixes ⲉϥ, masc. ⲉⲥ, fem. and ⲉⲩ plur, as ⲉϥⲉⲙⲡϣⲁ, *worthy,* m. ⲉⲥⲉⲙⲡϣⲁ, *worthy,* fem. ⲉϥⲟⲕⲙ̄. *sad,* m. Sah. ⲉⲩⲟⲕⲙ̄, *sad,* plur. Sah. The adjectives which have the suffixes ϥ and ⲥ singular, have the plural in ⲟⲩ, which variously is contracted with the preceding vowel, as ⲡⲉⲑⲛⲁⲛⲉϥ, *good.* ⲡⲉⲑⲛⲁⲛⲉⲩ, *good,* plur. ⲡⲉⲑⲛⲁⲁϥ, *great.* ⲡⲉⲑⲛⲁⲁⲩ, *great,* plur. ⲛⲁϣⲱϥ, *much.* ⲛⲁϣⲱⲟⲩ, *much,* plur.

9. There are a considerable number of Nouns in each dialect, which form their plural differently, which we shall here endeavour to class according to their termination.

10. Coptic Plurals which end in ⲓ. ⲁⲃⲱⲕ, *a crow.* ⲁⲃⲱⲕⲓ, *crows.* ⲁⲫⲱⲫ, *a giant.* ⲁⲫⲱⲫⲓ, *giants.* ⲙⲁ, *a place.* ⲙⲁⲓ, *places.* ⲙ̄ⲛⲟⲧ *a breast.* ⲙ̄ⲛⲟϯ, *breasts.* ⲣⲁⲙⲁⲟ̀, *rich.* ⲣⲁⲙⲁⲟⲓ̀, *rich,* plur. ϣⲫⲉⲣ, *a companion.* ϣⲫⲉⲣⲓ, *companions.* ⲃⲉⲗⲗⲟ, *old.* ⲃⲉⲗⲗⲟⲓ, *old,* plur.

11. Coptic Plurals which end in ⲩ and their sing. in ⲉ. ϭⲁⲗⲉ, *lame.* ϭⲁⲗⲉⲩ, *lame,* plur. ⲃⲉⲗⲗⲉ, *blind.* ⲃⲉⲗⲗⲉⲩ, *blind,* plur. ⲑⲉϣⲉ, *neighbour.* ⲑⲉϣⲉⲩ, *a neighbours.* ⲙⲉⲑⲣⲉ, *a witness.* ⲙⲉⲑⲣⲉⲩ, *witnesses.* ⲣⲉⲙⲅⲉ, *free.* ⲣⲉⲙⲅⲉⲩ, *free,* plur. ⲥⲁⲃⲉ, *prudent.* ⲥⲁⲃⲉⲩ, *prudent,* plur. ⲃⲁⲉ̀, *last,* ⲃⲁⲉⲩ, *last,* plur. ⲝⲁⲛⲉ, *humble.* ⲝⲁⲛⲉⲩ, *humble,* plur.

12. Coptic Plurals which end in ⲟⲩ, and their sing. in ⲉ and ⲟ; but which change them into ⲛⲟⲩ and ⲱⲟⲩ in the plural. ⲉ̀ⲃⲟ, *mute.* ⲉ̀ⲃⲱⲟⲩ, *mute,* plur. ⲉ̀ⲅⲉ, *an ox.* ⲉ̀ⲅⲏⲟⲩ and ⲉ̀ⲅⲱⲟⲩ, *oxen.* ⲓⲁⲣⲟ, *a river.* ⲓⲁⲣⲱⲟⲩ, *rivers.* ⲟⲩⲣⲟ, *a king.* ⲟⲩⲣⲱⲟⲩ, *kings.* ⲣⲁⲙⲁⲟ̀, *rich.* ⲣⲁⲙⲁⲱⲟⲩ, *rich,* plur. ⲣⲟ, *a door.* ⲣⲱⲟⲩ, *doors.* ⲥⲁⲓⲉ, *fair.* ⲥⲁⲓⲱⲟⲩ, *fair,* pl. ϣⲉⲙⲙⲟ, *a stranger.* ϣⲉⲙⲙⲱⲟⲩ, *strangers.* ϣⲛⲉ, *a net.* ϣⲛⲏⲟⲩ, *nets.* ϣⲧⲉⲕⲟ, *a prison.* ϣⲧⲉⲕⲱⲟⲩ, *prisons.* ϣϫⲉ, *a locust.* ϣϫⲏⲟⲩ, *locusts.* To these may be added ⲁⲡⲏ, *head,* Bash. ⲁⲡⲛⲟⲩ, *heads.*

13. Coptic Plurals which end in ⲟⲩⲓ, and their singulars ending with a consonant, or with ⲱ.

ⲁϥ, *flesh.* ⲁϥⲟⲩⲓ, *flesh,* plur. ⲁⲭⲱ, *magician.* ⲁⲭⲱⲟⲩⲓ, *magicians.* ⲉⲧⲫⲱ, *a burden.* ⲉⲧⲫⲱⲟⲩⲓ, *burdens.* ⲣⲉϥϫⲱ, *a singer.* ⲣⲉϥϫⲱⲟⲩⲓ, *singers.* ⲥⲃⲱ, *a doctrine.* ⲥⲃⲱⲟⲩⲓ, *doctrines.* ⲥϥⲓⲣ, *a side.* ⲥϥⲓⲣⲱⲟⲩⲓ, *sides.*

14. Of Coptic Plurals which end in ⲟⲩⲓ, and their singulars in ⲉ, ⲉⲓ, ⲏ or ⲟⲩ, which are changed into ⲛⲟⲩⲓ or ⲱⲟⲩⲓ in the plural: as

ⲁⲫⲉ, *a head.* ⲁⲫⲛⲟⲩⲓ, *heads.* ⲁⲗⲟⲩ, *a boy.* ⲁⲗⲱⲟⲩⲓ, *boys.* ⲃⲉⲭⲉ, *wages.* ⲃⲉⲭⲛⲟⲩⲓ, *wages,* plur. ⲉⲣⲙⲏ, *a tear.* ⲉⲣⲙⲱⲟⲩⲓ, *tears.* ⲉⲣⲫⲉⲓ, *a temple.* ⲉⲣⲫⲛⲟⲩⲓ, *temples.* ⲟⲩⲛⲟⲩ, *an hour.* ⲟⲩⲛⲱⲟⲩⲓ, *hours.* ⲧⲉⲃⲛⲏ, *a labouring beast.* ⲧⲉⲃⲛⲱⲟⲩⲓ, *beasts.* ϥⲉ, *heaven.* ϥⲛⲟⲩⲓ, *heavens.* ⳉⲣⲉ, *food.* ⳉⲣⲛⲟⲩⲓ, *food,* plur.

15. Sahidic Plurals which end in ⲉ.

ⲁⲃⲱⲕ, *a crow.* ⲁ̀ⲃⲱⲕⲉ, *crows.* ⲗⲟⲟⲩ, *an ornament.* ⲗⲟⲟⲩⲉ, *ornaments.*

16. Sahidic Plurals which end in ⲉⲩ, and ⲏⲩ, and their singulars in ⲉ, as

ⲃⲁⲗⲉ, *blind.* ⲃⲁⲗⲉⲩ. *blind,* pl. ⲥⲁⲃⲉ, *prudent.* ⲥⲁⲃⲉⲉⲩ, *prudent,* plur. ⲱⲁϥⲉ, *a desert.* ⲱⲁϥⲉⲉⲩ, *deserts.* ⲝⲓⲝⲉ, *an enemy.* ⲝⲓⲝⲉⲉⲩ, *enemies.* ϯⲙⲉ, *a village.* ϯⲙⲉⲉⲩ, *villages.* ⲅⲁⲉ, *last.* ⲅⲁⲉⲉⲩ and ⲅⲁⲉⲩⲉ, *last,* plur.

17. Sahidic Plur. which change the ⲉ sing. into ⲏⲩ pl. ⲁⲙⲣⲉ, *a baker.* ⲁⲙⲣⲏⲩ, *bakers.* ⲉⲅⲉ, *an ox.* ⲉⲅⲏⲩ, *oxen.* ⲱⲛⲉ, *a net.* ⲱⲛⲏⲩ, *nets.*

18. Sahidic Plurals which end in ⲉⲩⲉ, ⲏⲩⲉ, and ⲏⲟⲩⲉ, and their singulars in ⲉ, as

ⲁⲡⲉ, *a head.* ⲁⲡⲏⲩⲉ, *heads.* ⲡⲉ, *heaven.* ⲡⲏⲩⲉ, *heavens.* ⲅⲁⲉ, *last.* ⲅⲁⲉⲉⲩⲉ, *last,* plur. ⲅⲣⲉ, *food.* ⲅⲣⲏⲩⲉ, and ⲅⲣⲏⲟⲩⲉ, *food,* plur. ϭⲁⲗⲉ, *lame.* ϭⲁⲗⲉⲉⲩⲉ, *lame,* plur. The short ⲉ is changed into ⲏ when the plurals ends in ⲏⲩⲉ.

19. Sahidic Plurals which end in ⲟⲩ, and their singulars in ⲟ, which are changed into ⲱⲟⲩ, as

ⲓⲉⲣⲟ, *a river.* ⲓⲉⲣⲱⲟⲩ, *rivers.* ⲕⲣⲟ, *the shore.* ⲕⲣⲱⲟⲩ, *shores.* ⲙ̄ⲛⲧⲣ̄ⲣⲟ, *a kingdom.* ⲙ̄ⲛⲧⲣ̄ⲣⲱⲟⲩ, *kingdoms.* ⲣⲟ, *a door.* ⲣⲱⲟⲩ, *doors.* ⲣ̄ⲣⲟ, *a king.* ⲣ̄ⲣⲱⲟⲩ, *kings.* The following is formed not quite regularly: ⲉⲅⲉ, *an ox.* ⲉⲅⲟⲟⲩ, *oxen.*

20. Sahidic Plurals which end in ⲟⲩⲉ.

ⲉⲓⲱ, *an ass.* ⲉⲓⲱⲟⲩⲉ, *asses.* ⲉⲙⲣⲱ, *a harbour.* ⲉⲙⲣⲟⲟⲩⲉ, *harbours.* ⲉⲱ, *an ass.* ⲉⲟⲟⲩⲉ, *asses.* ⲕⲉ, *another.* ⲕⲟⲟⲩⲉ, *others.* ⲟⲩⲛⲟⲩ, *an hour.* ⲟⲩⲛⲟⲟⲩⲉ, *hours.* ⲟⲩⲱⲏ, *night.* ⲟⲩⲱⲟⲟⲩⲉ, *nights.* ⲣⲓⲙⲉ, ⲣⲙⲉⲓⲏ, *weeping.* ⲣⲙ̄ⲉⲓⲟⲟⲩⲉ, ⲣⲙⲉⲓⲟⲩⲉ, *tears.* ⲣⲟⲙⲡⲉ, *a year.* ⲣⲙ̄ⲡⲟⲟⲩⲉ, *years.* ⲥⲃⲱ, *a doctrine.* ⲥⲃⲟⲟⲩⲉ, *doctrines.* ⲥⲡⲓⲣ, *a side.* ⲥⲡⲓⲣⲟⲟⲩⲉ,

sides. ⲦⲂⲚⲎ, *a beast.* ⲦⲂⲚⲞⲞⲨⲈ, *beasts,* plur. ⳪ⲓⲎ, *a way.*
⳪ⲓⲞⲞⲨⲈ, *ways.* ⳪ⲣⲈ, *food.* ⳪ⲣⲈⲞⲨⲈ, *food,* plur.

21. Coptic and Sahidic Plurals of a more irregular
character.

Coptic.

Sing.	Plur.
Ⲁ⳪Ⲟ, *a treasure.*	Ⲁ⳪Ⲱⲣ, *treasures.*
ⲀⲂⲞⲦ, *a month.*	ⲀⲂⲎⲦ, *months.*
ⲀⲚⲀⲱ, *an oath.*	ⲀⲚⲀⲨⲱ, *oaths.*
ⲂⲎⲦ, *a palmwood.*	ⲂⲀ†, *palmwoods.*
ⲂⲰⲔ, *a servant.*	Ⲉ̀ⲂⲓⲀⲔ, *servants.*
ⲈⲐⲞⲱ, *an Ethiopian.*	ⲈⲐⲀⲨⲱ, *Ethiopians.*
ⲈⲘⲔⲀ⳪, *grief.*	ⲈⲘⲔⲀⲨ⳪, *griefs.*
ⲈⲰ, *an ass.*	ⲈⲈⲨ, *asses.*
ⲪⲱⲰ, *a pig.*	ⲈⲱⲀⲨ, *pigs.*
ⲈⲱⲰⲦ, *a merchant.*	ⲈⲱⲞ†, *merchants.*
Ⲏⲓ, *a house.*	ⲎⲞⲨ, *houses.*
ⲓⲞⲘ, *the sea.*	ⲀⲘⲀⲓⲞⲨ, *seas.*
ⲓⲰⲦ, *a father.*	ⲓⲟ†, *fathers.*
ⲘⲈⲚⲡⲓⲦ, *beloved.*	ⲘⲈⲚⲡⲀ†, *beloved.*
ⲘⲈⲱⲰⲦ, *a plain.*	ⲘⲈⲱⲞ†, *plains.*
ⲘⲰⲓⲦ, *a way.*	ⲘⲓⲦⲰⲞⲨⲓ, *ways.*
ⲞⲨⲡⲓⲦ, *a keeper.*	ⲞⲨⲣⲀ†, *keepers.*
ⲡⲈⲘⲎⲦ, *a tenth.*	ⲡⲈⲘⲀ†, *tenths.*
ⲤⲀⲃ, *a scribe.*	ⲤⲃⲞⲨⲓ, *scribes.*
ⲤⲞⲂⲦ, *a wall.*	ⲤⲈⲂⲐⲀⲓⲞⲨ, *walls.*
ⲤⲞⲚⲓ, *a robber.*	ⲤⲓⲚⲰⲞⲨⲓ, *robbers.*
ⲤⲞⲚ, *a brother.*	ⲤⲚⲎⲞⲨ, *brothers.*
Ⲥ⳪ⲓⲘⲓ, *a woman.*	⳪ⲓⲞⲘⲓ, *women.*

3*

ϣⲟⲙ, *a father in law.*	ϣⲙⲱⲟⲩ, *fathers in law.*
ϣⲃⲱⲧ, *a rod.*	ϣⲃⲟϯ, *rods.*
ϩⲃⲱ, *a viper.*	ϩⲃⲟⲩⲓ, *vipers.*
ϩⲑⲟ, *a horse.*	ϩⲑⲱⲣ, *horses.*
ϩⲁⲗⲏⲧ, *a bird.*	ϩⲁⲗⲁϯ, *birds.*
ϩⲟⲩⲓⲧ, *the first.*	ϩⲟⲩⲁϯ, *first,* plur.
ϩⲱⲃ, *a work.*	ϩⲃⲏⲟⲩⲓ, *works.*
ϫⲁⲙⲟⲩⲗ, *a camel.*	ϫⲁⲙⲁⲩⲗⲓ, *camels.*
ϫⲟⲓ, *a ship.*	ⲉϫⲏⲟⲩ, *ships.*
ϭⲁⲗⲟϫ, *a foot.*	ϭⲁⲗⲁⲩϫ, *feet.*
ⲟ̄ⲥ̄, *a Lord.*	ϭⲓⲥⲉⲩ, *Lords.*

Sahidic.

Sing.	Plur.
ⲁϩⲟ, *a treasure.*	ⲁϩⲱⲱⲣ, *treasures.*
ⲃⲓⲣ, *a basket.*	ⲃⲣⲏⲟⲩⲉ, *baskets.*
ⲉⲃⲟⲧ, *a month.*	ⲉⲃⲁⲧⲉ, *months.*
ⲫⲓⲱⲧ, *a father.*	ⲉⲓⲟⲧⲉ, *fathers.*
ⲟⲩⲣⲓⲧ, *a keeper.*	ⲟⲩⲣⲁⲧⲉ, *keepers.*
ⲥⲟⲛ, *a brother.*	ⲥⲛⲏⲩ, *brothers.*
ⲥϩⲓⲙⲉ, *a woman.*	ϩⲓⲟⲙⲉ, *women.*
ⲟⲩϩⲟⲣ, *a dog.*	ⲟⲩϩⲟⲟⲣ, *dogs.*
ϩⲁⲗⲏⲧ, *a bird.*	ϩⲁⲗⲁⲁⲧⲉ, *birds.*
ϩⲃⲱ, *a viper.*	ϩⲃⲟⲩⲓ, *vipers.*
ϩⲧⲟ, *a horse.*	ϩⲧⲱⲣ, ϩⲧⲱⲱⲣ, *horses.*
ϩⲱⲃ, *a work.*	ϩⲃⲏⲩ, ϩⲃⲏⲩⲉ, *works.*
ϫⲟⲓ, *a ship.*	ⲉϫⲏⲩ, *ships.*
ϫⲟⲉⲓⲥ, *Lord.*	ϫⲉⲓⲥⲟⲟⲩⲉ, *Lords.*

Of Cases of Nouns.

22. Strictly speaking the three Dialects of Egypt have no cases of nouns. But these are indicated by certain particles which precede, or are prefixed to the nouns, or by prepositions, as,

	Coptic.	Sahidic and Bashmuric.
Nom.	ⲛ̀ⲝⲉ.	ⲛ̄ϭ︦ⲓ.
Gen.	ⲛ̀ⲧⲉ, ⲙ̀, ⲛ̀.	ⲛ̄ⲧⲉ, ⲙ̄, ⲛ̄.
Dat.	ⲉ̀, ⲙ̀, ⲛ̀.	ⲉ̄, ⲙ̄, ⲛ̄.
Acc.	ⲉ̀, ⲙ̀, ⲛ̀.	ⲉ, ⲙ̄, ⲛ̄.
Voc.	ⲱ̀, ⲡⲓ.	ⲱ, ⲡⲉ.
Abl.	ⲉ̀, ⲙ̀, ⲛ̀, or a preposition.	ⲉ, ⲙ̄, ⲛ̄, or a preposition.

23. It will be seen that what are called cases in Greek and Latin are here denoted by particles which precede the noun, as in the nominative and genitive, or by particles prefixed.

The Nominative Case.

24. The sign of the nominative case is ⲛ̀ⲝⲉ in Coptic, and ⲛ̄ϭ︦ⲓ in Sahidic and Bashmuric, as ⲁϥⲉⲣⲟⲩⲱ̀ ⲛ̀ⲝⲉ ⲓ̄ⲏ̄ⲥ̄, ⲡⲉⲝⲁϥ ⲛⲱⲟⲩ, *Jesus answered (and) said to them,* Luke VI, 3. ⲁⲥⲓ̀ ⲇⲉ ⲛ̀ⲝⲉ ⲙⲁⲣⲓⲁ̀ ϯⲙⲁⲅⲇⲁⲗⲓⲛⲏ, *But Mary Magdalen came.* John XX, 18. ⲁϥⲉⲓ̂ ⲛ̄ϭ︦ⲓ ⲓ̈ⲱⲁⲛⲛⲏⲥ, *John came.* Mat. III, 1. Sah. ⲧⲟⲧⲉ ⲁϥⲉⲓ̂ ⲛ̄ϭ︦ⲓ ⲓ̄ⲥ̄ ⲉⲃⲟⲗϩⲛ̄, ⲧⲅⲁⲗⲓⲗⲁⲓⲁ, *than Jesus came out of Galilee.* Mat. III, 13. Sah.

The Genitive Case.

25. The genitive case is indicated by ⲛ̀ⲧⲉ preceding the noun, as ⲟⲩⲃⲁⲕⲓ ⲛ̀ⲧⲉ ⲧⲥⲁⲙⲁⲣⲓⲁ̀, *a city of Samaria.* John IV, 4. ⲫⲟⲩⲱⲓⲛⲓ ⲛ̀ⲧⲉ ⲡⲉⲕⲍⲟ, *the light of thy face.* Ps. XLIV, 3. ⲟⲩϣⲁⲝⲉ ⲛ̄ⲧⲉ ⲧⲙⲉ, *the word of truth,* Sah. 2. Cor. VI, 7. Sah. But the prefix ⲙ̀ or ⲛ̀, is frequently used as the sign of the genitive case, especially in the Sahidic, as ⲫⲣⲁⲛ ⲙ̀ⲡⲁⲓⲱⲧ, *the name of my father.* John V, 44. ⲟⲩⲥⲁⲝⲓ ⲛ̀ⲉⲙⲓ, *the word of knowledge.* 1. Cor. XII, 8. ⲧϣⲉⲉⲣⲉ ⲛ̄ⲥⲓⲱⲛ, *the daughter of Sion.* Mat. XXI, 5. Sah. ⲡϣⲏⲣⲉ ⲛ̄ⲇⲁⲩⲉⲓⲇ, *the son of David.* Mat. XXI, 9. Sah. ⲡϣⲏⲣⲉ ⲙ̄ⲡⲣⲱⲙⲉ, *the son of man.* Luke XXII, 48. Sah. ⲧϭⲟⲙ ⲙ̄ⲡⲛⲟⲩⲧⲉ, *the power of God.* Luke XXII, 69. Sah. The prefix ⲙ̀ is used principally before ⲃ, ⲙ and ⲫ, and always before ⲡ, but seldom before ⲗ and ⲣ.

The Dative Case.

26. The dative case takes the prefix ⲙ̀ or ⲛ̀, and sometimes ⲉ̀, as ⲁϥ†ⲧⲟⲧϥ ⲙ̄ⲡⲓⲥ̄ⲗ̄, *he hath given help* (his hand) *to Israel.* ⲡⲉⲭⲁϥ ⲛ̀ⲥⲓⲙⲱⲛ, *he said to Simon.* ⲁϥⲓ̀ ⲉ̀ⲡⲏⲓ ⲙ̀ⲙⲁⲣⲓⲁ̀, *he came to the house of Mary.* ⲛ̄† ϣⲱⲙ ⲙ̄ⲡⲣ̄ⲣⲟ, *to give tribute to the king,* Luke XXIII, 2. Sah. † ⲛ̄ⲛⲉⲍⲏⲕⲉ, *to give to the poor,* Luke XIX, 8. Sah. ⲛⲉⲕⲝⲱ ⲙ̄ⲙⲟⲥ ⲉⲟⲩⲟⲛ ⲛⲓⲙ, *sayest thou it to all?* Luke XII, 41. Sah. When ⲉ is prefixed to the indefinite article ⲟⲩ, the ⲉⲟⲩ are frequently contracted into ⲉⲩ, as ⲉⲥⲧⲛ̄ⲧⲱⲛ ⲉⲩⲃⲗ̄ⲃⲓⲗⲉ ⲛ̄ϣⲗ̄ⲧⲙ̄, *it is like to a grain of mustard seed.* Luke XIII, 19. Sah.

The Accusative Case.

27. The signs of the accusative case are ⲙ̄, ⲛ̄ or
ⲉ̀, as ⲁⲛⲝⲓⲙⲓ ⲙ̀ⲡⲓⲙⲁⲛⲥⲱⲛ2, *we found the prison*, Acts
V, 21. ⲁϥⲣⲱⲃⲧ ⲛ̄2ⲁⲛⲝⲱⲣⲓ, *he hath cast down the strong*,
Luke I, 52. ⲁⲗⲗⲁ ⲉ̀ⲣⲉⲧⲉⲛⲉ̀ϭⲓ ⲛ̄ⲟⲩⲝⲟⲙ, *but ye shall re-
ceive power*. Acts I, 8. ⲁⲛⲛⲁⲩ ⲉ̀ⲡⲟ̄ⲥ̄, *we have seen the
Lord*. John XX, 25. ⲁ ⲙⲱⲩⲥⲏⲥ ⲝⲉⲥⲧ̄ ⲙ̀ⲡ2ⲟϥ. *Moses
lifted up the serpent*. John I, 14. Sah. ⲡⲁⲓ ⲉⲧⲉ ⲣ̄ⲟⲩⲟⲉⲓⲛ
ⲉⲣⲱⲙⲉ ⲛⲓⲙ, *which enlighteneth every man*. John I, 9. Sah.
But the ⲉ is most frequently used as the sign of the
accusative.

The Vocative Case.

28. The sign of the vocative case is ⲱ̀ preceding
the noun, as ⲱ̀ ⲑⲉⲟϥⲓⲗⲉ, *o Theophilus*. Acts I, 1., but
it does not often occur. The definite article is used as
the sign of the vocative, as ϥⲣⲉϥ†ⲥⲃⲱ ⲛ̄ⲁⲅⲁⲑⲟⲥ, Copt.
ⲡⲥⲁ2 ⲛ̄ⲁⲅⲁⲑⲟⲥ, *o good Master!* Sah. Mat. XIX, 16.
ⲡⲁⲱϥⲏⲣ, *O my friend!* Copt. ⲡⲉⲱⲃⲉⲉⲣ, *O friend!* Sah.
Mat. XX, 13. ⲉⲩⲝⲱ ⲙ̄ⲙⲟⲥ ⲝⲉ ⲡⲝⲟⲉⲓⲥ ⲛⲁ ⲛⲁⲛ ⲡⲱⲏⲣⲉ
ⲛ̄ⲇⲁⲩⲉⲓⲇ. *saying, O Lord thou son of David, have mercy
on us*, Sah. Mat. XX, 30. ⲧⲱⲉⲣⲓ ⲛ̄ⲥⲓⲱⲛ, Copt. ⲧⲱⲉⲉⲣⲉ
ⲛ̄ⲥⲓⲱⲛ, *O daughter of Sion!* John XII, 15. Sah.

The Ablative Case.

29. This case sometimes takes the prefix ⲙ̄, ⲛ̄ or
ⲉ̀, as ⲉⲛⲟⲃⲉ ⲛⲓⲙ, *from all sin*. Sah. ⲉⲡⲛⲟⲩⲧⲉ, *from God*.

Ⲛ̄ Ⲙ̄ⲙⲟⲕⲙⲉⲕ. *from the thoughts.* Sah. But the ablative is generally represented by some preposition.

The Bashmuric takes the same particles as the Sahidic to all the cases, except the Ablative.

CHAP. V.

Of Adjectives.

1. There are some adjectives, the number and gender of which are known by the suffixes, or the articles, as ⲡⲓⲛⲓϣϯ, *great,* m. ϯⲛⲓϣϯ, *great,* f. and ⲉⲑⲛⲁⲛⲉϥ, *good,* m. ⲉⲑⲛⲁⲛⲉⲥ, *good,* f. ⲛⲁⲁϥ or ⲉⲑⲛⲁⲁϥ, *great,* m. Sah. ⲛⲁⲁⲥ, *great,* f. Sah. ⲉⲑⲛⲁⲁⲩ, *great,* plur. Sah.

ⲉ, ⲉⲧ, or ⲉⲑ united to verbs forms adjectives, as ⲟⲩⲁⲃ *to be clean, holy.* ⲉⲑⲟⲩⲁⲃ, *clean, holy.*

ⲛⲁϣⲉ or ⲉⲛⲁϣⲉ, Sah. *much.* ⲛⲁϣⲱϥ or ⲉⲛⲁϣⲱϥ, Sah. *much,* m. ⲛⲁϣⲱⲥ or ⲉⲛⲁϣⲱⲥ, Sah. *much,* f. ⲛⲁϣ-ⲱⲟⲩ or ⲉⲛⲁϣⲱⲟⲩ, Sah. *much,* plur.

ⲛⲁⲛⲉ and ⲛⲁⲛⲟⲩ, ⲉⲛⲁⲛⲟⲩ, Sah. *good.* ⲛⲁⲛⲉϥ, ⲛⲁⲛⲟⲩϥ, ⲉⲛⲁⲛⲟⲩϥ, Sah. *good,* m. ⲛⲁⲛⲉⲥ; and ⲛⲁⲛⲟⲩⲥ, ⲉⲛⲁⲛⲟⲩⲥ, Sah. *good,* f. ⲉⲑⲛⲁⲛⲉⲩ, ⲉⲧⲛⲁⲛⲟⲩⲟⲩ, Sah. *good,* plur.

ⲛⲁⲉⲓⲁⲧ or ⲛⲁⲓⲁⲧ, Sah. *blessed.* ⲛⲁⲓⲁⲧⲕ, *blessed thou,* m. ⲛⲁⲓⲁⲧϥ; *blessed he.* ⲛⲁⲓⲁⲧⲥ, *blessed she.* ⲛⲁⲓⲁⲑⲏⲩⲧⲛ̄, *blessed ye.* ⲛⲁⲓⲁⲧⲟⲩ, *blessed they.*

ⲛⲉⲥⲉ or ⲉ̀ⲛⲉⲥⲉ, *fair, beautiful.* ⲛⲉⲥⲱⲓ, *fair I.* ⲛⲉⲥⲱϥ, ⲉⲑⲛⲉⲥⲱϥ or ⲉ̀ⲛⲉⲥⲱϥ, *fair he.* ⲛⲉⲥⲱⲥ, ⲉⲑⲛⲉⲥⲱⲥ or ⲉ̀ⲛⲉⲥⲱⲥ, *fair she.* ⲉ̀ⲛⲉⲥⲱⲟⲩ or ⲉⲛⲉⲥⲟⲟⲩ, *fair they.*

ⲥⲙⲁⲣⲱⲟⲩⲧ, and ⲥⲙⲁⲙⲁⲁⲧ, Sah. *blessed.* ⲕⲥⲙⲁ-
ⲣⲱⲟⲩⲧ, *blessed thou.* ϥⲥⲙⲁⲣⲱⲟⲩⲧ, ϥⲥⲙⲁⲙⲁⲁⲧ, Sahidic.
blessed he. ⲛⲏⲉⲧⲥⲙⲁⲣⲱⲟⲩ, ⲛⲉⲧⲥⲙⲁⲙⲁⲁⲧ, Sah. *blessed*
they.

ⲟⲩⲁⲁ, Sah. *alone.* ⲟⲩⲁⲁⲕ, *alone thou.* ⲟⲩⲁⲁϥ, *alone*
he. ⲟⲩⲁⲁⲧⲟⲩ, *alone they.*

ⲙ̇ⲙⲁⲩⲁⲧ, and ⲙⲁⲩⲁⲁⲧ, Sah. *alone.* ⲙ̇ⲙⲁⲩⲁⲧⲕ,
ⲙⲁⲩⲁⲁⲕ, Sah. *alone thou.* m. ⲙ̇ⲙⲁⲩⲁϯ, *alone thou* f.
ⲙ̇ⲙⲁⲩⲁⲧϥ. ⲙⲁⲩⲁⲁϥ, Sah. *alone he.* ⲙ̇ⲙⲁⲩⲁⲧⲥ, ⲙⲁⲩ-
ⲁⲁⲥ, Sah. *alone she.* ⲙⲁⲩⲁⲁⲛ, Sah. ⲙ̇ⲙⲁⲩⲁⲧⲉⲛ, *alone*
we. ⲙ̇ⲙⲁⲩⲁⲧⲟⲩ, ⲙⲁⲩⲁⲁⲩ, Sah. *alone they.*

ⲧⲏⲣ, *all.* ⲧⲏⲣⲕ, *the whole thou,* m. ⲧⲏⲣϥ, ⲧⲏⲣⲉϥ,
Sah. *all he.* ⲧⲏⲣⲥ, ⲧⲏⲣⲉⲥ, Sah. *all she.* ⲧⲏⲣⲉⲛ, ⲧⲏⲣⲛ̄,
all we. ⲧⲏⲣⲧⲛ̄, Sah. *all ye.* ⲧⲏⲣⲟⲩ, *all they.*

Of the Comparison of Adjectives.

2. Comparatives are formed by ⲉⲟⲩⲟ, Copt. ⲉⲟⲩⲟ,
ⲉⲟⲩⲉ, Sah. ⲉⲟⲩⲁ, ⲉⲩⲉ, Bash. *more,* as ⲉⲟⲩⲟ̇ ⲧⲁⲓⲟ̇
ⲉ̇ⲉⲟⲧⲉ ⲙⲱⲩⲥⲏⲥ, *more (greater) honour than Moses.*
ⲟⲩⲉⲟⲩⲟ̇ ⲧⲁⲓⲟ̇ ⲉ̇ⲉⲟⲧⲉ ⲡⲓⲏⲓ, *more (greater) honour than*
the house. Heb. III, 3. ⲙⲛ̄ⲧⲁⲛ ⲉⲟⲩⲟ ⲉϯⲟⲩ ⲛⲟⲉⲓⲕ,
Sah. *we have not more than five breads loaves.* Luc. IX, 13.

ⲉ̇ⲉⲟⲧⲉ is also a sign of the comparative, as ⲉ̇ⲉⲟⲧⲉ-
ⲣⲟⲓ, *more than me,* Mat. X, 37. and with ⲉ̇, as ϯⲙⲉⲧⲥⲟⲝ
ⲛ̄ⲧⲉ ⲫϯ ⲉⲥⲟⲓ ⲛ̄ⲥⲁⲃⲉ ⲉ̇ⲉⲟⲧⲉ ⲉ̇ⲛⲓⲣⲱⲙⲓ, *the foolishness of*
God is wise more (wiser) than men. 1. Cor. I, 25.

3. The comparative is also expressed by adding
ⲛ̄ⲉⲟⲩⲟ to the positive; as ϯⲙⲉⲧⲙⲉⲑⲣⲉ ⲛ̄ⲧⲉ ⲫϯ ⲟⲩⲛⲓϣϯ ⲧⲉ ⲛ̄ⲉⲟⲩⲟ, *the witness of God is greater.* 1. John

4

V, 9. It is also expressed by adding ε, or ⲛ to the positive, as ⲙⲏ ⲛ̄ⲧⲟⲕ ⲉⲕⲛⲁⲁⲕ ⲉⲡⲛ̄ⲓⲱⲧ ⲓⲁⲕⲱⲃ, *art thou greater than our father Jacob?* John IV, 12. Sah. ⲟⲩⲛⲟϭ ⲛ̄ⲛⲟⲃⲉ, *greater sin.* John XIX, 11. Sah. ⲛ̄ⲛⲟϭ ⲉⲡⲉⲛϩⲏⲧ, *greater than our heart.* 1. John III, 20. Sah. ⲙⲏ ⲉⲛϫⲟⲟⲣ ⲉⲣⲟϥ, *are we stronger than he?* 1. Cor. X, 22. Sah.

4. Sometimes there is no word to express the comparative, and it can only be collected from the sense of the passage; as ⲛⲓⲙ ⲅⲁⲣ ⲡⲉ ⲡⲓⲛⲓϣϯ, *for which is great (greater)* Luke XXII, 27. ⲧⲙⲛ̄ⲧⲙⲛ̄ⲧⲣⲉ ⲛ̄ⲡⲛⲟⲩⲧⲉ ⲛⲁⲁⲁⲥ, *the witness of God is great (greater)* 1. John V, 9. Sah.

5. The positive is sometimes used for the superlative as ⲛⲓⲙ ⲡⲉ ⲡⲓⲛⲓϣϯ ϧⲉⲛ ϯⲙⲉⲧⲟⲩⲣⲟ ⲛ̄ⲧⲉ ⲛⲓⲫⲏⲟⲩⲓ, ⲛⲓⲙ ⲡⲉ ⲡⲛⲟϭ ϩⲛ̄ ⲧⲙⲛ̄ⲧⲉⲣⲟ ⲛ̄ⲙ̄ⲡⲏⲩⲉ, Sah. *who is the great (greatest) in the kingdom of heaven?* Mat. XVIII, 1. Sah.

6. The superlative is formed by adding ⲉ̀, ⲉ̀ⲃⲟⲗ, ⲉ̀ⲃⲟⲗⲟⲩⲧⲉ, or some such word to the positive, as ⲁⲛⲟⲕ ⲅⲁⲣ ⲡⲉ ⲡⲓⲕⲟⲩϫⲓ ⲉ̀ⲃⲟⲗⲟⲩⲧⲉ ⲛⲓⲁ̀ⲡⲟⲥⲧⲟⲗⲟⲥ ⲧⲏⲣⲟⲩ, and Bash. ⲁⲛⲟⲕ ⲅⲁⲣ ⲡⲉ ⲡⲕⲟⲩⲓ ⲟⲩⲧⲉ ⲛⲓⲁⲡⲟⲥⲧⲟⲗⲟⲥ ⲧⲏⲣⲟⲩ, *for I am the least of all the Apostles.* 1. Cor. XV, 9.

7. The superlative is more often formed by adding ⲉ̀ⲙⲁϣⲱ, Copt. ⲉⲙⲁⲧⲉ, Sah. ⲉⲙⲁϣⲁ, Bash. *greatly, very much,* to the positive, as ⲁⲧⲁⲯⲩⲭⲏ ϣⲑⲟⲣⲧⲉⲣ ⲉ̀ⲙⲁϣⲱ, *my soul is exceedingly troubled.* Ps. VI, 3. ⲉ̀ⲙⲁϣⲱ, ⲉⲙⲁⲧⲉ and ⲉⲙⲁϣⲁ are also repeated; as ⲁϥⲉⲣ ⲣⲁⲙⲁ̀ⲟ ⲛ̄ϫⲉ ⲡⲓⲣⲱⲙⲓ ⲉ̀ⲙⲁϣⲱ ⲉ̀ⲙⲁϣⲱ, *the man was exceeding rich.* Gen. XXX, 43. ϫⲉⲕⲁⲥ ⲉⲣⲉ ⲧⲉⲧⲛ̄ⲁⲅⲁⲡⲏ ⲣ̄ϩⲟⲩⲟ ⲉⲙⲁⲧⲉ ⲉⲙⲁⲧⲉ, *that your love may abound exceedingly.* Sahidic.

Phil. I, 9. and in Bash. ⲭⲉⲕⲉⲥ ⲉⲣⲉ ⲧⲉⲧⲉⲛⲁⲅⲁⲡⲏ ⲉⲗ-
ⲋⲟⲩⲁ ⲉⲙⲁϣⲁ. The superlative is also formed by ⲛ̀ⲋⲟⲩⲟ
repeated, as ⲟⲩⲟⲋ ⲛ̀ⲋⲟⲩⲟ̀ ⲛ̀ⲋⲟⲩⲟ̀ ⲛⲁⲩⲉⲣϣⲫⲏⲣⲓ, *and they
were exceedingly astonished.* Mark VII, 37.

CHAP. VI.

Of Personal Pronouns.

Singular.

Coptic.	Sahidic.	Bash.	
ⲁ̀ⲛⲟⲕ	ⲁ̅ⲛⲟⲕ	ⲁ̀ⲛⲟⲕ	*I.*
	ⲁ̅ⲛⲅ̅	ⲁ̀ⲛⲁⲕ	
	ⲁ̅ⲛⲕ̅		
ⲛ̀ⲑⲟⲕ	ⲛ̅ⲧⲟⲕ	ⲛ̀ⲧⲁⲕ	*thou,* m.
	ⲛ̅ⲧⲕ̅		
ⲛ̀ⲑⲟ	ⲛ̅ⲧⲟ	ⲛ̀ⲧⲁ	*thou,* f.
ⲛ̀ⲑⲟϥ	ⲛ̅ⲧⲟϥ	ⲛ̀ⲧⲁϥ	*he.*
ⲛ̀ⲑⲟⲥ	ⲛ̅ⲧⲟⲥ	ⲛ̀ⲧⲁⲥ	*she.*

Plural.

Coptic.	Sahidic.	Bash.	
ⲁ̀ⲛⲟⲛ	ⲁ̅ⲛⲟⲛ	ⲁ̀ⲛⲁⲛ	*we.*
	ⲁ̅ⲛⲛ̅		
ⲛ̀ⲑⲱⲧⲉⲛ	ⲛ̅ⲧⲱⲧⲛ̅	ⲛ̀ⲧⲁⲧⲉⲛ	*ye.*
	ⲛ̅ⲧⲉⲧⲉⲛ	ⲛ̀ⲧⲁⲧⲛ̀	
	ⲛ̅ⲧⲉⲧⲛ̅		
ⲛ̀ⲑⲱⲟⲩ	ⲛ̅ⲧⲟⲟⲩ	ⲛ̀ⲧⲁⲩ	*they.*

4·

Personal Pronouns.

2. Of the Genitive Case.

Singular.

Coptic.	Sahidic.	Bash.
ⲚⲐⲒ	ⲚⲦⲀⲒ	ⲈⲚⲐⲒ *mei, of me.*
ⲚⲦⲀⲔ	ⲚⲦⲀⲔ	ⲚⲐⲎⲔ *of thee,* m.
ⲚⲦⲈ	ⲚⲦⲈ	ⲚⲦⲈ *of thee,* f.
ⲚⲦⲀϥ	ⲚⲦⲀϥ ⲚⲦϥ	ⲚⲐⲎϥ ⲚⲦⲈϥ } *of him.*
ⲚⲦⲀⲤ	ⲚⲦⲀⲤ ⲚⲦⲤ̅	ⲚⲐⲎⲤ } *of her.*

Plural.

ⲚⲦⲀⲚ	ⲚⲦⲀⲚ ⲚⲦⲚ̅	ⲚⲐⲎⲚ̅ } *of us.*
ⲚⲐⲰⲦⲈⲚ	ⲚⲦⲈⲦⲚ̅	ⲚⲐⲎⲦⲈⲚ
ⲚⲦⲰⲦⲈⲚ	ⲚⲦⲈⲦⲎⲦⲚ̅	ⲚⲦⲈⲦⲈⲚ } *of you*
ⲚⲦⲈⲐⲎⲚⲞⲨ		ⲚⲦⲈⲦⲎⲚⲞⲨ
ⲚⲦⲰⲞⲨ	ⲚⲦⲀⲨ	ⲚⲐⲞⲨ, *of them.*

Of the Dative Case.

Singular.

Coptic.	Sahidic.	Bash.
ⲚⲎⲒ	ⲚⲀⲒ	ⲚⲎⲒ *mihi, to me.*
ⲚⲀⲔ	ⲚⲀⲔ	ⲚⲎⲔ *to thee,* m.
ⲚⲈ	ⲚⲈ	*to thee,* f.
ⲚⲀϥ	ⲚⲀϥ	ⲚⲎϥ ⲚⲈϥ } *to him*
ⲚⲀⲤ	ⲚⲀⲤ	ⲚⲎⲤ *to her.*

Plural.

ⲚⲀⲚ	ⲚⲀⲚ	ⲚⲎⲚ *to us.*
ⲚⲰⲦⲈⲚ	ⲚⲎⲦⲚ̄	ⲚⲎⲦⲈⲚ *to you.*
ⲐⲎⲚⲞⲨ	ⲦⲎⲚⲞⲨ·	ⲦⲎⲚⲞⲨ *with an accus.*
ⲚⲰⲞⲨ	ⲚⲀⲨ	ⲚⲎⲞⲨ, ⲚⲎⲨ ⲚⲈⲨ } *to them.*

3. The dative is also formed by the word ⲡⲟ Copt. and ⲗⲁ Bash. by prefixing ⲉ̀ to them: and by ⲦⲞⲦ, Copt. ⲦⲞⲞⲦ, Sah. ⲦⲀⲀⲦ, Bash. by prefixing ⲉ̀ or ⲛ̄ to them.

Singular.

Coptic.	Sahidic.	Bash.
ⲉ̀ⲣⲟⲓ	ⲈⲢⲞⲒ, ⲈⲢⲀⲒ	ⲈⲖⲀⲒ *to me.*
ⲉ̀ⲣⲟⲕ	ⲈⲢⲞⲔ, ⲈⲢⲀⲔ	ⲈⲖⲀⲔ *to thee,* m.
ⲉ̀ⲣⲟ	ⲈⲢⲞ, ⲈⲢⲀ	ⲈⲖⲀ *to thee,* f.
ⲉ̀ⲣⲟϥ	ⲈⲢⲞϥ, ⲈⲢⲀϥ	ⲈⲖⲀϥ *to him.*
ⲉ̀ⲣⲟⲥ	ⲈⲢⲞⲤ, ⲈⲢⲀⲤ	ⲈⲖⲀⲤ *to her.*

Plural.

ⲉ̀ⲡⲟⲚ	ⲈⲢⲞⲚ, ⲈⲢⲀⲚ	ⲈⲖⲀⲚ *to us.*
ⲉ̀ⲣⲱⲦⲈⲚ	ⲈⲢⲰⲦⲚ̄	ⲈⲖⲀⲦⲈⲚ } *to you.*
ⲉ̀ⲣⲱⲦⲈⲚ ⲐⲎⲚⲞⲨ	ⲈⲢⲀⲦ ⲦⲎⲨⲦⲚ̄	ⲈⲖⲀⲦⲦⲎⲚⲞⲨ }
ⲉ̀ⲣⲱⲞⲨ	ⲈⲢⲞⲞⲨ	ⲈⲖⲀⲨ *to them.*

Singular.

Coptic.	Sahidic.	Bash.
ⲉ̀ or ⲛ̀ⲦⲞⲦ	ⲉ̀ or Ⲛ̄ⲦⲞⲞⲦ	ⲉ̀ or Ⲛ̄ⲦⲀⲀⲦ *to me.*
ⲛ̀ⲦⲞⲦⲔ	Ⲛ̄ⲦⲞⲞⲦⲔ	ⲚⲦⲀⲀⲦⲔ *to thee,* m.
ⲛ̀Ⲧⲟϯ	Ⲛ̄ⲦⲞⲞⲦⲈ	*to thee,* f.
ⲛ̀ⲦⲞⲦϥ	Ⲛ̄ⲦⲞⲞⲦϥ	Ⲛ̄ⲦⲀⲀⲦϥ *to him.*
ⲛ̀ⲦⲞⲦⲤ	Ⲛ̄ⲦⲞⲞⲦⲤ	Ⲛ̄ⲦⲀⲀⲦⲤ *to her.*

Plural.

ⲉ̀ or ⲚⲦⲞⲦⲈⲚ	Ⲉ̄ or ⲚⲦⲞⲞⲦⲚ̄	ⲉ̀ or ⲚⲦⲀⲀⲦⲈⲚ	*to us.*
Ⲉ̀ⲦⲈⲚⲐⲎⲚⲞⲨ	Ⲉ̄ⲦⲞⲞⲦ ⲦⲎⲨⲦⲚ̄		*to you.*
Ⲉ̀ⲦⲞⲦⲞⲨ ⎫ Ⲛ̀ⲦⲀⲦⲞⲨ ⎭	ⲚⲦⲞⲞⲦⲞⲨ	ⲚⲦⲀⲀⲦⲞⲨ	*to them.*

4. The accusative Pronoun is formed by ⲘⲘⲞ Copt. and Sah., ⲘⲘⲀ and ⲘⲀ Bash.

Singular.

Coptic.	Sahidic.	Bash.	
ⲘⲘⲞⲒ	ⲘⲘⲞⲒ, ⲘⲘⲞⲈⲒ	ⲘⲘⲀⲒ	*me.*
ⲘⲘⲞⲔ	ⲘⲘⲞⲔ	ⲘⲘⲞⲔ	*thee*, m.
ⲘⲘⲞ	ⲘⲘⲞ		*thee*, f.
ⲘⲘⲞϥ	ⲘⲘⲞϥ	ⲘⲘⲀϥ	*him.*
ⲘⲘⲞⲤ	ⲘⲘⲞⲤ	ⲘⲘⲀⲤ	*her.*

Plural.

ⲘⲘⲞⲚ	ⲘⲘⲞⲚ	ⲘⲘⲀⲚ	*us.*
ⲘⲘⲰⲦⲈⲚ	ⲘⲘⲰⲦⲚ̄	ⲘⲘⲀⲦⲈⲚ	*you.*
ⲘⲘⲰⲞⲨ	ⲘⲘⲞⲞⲨ	ⲘⲘⲀⲨ	*them.*

ⲘⲘⲞ with other words sometimes expresses the various cases of the personal pronoun, as ⲚⲒⲘ ⲘⲘⲰⲞⲨ *some of them.* 1. Cor. X, 10. ⲈⲂⲞⲖ ⲘⲘⲞϥ, *from him.*

5. Another form of the accusative is ⲂⲎ, Copt. ⲈⲎ, Sah., which take Ⲧ with the suffixes.

Singular.

Coptic.	Sahidic.
ⲃⲏⲧ	ⲍⲏⲧ *my face, me.*
ⲃⲏⲧⲕ	ⲍⲏⲧⲕ *thee,* m.
ⲃⲏϯ	ⲍⲏⲧⲉ *thee,* f.
ⲃⲏⲧϥ	ⲍⲏⲧϥ *him.*
ⲃⲏⲧⲥ	ⲍⲏⲧⲥ *her.*

Plural.

ⲃⲏⲧⲉⲛ	ⲍⲏⲧⲛ̅ *us.*
ⲃⲏⲧⲟⲩ	ⲍⲏⲧⲟⲩ *them.*

6. The ablative case is formed by the following prepositions with the suffixes.

	Coptic.	Sahidic.	Bash.
ⲛ̀ⲧⲉ	ⲛ̀ⲧⲟⲧ	ⲛ̅ⲧⲟⲟⲧ	ⲛ̀ⲧⲁⲁⲧ
ⲉ̀ⲃⲟⲗ	ⲉ̀ⲃⲟⲗⲙ̀ⲙⲟ	ⲉ̅ⲃⲟⲗⲙ̅ⲙⲟ	ⲉ̀ⲃⲁⲗⲙ̀ⲙⲁ
	ⲉ̀ⲃⲟⲗⲛ̀ⲃⲏⲧ	ⲉ̅ⲃⲟⲗⲛ̅ⲍⲏⲧ	ⲉ̀ⲃⲁⲗⲛ̀ⲍⲏⲧ
ⲉ̀ⲃⲟⲗⲍⲁ	ⲉ̀ⲃⲟⲗⲍⲁⲣⲟ		
ⲉ̀ⲃⲟⲗⲍⲓ	ⲉ̀ⲃⲟⲗⲍⲓⲱⲧ	ⲉ̅ⲃⲟⲗⲍⲓⲱⲱ	
ⲉ̀ⲃⲟⲗⲍⲓⲧⲉⲛ	ⲉ̀ⲃⲟⲗⲍⲓⲧⲟⲧ	ⲉ̅ⲃⲟⲗⲍⲓⲧⲟⲟⲧ	ⲉ̀ⲃⲁⲗⲍⲓⲧⲁⲁⲧ
ⲉ̀ⲃⲟⲗⲍⲓⲭⲉⲛ	ⲉ̀ⲃⲟⲗⲍⲓⲭⲱ		
ⲍⲓⲧⲉⲛ	ⲍⲓⲧⲟⲧ	ⲍⲓⲧⲟⲟⲧ	ⲍⲓⲧⲁⲁⲧ &c.

Possessive Pronouns.

7. The possessive pronouns are sometimes expressed by the genitive personal pronouns, as ⲛ̀ⲧⲏⲓ, Copt. ⲛ̅ⲧⲁⲓ, Copt. ⲛ̀ⲧⲁⲕ, Copt. and Sah. ⲛ̀ⲧⲁϥ. Copt. and Sah. &c. yet they are formed of the definite article with ⲱ in the singular and ⲟⲩ in the plural, as

Sing. Masc.		Sing. Fem.	
Coptic.	Sahidic.	Coptic.	Sahidic.
ϥⲱⲓ	ⲡⲱⲓ *mine.*	ⲑⲱⲓ	ⲧⲱⲓ
ϥⲱⲕ	ⲡⲱⲕ *thine,* m.	ⲑⲱⲕ	ⲧⲱⲕ
ϥⲱ	ⲡⲱ *thine,* f.	ⲑⲱ	ⲧⲱ
ϥⲱϥ	ⲡⲱϥ *his.*	ⲑⲱϥ	ⲧⲱϥ
ϥⲱⲥ	ⲡⲱⲥ *her.*	ⲑⲱⲥ	ⲧⲱⲥ
ϥⲱⲛ	ⲡⲱⲛ *our.*	ⲑⲱⲛ	ⲧⲱⲛ
ϥⲱⲧⲉⲛ	ⲡⲱⲧⲛ̄ *your.*	ⲑⲱⲧⲉⲛ	ⲧⲱⲧⲛ̄
ϥⲱⲟⲩ	ⲡⲱⲟⲩ *their.*	ⲑⲱⲟⲩ	ⲧⲱⲟⲩ

Plural Common.

ⲛⲟⲩⲓ *mine.*

ⲛⲟⲩⲕ *thine,* m.

ⲛⲟⲩ *thine,* f.

ⲛⲟⲩϥ }
ⲛⲱϥ } *his.*

ⲛⲟⲩⲥ *her.*

ⲛⲟⲩⲛ *our.*

ⲛⲟⲩⲧⲉⲛ }
ⲛⲱⲧⲉⲛ } *your.*

ⲛⲟⲩⲟⲩ }
ⲛⲱⲟⲩ } *their.*

Demonstrative Pronouns.

Singular.

Masc.			Fem.		
Coptic.	Sahidic.	Bash.	Coptic.	Sahidic.	Bash.
ϥⲁⲓ	ⲡⲁⲓ	ⲡⲉⲓ	ⲑⲁⲓ	ⲧⲁⲓ	ⲧⲉⲓ *this.*

Plural.

Coptic and Sahidic.	Bashmuric.
ⲛⲁⲓ	ⲛⲉⲓ *these.*

Another form of the demonstrative pronoun is as follows.

Masc.		Fem.	
Coptic.	Sahidic.	Coptic.	Sahidic.
ⲫⲏ	ⲡⲏ *he.*	ⲑⲏ	ⲧⲏ *she.*

Plural.

ⲛⲏ *they.*

8. The demonstrative pronoun is often joined with the relative pronoun ⲉⲧ, as

Singular.

Masc.		Fem.	
Coptic.	Sahidic.	Coptic.	Sahidic.
ⲫⲏⲉⲧ	ⲡⲏⲉⲧ *he, who.*	ⲑⲏⲉⲧ	ⲧⲏⲉⲧ *she, who.*

Plural.

ⲛⲏⲉⲧ *they, who.*

ⲙ̀ⲙⲁⲩ is frequently united with the demonstrative and relative pronouns both singular and plural, as ⲫⲏ-ⲉ̀ⲧⲉⲙ̀ⲙⲁⲩ, *he.* Luke XXII, 12. Copt. ⲛⲓⲟⲩⲇⲁⲓ ⲉⲧϣⲟⲡ ⲙ̀ⲡⲓⲙⲁ ⲉ̀ⲧⲉⲙ̀ⲙⲁⲩ, *the jews dwelling in that place,* Acts XVI, 3. Copt. ϧⲉⲛ ϯⲟⲩⲛⲟⲩ ⲉ̀ⲧⲉⲙ̀ⲙⲁⲩ, *in that hour.* Copt. ⲟⲩⲟϩ ⲁ̀ ⲧⲉⲥⲥⲙⲏ ϣⲉⲛⲁⲥ ⲉ̀ⲃⲟⲗ ϩⲓϫⲉⲛ ⲡⲓⲕⲁϩⲓ ⲧⲏⲣϥ ⲉ̀ⲧⲉⲙⲙⲁⲩ, *and the fame of it went out through all that land.* Mat. IX, 26.

Relative Pronouns.

9. The relative pronoun is ⲉ. ⲉⲧ, ⲉⲧⲉ. or ⲉⲑ before the letters ⲙ, ⲛ and ⲟ in Copt.; and ⲉⲛⲧ. *qui, quae, quod,* and likewise ⲉ, ⲉⲧ, ⲉⲧⲉ, ⲛⲧ, in Sahidic and Bashmuric. ⲛ̀ⲛⲏ̀ⲧ ⲁⲩⲧⲁⲟⲅⲟⲛ, *to those who sent us.* John I, 22. ⲫⲏ̀ⲧ ⲥⲱⲧⲉⲙ ⲛ̀ⲥⲱⲧⲉⲛ, *he who heareth you.* ⲫⲏ̀ⲧ ϣⲱϣ ⲙ̀ⲙⲱⲧⲉⲛ, *he who despiseth you.* Luke X, 16.

10. The interrogative pronouns undergo no variation, which are these, ⲛⲓⲙ, *who?* ⲁϣ, ⲉϣ, *who? what?* ⲟⲩ, *who?* ⲟⲩⲏⲣ, *how many?*

Of Prepositions.

11. There are some substantives which are used as prepositions, as ⲣⲁⲧ Copt. ⲗⲉⲧ, Bash. *a foot.* ⲣⲟ, *a mouth.* ⲧⲟⲧ, *a hand.* ⲃⲏⲧ, *a neck.* ⲋⲏⲧ, *a heart.* ⲋⲣⲁ, *a face.* ⲭⲱ, *a head.* These, being united with some particles become prepositions, as ⲉ̀ⲣⲁⲧ *to me.* Mat. VI, 18. ⲃⲁⲣⲁⲧ, Copt. ⲋⲁⲣⲁⲧ, Sah. *under me.* Mat. VIII, 9. ⲉ̀ⲣⲟ, ⲃⲁⲣⲟ, *under thee.* Ezech. XXVII, 30. ⲃⲁⲣⲟϥ, *against him.* Ex. XVI, 8. ⲛ̀ⲧⲟⲧϥ *from him.* Deut. XV, 3. ⲛ̀ⲃⲏⲧⲟⲩ, *in them.* Psalm V, 10. ⲛⲋⲏⲧⲕ, Sah. *in thee.* Ezech. XXVIII, 15. ⲉ̀ⲋⲣⲁⲓ, *against me.* Ps. CI, 8. ⲉ̀ⲋⲣⲏⲓ ⲉ̀ⲭⲱⲓ, *against me.* Ps. III, 1. &c.

Prepositions.

ⲉ̀, acc., dat., *ad, in* &c.
ⲉ̀ⲃⲟⲗⲛ̀ⲃⲏⲧ, Copt. *from, e.r.* ⲉ̀ⲃⲟⲗⲛ̀ⲃⲏⲧϥ, ⲉ̀ⲃⲟⲗⲛ̀ⲃⲏⲧⲟⲩ &c.
ⲉⲃⲟⲗⲛ̄ⲋⲏⲧ, Sah. *from, e.r.* ⲉⲃⲟⲗⲛ̄ⲋⲏⲧϥ, ⲉⲃⲟⲗⲛ̄ⲋⲏⲧⲛ̄ &c.
ⲉ̀ⲃⲟⲗⲋⲁ, *from, ab, e.r.*

ⲉⲃⲟⲗϩⲁⲣⲟ, *a*, *ab*. ⲉ̀ⲃⲟⲗϩⲁⲣⲟϥ, ⲉ̀ⲃⲟⲗϩⲁⲣⲟⲛ &c.

ⲉⲃⲟⲗϩⲓⲧⲛ̄, Sah. *a*, *ab*.

ⲉⲃⲟⲗϩⲓⲧⲙ̄, Sah. *a*, *ab*.

ⲉ̀ⲃⲟⲗϩⲓⲧⲟⲧ, *per*, *a*, *ab*. ⲉ̀ⲃⲟⲗϩⲓⲧⲟⲧⲕ, ⲉ̀ⲃⲟⲗϩⲓⲧⲟⲧϥ, &c.

ⲉⲃⲟⲗϩⲓⲧⲟⲟⲧ, S. *per*, *a*, *ab*. ⲉⲃⲟⲗϩⲓⲧⲟⲟⲧⲕ, ⲉ̀ⲃⲟⲗϩⲓⲧⲟⲟⲧϥ.

ⲉ̀ϩⲟⲧⲉⲣⲟ, *supra*, *plus quam*. ⲉ̀ϩⲟⲧⲉⲣⲟⲕ, ⲉ̀ϩⲟⲧⲉⲣⲟϥ, &c.

ⲛ̇, acc., dat., *ad*, *ab*, *from*, &c.

ⲛ̇ⲧⲉⲛ, ⲛ̄ⲧⲛ̄, Sah. *from*.

ϣⲁ, *ad*, *usque ad*, ϣⲁⲣⲟⲓ, ϣⲁⲣⲟⲕ, ϣⲁⲗⲁⲕ, Bash. &c.

ⲃⲁ, Copt. *sub*, *contra*, ⲃⲁⲧⲟⲧⲕ. *apud te*, ⲃⲁⲧⲟⲧϥ, *apud eum*.

ϩⲁ, Sah. *sub*, *ad*, *pro*. ϩⲁⲧⲟⲧⲕ, etc.

ϩⲁⲧⲙ̄, Sah. *apud*, *ad*, &c.

ϩⲁⲧⲛ̄, Sah. *apud*, &c.

ϩⲓ, *in*, *cum*, ϩⲓⲧⲟⲧ, ϩⲓⲧⲟⲟⲧ, Sah. ϩⲓⲧⲟⲟⲧⲥ, Sah. &c.

To these may be added ⲁⲧⲟ̄ⲛⲉ, ⲉⲑⲃⲉ, ⲉⲧⲃⲉ, Sah.
ⲟⲩⲃⲉ, ⲟⲩⲧⲉ and others.

The Pronoun Infixes and Suffixes.

12. The pronoun infixes and suffixes are added to words, instead of the possessive and personal pronouns.

13. The pronoun infixes are inserted between the article and the noun, and used instead of the possessive pronouns. They are the following: ⲁ, *my*. ⲉⲕ, *thy*. ⲉ or ⲟⲩ, *thy*, f. ⲉϥ, *his*. ⲉⲥ, *her*. ⲉⲛ or ⲛ̄, *our*. ⲉⲧⲉⲛ or ⲉⲧⲛ̄ *your*. ⲟⲩ or ⲉⲩ, *their*.

An example of the infixes with the articles is here given.

The Infixes.

<table>
<tr><td colspan="2" align="center">Singular.</td><td align="center">Plural.</td></tr>
<tr><td>with artic. masc.</td><td>with artic. fem.</td><td></td></tr>
<tr><td>ⲡ-ⲁ,</td><td>ⲧ-ⲁ,</td><td>ⲛ-ⲁ, my.</td></tr>
<tr><td>ⲡ-ⲉⲕ,</td><td>ⲧ-ⲉⲕ,</td><td>ⲛ-ⲉⲕ, thy, m.</td></tr>
<tr><td>ⲡ-ⲉ,</td><td>ⲧ-ⲉ,</td><td>ⲛ-ⲉ, thy, f.</td></tr>
<tr><td>ⲡ-ⲟⲩ,</td><td>ⲧ-ⲟⲩ,</td><td>ⲛ-ⲟⲩ, thy, f. Sah.</td></tr>
<tr><td>ⲡ-ⲉϥ,</td><td>ⲧ-ⲉϥ,</td><td>ⲛ-ⲉϥ, his.</td></tr>
<tr><td>ⲡ-ⲉⲥ,</td><td>ⲧ-ⲉⲥ,</td><td>ⲛ-ⲉⲥ, her.</td></tr>
<tr><td>ⲡ-ⲉⲛ,</td><td>ⲧ-ⲉⲛ,</td><td>ⲛ-ⲉⲛ, our.</td></tr>
<tr><td>ⲡ-ⲛ̄,</td><td>ⲧ-ⲛ̄,</td><td>ⲛ-ⲛ̄, our, Sah.</td></tr>
<tr><td>ⲡ-ⲉⲧⲉⲛ,</td><td>ⲧ-ⲉⲧⲉⲛ,</td><td>ⲛ-ⲉⲧⲉⲛ, your.</td></tr>
<tr><td>ⲡ-ⲉⲧⲛ̄,</td><td>ⲧ-ⲉⲧⲛ̄,</td><td>ⲛ-ⲉⲧⲛ̄, your.</td></tr>
<tr><td>ⲡ-ⲟⲩ,</td><td>ⲧ-ⲟⲩ,</td><td>ⲛ-ⲟⲩ, their.</td></tr>
<tr><td>ⲡ-ⲉⲩ,</td><td>ⲧ-ⲉⲩ,</td><td>ⲛ-ⲉⲩ, their, Sah.</td></tr>
</table>

ⲟⲩ is sometimes used for the infix of the second person feminine, instead of ⲉ in Coptic, but it seldom occurs.

14. The suffixes are used with words instead of the infixes, and are these which follow.

The Suffixes.

<table>
<tr><td align="center">Singular.</td><td align="center">Plural.</td></tr>
<tr><td>ⲓ or ⲧ, me, or my.</td><td>ⲛ or ⲉⲛ, us, or our.</td></tr>
<tr><td>ⲕ, thee, or thy, m.</td><td>ⲧⲉⲛ, you, or your.</td></tr>
<tr><td>ⲉ or ⲓ,*) thee, or thy, f.</td><td>ⲧⲛ̄, you, or your, Sah.</td></tr>
</table>

---

*) The ⲓ following ⲧ is changed into ϯ.

<table>
<tr><td>Singular.</td><td>Plural.</td></tr>
</table>

Ⲉ, *thee*, or *thy*, f.   ⲞⲨ. ⲀⲨ, *they*, or *their*.

ϥ, *him*, or *his*.   ⲈⲞⲨ or ⲎⲨ, *they*, or *their*, Sah.

ⲥ, *her*, or *hers*.

-A small number of words vary from the general rule.

The Infixes.

15. The infixes to nouns will be understood by the following examples.

ϣⲎⲣⲓ, *a son*, with the m. article, and infixes.

<table>
<tr><td>Singular.</td><td>Plural.</td></tr>
<tr><td>Artic. and Infixes to a noun masc.</td><td>Artic. and Infixes to a noun masc.</td></tr>
</table>

ⲠⲀ-ϣⲎⲣⲓ, *my son*.	ⲚⲀ-ϣⲎⲣⲓ, *my sons*.
ⲠⲈⲔ-ϣⲎⲣⲓ, *thy son*, m.	ⲚⲈⲔ-ϣⲎⲣⲓ, *thy sons*, m.
ⲠⲈ-ϣⲎⲣⲓ, *thy son*, f.	ⲚⲈ-ϣⲎⲣⲓ, *thy sons*, f.
ⲠⲞⲨ-ϣⲎⲣⲈ, *thy son*, f. Sah.	ⲚⲞⲨ-ϣⲎⲣⲈ, *thy sons*, f. Sah.
ⲠⲈϥ-ϣⲎⲣⲓ, *his son*.	ⲚⲈϥ-ϣⲎⲣⲓ, *his sons*.
ⲠⲈⲥ-ϣⲎⲣⲓ, *her son*.	ⲚⲈⲥ-ϣⲎⲣⲓ, *her sons*.
ⲠⲈⲚ-ϣⲎⲣⲓ, *our son*.	ⲚⲈⲚ-ϣⲎⲣⲓ, *our sons*.
ⲠⲚ̅-ϣⲎⲣⲈ, *our son*, Sah.	ⲚⲚ̅-ϣⲎⲣⲈ, *our sons*, Sah.
ⲠⲈⲦⲈⲚ-ϣⲎⲣⲓ, *your son*.	ⲚⲈⲦⲈⲚ-ϣⲎⲣⲓ, *your sons*.
ⲠⲈⲦⲚ̅-ϣⲎⲣⲈ, *your son*, Sah.	ⲚⲈⲦⲚ̅-ϣⲎⲣⲈ, *your sons*, Sah.
ⲠⲞⲨ-ϣⲎⲣⲓ, *their son*.	ⲚⲞⲨ-ϣⲎⲣⲓ, *their sons*.
ⲠⲈⲨ-ϣⲎⲣⲈ, *their son*, Sah.	ⲚⲈⲨ-ϣⲎⲣⲈ, *their sons*, Sah.

ⲤⲰⲚⲒ, *a sister*, with the fem. article and infixes.

<table>
<tr><td colspan="2" align="center">Singular.</td><td colspan="2" align="center">Plural.</td></tr>
<tr><td colspan="2">Artic. and Infixes to a noun fem.</td><td colspan="2">Artic. and Infixes to a noun fem.</td></tr>
</table>

ⲦⲀ-ⲤⲰⲚⲒ, *my sister*.	ⲚⲀ-ⲤⲰⲚⲒ, *my sisters*.
ⲦⲈⲔ-ⲤⲰⲚⲒ, *thy sister*, m.	ⲚⲈⲔ-ⲤⲰⲚⲒ, *thy sisters*, m.
ⲦⲈ-ⲤⲰⲚⲒ, *thy sister*, f.	ⲚⲈ-ⲤⲰⲚⲒ, *thy sisters*, f.
ⲦⲞⲨ-ⲤⲰⲚⲈ, *thy sister*, f. Sah.	ⲚⲞⲨ-ⲤⲰⲚⲈ, *thy sisters*, f. Sah.
ⲦⲈϥ-ⲤⲰⲚⲒ, *his sister*.	ⲚⲈϥ-ⲤⲰⲚⲒ, *his sisters*.
ⲦⲈⲤ-ⲤⲰⲚⲒ, *her sister*.	ⲚⲈⲤ-ⲤⲰⲚⲒ, *her sisters*.
ⲦⲈⲚ-ⲤⲰⲚⲒ, *our sister*.	ⲚⲈⲚ-ⲤⲰⲚⲒ, *our sisters*.
ⲦⲚ̄-ⲤⲰⲚⲈ, *our sister*, Sah.	ⲚⲚ̄-ⲤⲰⲚⲈ, *our sisters*, Sah.
ⲦⲈⲦⲈⲚ-ⲤⲰⲚⲒ, *your sister*.	ⲚⲈⲦⲈⲚ-ⲤⲰⲚⲒ, *your sisters*.
ⲦⲈⲦⲚ̄-ⲤⲰⲚⲈ, *your sister*, Sah.	ⲚⲈⲦⲚ̄-ⲤⲰⲚⲈ, *your sisters*, Sah.
ⲦⲞⲨ-ⲤⲰⲚⲒ, *their sister*.	ⲚⲞⲨ-ⲤⲰⲚⲒ, *their sisters*.
ⲦⲈⲨ-ⲤⲰⲚⲈ, *their sister*, Sah.	ⲚⲈⲨ-ⲤⲰⲚⲈ, *their sisters*, Sah.

16. It will be seen from the foregoing examples, that the *infixes* are the same to a masculine and feminine noun, singular and plural.

The Suffixes.

17. The following examples will show the position of the suffixes.

Adjectives with the Suffixes.

ⲈⲚⲈⲤⲈ or ⲚⲈⲤⲈ, *fair*.	ⲦⲎⲢ. *all*.
ⲈⲚⲈⲤⲰⲒ. *fair*, *I*.	ⲦⲎⲢⲔ, *all*, *thou*, m.
ⲈⲚⲈⲤⲰⲔ. *fair*, *thou*, m.	ⲦⲎⲢⲔ̄, *all*, *thou*, m. Sah.
ⲈⲚⲈⲤⲰϥ, *fair*, *he*.	ⲦⲎⲢϥ, *all*, *he*.
ⲈⲚⲈⲤⲰⲤ, *fair*, *she*.	ⲦⲎⲢⲤ, *all*, *she*.
ⲈⲚⲈⲤⲰⲚ, *fair*, *we*.	ⲦⲎⲢⲈⲚ, *all*, *we*.

ⲉⲛⲉⲥⲱⲟⲩ, *fair, they.*　　ⲧⲏⲣⲛ̄, *all, we,* Sah.

ⲉⲛⲉⲥⲟⲟⲩ, *fair, they,* Sah.　　ⲧⲏⲣⲧⲉⲛ, *all, ye.*

　　　　　　　　　　　　ⲧⲏⲣⲧⲛ̄, *all, ye,* Sah.

　　　　　　　　　　　　ⲧⲏⲣⲟⲩ, *all, they.*

ⲛⲁⲁ or ⲉⲛⲁⲁ, *great.*　　ⲛⲁⲛⲉ or ⲛⲁⲛⲟⲩ, *good.*

ⲛⲁⲁⲓ, *great, I.*　　ⲛⲁⲛⲟⲩⲓ, *good, I.*

ⲛⲁⲁⲕ, *great, thou,* m.　　ⲛⲁⲛⲉϥ, *good, he.*

ⲛⲁⲁϥ, *great, he.*　　ⲛⲁⲛⲉⲥ, *good, she.*

ⲛⲁⲁⲥ, *great, she.*　　ⲛⲁⲛⲉⲩ, *good, they.*

ⲛⲁⲁⲩ, *great, they.*

ⲙⲁⲩⲁⲧ, *alone.* ⲙⲁⲩⲁⲧⲕ, *alone, thou,* m. ⲙⲁⲩⲁⲧ̄, *alone, thou,* f. ⲙⲁⲩⲁⲧϥ, *alone, he.* ⲙⲁⲩⲁⲧⲥ, *alone, she.* ⲙⲁⲩⲁⲧⲉⲛ, *alone, we.* ⲙⲁⲩⲁⲧⲉⲛⲑⲏⲛⲟⲩ, *alone, ye.* ⲙⲁⲩⲁⲧⲟⲩ, *alone, they.*

Prepositions with the Suffixes.

Coptic and Sahidic.	Bash.	
ⲉⲣⲁⲧ,	ⲉⲗⲉⲧ,	*to me.*
ⲉⲣⲁⲧⲕ,	ⲉⲗⲁⲧⲕ,	*to thee,* m.
ⲉⲣⲁⲧ̄,	ⲉⲗⲉⲧⲓ,	*to thee,* f.
ⲉⲣⲁⲧⲉ, ·		*to thee,* f. Sah.
ⲉⲣⲁⲧϥ,	ⲉⲗⲉⲧϥ,	*to him.*
ⲉⲣⲁⲧⲥ,	ⲉⲗⲉⲧⲥ,	*to her.*
ⲉⲣⲁⲧⲉⲛ,	ⲉⲗⲉⲧⲉⲛ,	*to us.*
ⲉⲣⲁⲧⲛ̄,		*to us,* Sah.
ⲉⲣⲁⲧⲉⲛⲑⲏⲛⲟⲩ,	ⲉⲗⲉⲧⲧⲏⲛⲟⲩ,	*to you.*
ⲉⲣⲁⲧⲧⲏⲩⲧⲛ̄,		*to you,* Sah.
ⲉⲣⲁⲧⲟⲩ,	ⲉⲗⲉⲧⲟⲩ,	*to them.*

Coptic.	Sahidic.
ⲈⲐⲂⲈ,	ⲈⲦⲂⲈ, *de, ob.*
ⲈⲐⲂⲎⲦ,	ⲈⲦⲂⲎⲎⲦ, *of me.*
ⲈⲐⲂⲎⲦⲔ,	ⲈⲦⲂⲎⲎⲦⲔ, *of thee,* m.
ⲈⲐⲂⲎ†,	ⲈⲦⲂⲎⲎⲦⲈ, *of thee,* f.
ⲈⲐⲂⲎⲦϥ,	ⲈⲦⲂⲎⲎⲦϥ, *of him.*
ⲈⲐⲂⲎⲦⲤ,	ⲈⲦⲂⲎⲎⲦⲤ, *of her.*
ⲈⲐⲂⲎⲦⲈⲚ,	ⲈⲦⲂⲎⲎⲦⲚ, *of us.*
ⲈⲐⲂⲈⲐⲎⲚⲞⲨ,	ⲈⲦⲂⲈⲐⲎⲨⲦⲚ, *of you.*
ⲈⲐⲂⲎⲦⲞⲨ,	ⲈⲦⲂⲎⲎⲦⲞⲨ, *of them.*

Coptic.	Sahidic.
ⲚⲈⲘ,	ⲚⲘ̄, *with.*

Coptic.	Sahidic.	Bashmuric.
ⲚⲈⲘⲎⲒ,	ⲚⲘ̄ⲘⲀⲒ, ⲘⲞⲒ,	ⲚⲈⲘⲎⲒ, *with me.*
ⲚⲈⲘⲀⲔ,	ⲚⲘ̄ⲘⲀⲔ,	*with thee,* m.
ⲚⲈⲘⲈ,	ⲚⲘ̄ⲘⲈ,	*with thee,* f.
ⲚⲈⲘⲀϥ,	ⲚⲘ̄ⲘⲀϥ, Oϥ,	ⲚⲈⲘⲎϥ, *with him.*
ⲚⲈⲘⲀⲤ,	ⲚⲘ̄ⲘⲀⲤ,	ⲚⲈⲘⲎⲤ, *with her.*
ⲚⲈⲘⲀⲚ,	ⲚⲘ̄ⲘⲀⲚ, ⲞⲚ,	*with us.*
ⲚⲈⲘⲰⲦⲈⲚ,	ⲚⲘ̄ⲘⲎⲦⲚ̄,	ⲚⲈⲘⲎⲦⲈⲚ, *with you.*
ⲚⲈⲘⲰⲞⲨ,	ⲚⲘ̄ⲘⲀⲨ,	ⲚⲈⲘⲎⲞⲨ, *with them.*

Ⲛ̀ⲤⲀ, *after.*

Ⲛ̀ⲤⲰⲒ, *after me.* Ⲛ̀ⲤⲰⲔ, *after thee,* m. Ⲛ̀ⲤⲰ, *after thee,* f. Ⲛ̀ⲤⲰϥ, *after him.* Ⲛ̀ⲤⲰⲤ, *after her.* Ⲛ̀ⲤⲰⲚ, *after us.* ⲚⲤⲰ-ⲦⲈⲚ, Ⲛ̄ⲤⲰⲦⲚ̄, *after you,* S. Ⲛ̀ⲤⲰⲞⲨ, *after them.*

Of Numbers.

18. The Coptic Numbers are generally expressed by the letters of the Alphabet with a line above them,

as ⲅ̄ ⲛ̀ⲉⲅⲟⲟⲩ, *three days.* Matt. XII, 40. ⲇ̄ ⲛ̀ⲁ̀ⲃⲟⲧ, *four months.* John IV, 35; sometimes they are expressed by words, as ⲫⲧⲟⲩ-ⲫⲟⲟⲩ, *four days.* Acts V, 30. But the Sahidic numbers are usually expressed by words.

19. Numbers admit the articles, and are also found without them, as ⲡⲓⲓ̄ⲃ̄, *the twelve.* Matt. X, 2. 5. ⲡⲓⲥⲛⲁⲩ, *the two.* Deut. XVII, 6. ⲱⲑⲏⲛ ⲥⲛⲟⲩⲧ̄, *two tunics.* Luke III, 11.

The Cardinal Numbers.

	Coptic.		Sahidic.	
	Masc.	Fem.	Masc.	Fem.
ⲁ̄	ⲟⲩⲁⲓ,	ⲟⲩⲉ,	ⲟⲩⲁ,	ⲟⲩⲉⲓ,
	ⲟⲩⲱⲧ		ⲟⲩⲱⲧ	
ⲃ̄	ⲥⲛⲁⲩ,	ⲥⲛⲟⲩⲧ̄,	ⲥⲛⲁⲩ,	ⲥⲉⲛⲧⲉ, ⲥⲛ̄ⲧⲉ,
ⲅ̄	ⲱⲟⲙⲧ,	ⲱⲟⲙⲧ̄,	ⲱⲟⲙⲛ̄ⲧ, ⲱⲙ̄ⲛⲧ, ⲱⲟⲙⲧⲉ,
ⲇ̄	ⲫⲧⲱⲟⲩ, ·	ⲫⲧⲟⲉ,	ⲫⲧⲟⲟⲩ,	ⲫⲧⲟⲉ, ⲫⲧⲟ,
ⲉ̄	ⲧ̄ⲟⲩ,	ⲧ̄ⲉ, ⲧ̄,	ⲧ̄ⲟⲩ,	ⲧ̄ⲉ,
ⲋ̄	ⲥⲟⲟⲩ,	ⲥⲟ,	ⲥⲟⲟⲩ,	ⲥⲟⲟ, ⲥⲟⲉ,
ⲍ̄	ⲱⲁⲱϥ,	ⲱⲁⲱϥⲓ,	ⲥⲁⲱϥ, ⲥⲉⲱϥ, ⲥⲁⲱϥⲉ,
ⲏ̄	ⲱⲙⲏⲛ,	ⲱⲙⲏⲛⲓ,	ⲱⲙⲟⲩⲛ, ⲱⲙⲟⲩⲛⲉ,
ⲑ̄	ⲯⲓⲧ,	ⲯⲓⲧ̄,	ⲯⲓⲧ,	ⲡⲥⲓⲧⲉ,
ⲓ̄	ⲙⲉⲧ,	ⲙⲏⲧ̄,	ⲙⲏⲧ,	ⲙⲏⲧⲉ,
ⲕ̄	ⲭⲱⲧ,	ⲭⲟⲩⲱⲧ,	ⲭⲟⲩⲱⲧ,	ⲭⲟⲩⲱⲧⲉ,
ⲗ̄	ⲙⲁⲡ,		ⲙⲁⲁⲃ, ⲙⲁⲃ, ⲙⲁⲁⲃⲉ,
ⲙ̄	ⲥⲙⲉ,		ⲥⲙⲉ,	ⲥⲙⲏ,
ⲛ̄	ⲧⲁⲓⲟⲩ,		ⲧⲁⲓⲟ,	
ⲍ̄	ⲥⲉ,		ⲥⲉ,	

6

	Coptic.		Sahidic.	
	Masc.	Fem.	Masc.	Fem.
ⲟ̄	ⲱⲃⲉ		ⲱⲃⲉ, ⲱϥⲉ,	
ⲡ̄	ⳉⲁⲙⲛⲉ,		ⲥⲙⲉⲛⲉ,	
ϥ	ⲡⲓⲥⲧⲁⲩ,	ⲡⲓⲥⲧⲉⲟⲩⲓ.	ⲡⲥ̄ⲧⲁⲓⲟⲩ, ⲡⲉⲥⲧⲁⲓⲟⲩ,	
ⲣ̄	ⲱⲉ,		ⲱⲉ,	
ⲥ̄	ⲥⲛⲁⲩⲛ̀ⲱⲉ,	ⲥⲛⲁⲩⲱⲉ,	ⲱⲏⲧ,	
ⲧ̄	ⲱⲟⲙⲧⲛ̀ⲱⲉ,		ⲱⲙ̄ⲛⲧⲱⲉ, ⲱⲙ̄ⲧⲱⲉ, ⲱⲟⲙⲉⲧⲱⲉ,	
ⲩ̄	ϥⲧⲟⲟⲩⲛ̀ⲱⲉ,		ϥⲧⲟⲟⲩⲱⲉ, ϥⲧⲟⲩⲱⲉ, ϥⲧⲉⲩⲱⲉ,	
ⲫ̄	ϯⲟⲩⲛ̀ⲱⲉ,	ϯⲟⲩⲱⲉ,	ϯⲟⲩⲛ̄ⲱⲉ.	
ⲭ̄	ⲥⲟⲟⲩⲛ̀ⲱⲉ,	ⲥⲟⲟⲩⲱⲉ,	ⲥⲟⲟⲩⲛ̄ⲱⲉ, ⲥⲉⲩⲱⲉ,	
ⲯ̄	ⲱⲁⲱϥⲛ̀ⲱⲉ,		ⲥⲁⲱϥⲛ̄ⲱⲉ,	
ⲱ̄	ⲱⲙⲏⲛⲛ̀ⲱⲉ,		ⲱⲙⲟⲩⲛⲱⲉ,	
ⳇ			ⲯⲓⲥⲛ̄ⲱⲉ,	
ⲁ̿	ⲱⲟ,		ⲱⲟ,	
ⲃ̿	ⲱⲟⲥⲛⲁⲩ,		ⲥⲛⲁⲩⲛ̄ⲱⲟ.	
ⲧ̿	ⲑⲃⲁ.		ⲧⲃⲁ.	

20. The following numbers are prefixes to nouns, viz.
ⲱⲙ̄ⲛⲧ, ⲱⲙ̄ⲧ, ⲱⲟⲙⲧ, *three,* Sah. ⲱⲙ̄ⲧⲱⲟ, *three thousand.*
ϥⲧⲉ, Copt. ϥⲧⲟⲩ, ϥⲧⲉⲩ, Sah. *four.* ⲥⲉⲩ, Sah. *six.* ⲙⲏⲧ,
Sah. *ten.* ϫⲟⲩⲧ, Sah. *twenty.*

The following are suffixes to numbers: ⲟⲩⲉ, Sah.
one. ⲙⲛ̄ⲧⲟⲩⲉ, *eleven.* ⲥⲛⲟⲟⲩⲥ, ⲥⲛⲟⲩⲥ, m. ⲥⲛⲟⲟⲩⲥⲉ.
ⲥⲛⲟⲩⲉ, f. Sah. *two.* ⲙⲛ̄ⲧⲥⲛⲟⲟⲩⲥ, *twelve.* ⲱⲟⲙⲧ, Sahidic.
three. ⲧⲁϥⲧⲉ, ⲁϥⲧⲉ, Sah. *four.* ⲧⲏ, ⲧⲉ, Sah. *five.* ⲧⲁⲥⲉ,
ⲁⲥⲉ, Sah. *six.* ⲱⲙⲏⲛ, Copt. ⲱⲙⲏⲛⲉ, f. Sah. *eight.* ⲙ̄ⲛⲧⲟⲩⲉ.

The Bashmuric has the following variations, ⲟⲩⲉⲉⲓ,
m. ⲟⲩⲉⲓ. f. *one.* ⲱⲁⲙⲉⲛⲧ, *three.* ⲱⲁ, *a thousand.*

The Ordinal Numbers.

21. The *first*, in ordinal numbers is expressed differently from the others; as

Copt.		Sahidic.		Bash.	
Masc.	Fem.	Masc.	Fem.	Masc.	Fem.
ⲍⲟⲩⲓⲧ,	ⲍⲟⲩⲓⲧ,	ϣⲟⲣⲡ,	ϣⲟⲣⲡⲓ,	ϣⲁⲣⲉⲡ.	ϣⲁⲣⲡⲓ, *first*.
ϣⲟⲣⲡ,	ϣⲱⲣⲡ,				
ϣⲉⲣⲡ.					

22. The remaining cardinals are formed by putting ⲙⲁⲍ Copt. and ⲙⲉⲍ Sah. and Bash. before the cardinal numbers, as ⲡⲓⲙⲏⲓⲛⲓ ⲙ̄ⲙⲁⲍⲃ̄, *the second miracle.* John IV, 54. Copt. ⲡⲙⲉⲍ ϣⲟⲙⲛ̄ⲧ, *the third.* Matt. XXII, 26. Sah. ⲃⲉⲛ ⲧⲙⲁⲍ ⲥⲛⲟⲩⲧ ⲛ̄ⲣⲟⲙⲡⲓ, *in anno secundo,* Dan. II, 1. Coptic. ⲧⲙⲉⲍ ⲥⲛ̄ⲧⲉ, *the second,* f. Luke XII, 38. Sahidic.

ⲥⲟⲩ is used instead of ⲙⲁⲍ and ⲙⲉⲍ with the cardinal numbers when the days of the month are spoken of, as ⲥⲟⲩⲕ̄ⲉ ⲛ̄ⲁⲑⲱⲣ, *the twenty fifth day of Athor.* Exod. XII, 3. Copt. ⲛ̄ⲥⲟⲩⲕ̄ⲍ ⲙ̄ⲡⲓⲁⲃⲟⲧ, *the twenty seventh day of the month.* Gen. VIII, 4. ⲥⲟⲩⲝⲟⲩⲧ ⲯⲓⲥ ⲛ̄ⲍⲁⲑⲱⲣ. *the twenty ninth day of the month Athor.* Zoeg. Sah.

ⲁⲝⲡ Copt. and ⲝ̄ⲡ, Sah. occur with the cardinal numbers when hours are spoken of, as ⲛ̄ⲁⲝⲡ ⲑ̄ ⲙ̄ⲡⲓⲉⲍⲟⲟⲩ, *the ninth hour of the day.* Acts X, 3. ⲛ̄ⲡⲛⲁⲩ ⲛ̄ⲝ̄ⲡ ⲥⲟⲉ, *about the sixth hour.* Sah. Matt. XX, 5.

ⲣⲉ, Copt. and Sah. *part,* is used with numbers, as ⲡⲓⲣⲉ ⲉ̄, *the fifth part.* Gen. XLI, 34. ⲟⲩⲟⲍ ⲁϥⲣⲱⲕⲍ

ⲚϪⲈ ⲪⲢⲈ Ⲅ̅ ⲚⲚⲓϢϢⲎⲚ, *and the third part of the trees was burnt up.* Rev. VIII, 7. ⲠⲢⲈϢⲞⲘⲚⲦ, *the third part,* Numb. XXVIII, 5. Sah. The Copt. has also ⲦⲈⲢⲈ, or ⲦⲈⲢ, and the Sah. ⲦⲢⲈ. *part.*

ⲞⲨⲰⲚ, more often ⲞⲨⲚ̅, and sometimes ⲞⲨⲈⲚ, and ⲞⲨⲚⲈ, Sah. *a part*, is put before numbers, as ⲞⲨⲰⲚ ⲀⲨⲀⲀϤ ⲚϤⲦⲞⲞⲨ Ⲛ̅ⲞⲨⲰⲚ, ⲞⲨⲞⲨⲰⲚ Ⲙ̅ⲠⲞⲨⲀ ⲠⲞⲨⲀ, *they made four parts, a part to each one,* John XIX, 23. Sah. ⲠⲞⲨⲚ̅ Ⲛ̅ϤⲦⲞⲞⲨ, *fourth part,* Ezech. V, 2. Sah. ⲠⲞⲨⲈⲚ Ⲛ̅ⲦⲞⲨ, *the fifth part,* Zoeg. Sah. ⲠⲞⲨⲚⲈ ϢⲞⲘⲚ̅Ⲧ, *the third part,* Tukius.

ⲠⲈϤ Copt. and Sah. is prefixed to numbers signifying days, as ⲠⲈϤϤⲦⲞⲞⲨ ⲄⲀⲢ ⲠⲈ. *for it is four days.* John XI, 39. ⲈⲠⲈϤϤⲦⲞⲞⲨ ⲠⲈ ⲈⲨ Ⲉ̅Ⲙ̅ ⲦⲒⲦⲀⲪⲞⲤ, *it is four days he is in the sepulchre.* v. 17. Sah.

  Ⲁ, et ⲚⲀ *about.* Copt. and Sah. as ⲀϤⲦⲞⲨ ϢⲈ Ⲛ̅ⲢⲰⲘⲈ, *about four hundred men,* Acts V, 36. Sah. ⲚⲀ ϤⲦⲞⲨ ϢⲈ ⲦⲀⲒⲞⲨ Ⲛ̅ⲢⲞⲘⲠⲈ, *about four hundred and fifty years.* Acts XIII, 20. Sah.

  The plural of number is occasionally expressed by repeating the number, as, ⲔⲀⲦⲀ Ⲣ̅Ⲣ̅ ⲚⲈⲘ ⲔⲀⲦⲀ Ⲛ̅Ⲛ̅, *by hundreds, and by fifties.* Mark VI, 40.

CHAP. VII.

Of Verbs.

23. Egyptian verbs have no passive voice differing from the active, but the passive may be known thus, ⲀⲤ-ⲐⲀⲘⲒⲞ ⲚⲬⲈ Ⲧ-ⲤⲞⲫⲒⲀ ⲈⲂⲞⲖⲂⲈⲚ ⲚⲈⲤ-ⲄⲂⲎⲞⲨⲒ, *wisdom is justified of her works*, Matt. XI, 19. ⲞⲨⲞⲄ ⲀⲨⲞⲨⲰⲚ ⲚⲬⲈ ⲚⲈϤ-ⲤⲰⲦⲈⲘ, *and his ears were opened*, Mark VII, 35.

24. The passive is more commonly expressed by the verb in the third person plural of the verb active, as ⲠⲈⲚ-ⲢⲰⲘⲒ ⲚⲀⲠⲀⲤ ⲀⲨⲀϢϤ ⲚⲈⲘⲀϤ, *our old man was crucified with him*. Rom. VI, 6. ⲈⲨⲚⲀⲠⲰⲚⲄ ⲈⲂⲞⲖ ⲘⲠⲈⲤ-ⲚⲞϤ ⲚⲦⲈ ⲤⲦⲈⲫⲀⲚⲞⲤ, *the blood of Stephen was shed.* Acts XXII, 20. Sah. ⲞⲨⲞⲄ ⲞⲨⲘⲎⲒⲚⲒ ⲚⲚⲞⲨⲦⲎⲒϤ, *and no sign shall be given.* Matt. XII, 39. ⲀⲨ-ⲔⲞⲤⲈⲚ ⲚⲈⲘⲀϤ, *we are buried with him.* Rom. VI, 4.

25. But sometimes the passive voice can only be discovered by the sense of the passage read. But see further on verbs passive.

The Prefixes and Suffixes to Verbs.

	The Prefixes.		The Suffixes.
Person.	Coptic.	Sahidic.	
1.	Ⲧ	Ⲧ	ⲓ
2. m.	Ⲕ, Ⲭ	Ⲕ	Ⲕ
2. f.	ⲦⲈ	ⲦⲈ	Ⲉ

Person.	The Prefixes.		The Affixes.
	Coptic.	Sahidic.	
3. m.	ϥ	ϥ	ϥ
3. f.	c	c	c
1. plur.	ⲧⲉⲛ	ⲧⲛ̄, ⲧⲉⲛ	ⲛ
2.	ⲧⲉⲧⲉⲛ	ⲧⲉⲧⲛ̄, ⲧⲉⲧⲉⲛ	ⲧⲉⲛ
3.	ⲥⲉ	ⲥⲉ	ⲩ

Indicative Mood.

The 1st Present Tense.

Singular.

Coptic.	Sahidic.
ϯ	ϯ, *I do*, or *am doing*.
ⲕ, ⲝ	ⲕ, *thou art*, m.
ⲧⲉ	ⲧⲉ, *thou art*, f
ϥ	ϥ, *he is*.
ⲥ	ⲥ, *she is*.

Plural.

ⲧⲉⲛ	ⲧⲛ̄, ⲧⲉⲛ, *we are*.
ⲧⲉⲧⲉⲛ	ⲧⲉⲧⲛ̄, ⲧⲉⲧⲉⲛ, *ye are*.
ⲥⲉ	ⲥⲉ, *they are*.

The 2nd Present Tense.

Singular.

Coptic.	Sahidic.	Bash.
ⲉⲓ	ⲉⲓ	ⲉⲓ, *I am*, ⲟⲩⲣ.
ⲉⲕ	ⲉⲕ	ⲉⲕ, *thou art*, ⲃⲓ.

Coptic.	Sahidic.	Bash.
ⲉⲣⲉ	ⲉⲣⲉ	ⲉⲗⲉ; *thou art*, f.
ⲉϥ⎱ ⲉⲣⲉ	ⲉϥ⎱ ⲉⲣⲉ	ⲉϥ⎱ ⲉⲗⲉ. *he is.* *he* and *she.* *is.*
ⲉⲥ⎰	ⲉⲥ⎰	ⲉⲥ⎰

Plural.

| ⲉⲛ | ⲛ̄, ⲉⲛ | ⲉⲛ, *we are.* |
| ⲉⲧⲉⲧⲉⲛ | ⲉⲧⲉⲧⲛ̄ | ⲉⲧⲉⲧⲉⲛ, *ye are.* |

ⲉⲩ, ⲟⲩ, ⲉⲣⲉ   ⲉⲩ, ⲟⲩ, ⲉⲣⲉ   ⲉⲩ, ⲟⲩ ⲉⲗⲉ, *they are.*

The Imperfect Tense.

Singular.

Coptic.	Sahidic.	Bash.
ⲛⲁⲓ ⲡⲉ	ⲛⲉⲓ ⲡⲉ	ⲛⲁⲓ ⲡⲉ, *I was.*
ⲛⲁⲕ ⲡⲉ	ⲛⲉⲕ ⲡⲉ	ⲛⲁⲕ ⲡⲉ, *thou*, m.
ⲛⲁⲣⲉ ⲡⲉ	ⲛⲉⲣⲉ ⲡⲉ	ⲛⲁⲣⲉ ⲡⲉ; *thou*, f. *he.*
ⲛⲁϥ ⲡⲉ⎱ ⲛⲁⲣⲉ	ⲛⲉϥ ⲡⲉ⎱ ⲛⲉⲣⲉ	ⲛⲁϥ ⲡⲉ⎱ ⲛⲁⲣⲉ *he* and *she.*
ⲛⲁⲥ ⲡⲉ⎰ ⲡⲉ	ⲛⲉⲥ ⲡⲉ⎰ ⲡⲉ	ⲛⲁⲥ ⲡⲉ⎰ ⲡⲉ; *is.*

Plural.

| ⲛⲁⲛ ⲡⲉ | ⲛⲉⲛ ⲡⲉ | ⲛⲁⲛ ⲡⲉ, *we were.* |
| ⲛⲁⲣⲉⲧⲉⲛ ⲡⲉ | ⲛⲉⲧⲉⲧⲛ̄ ⲡⲉ | ⲛⲁⲣⲉⲧⲉⲛ ⲡⲉ, *ye.* |

ⲛⲁⲩ ⲡⲉ, ⲛⲁⲣⲉⲡⲉ   ⲛⲉⲩ ⲡⲉ, ⲛⲉⲣⲉⲡⲉ   ⲛⲁⲩⲡⲉ, ⲛⲁⲣⲉ ⲡⲉ, *they.*

The 1st Perfect Tense.

Singular.

Coptic.	Sahidic.	Bash.
ⲁⲓ	ⲁⲓ	ⲁⲓ; *I have.*
ⲁⲕ	ⲁⲕ	ⲁⲕ, *thou hast*, m.
ⲁⲣⲉ	ⲁⲣⲉ	ⲁⲣⲉ, *thou hast*, f.
ⲁϥ⎱ ⲁ̀	ⲁϥ⎱ ⲁ̀	ⲁϥ⎱ ⲁ̀ *he hath.* *he* and *she.*
ⲁⲥ⎰	ⲁⲥ⎰	ⲁⲥ⎰ *hath.*

Plural.

Coptic.	Sahidic.	Bash.
ⲁⲛ	ⲁⲛ	ⲁⲛ, *we have.*
ⲁⲡⲉⲧⲉⲛ	ⲁⲧⲉⲧⲛ̅	ⲁⲧⲉⲧⲛ̅, *ye have.*
ⲁⲩ, ⲁ̀	ⲁⲩ, ⲁ̀	ⲁⲩ, ⲁ̀, *they have.*

The 2nd Perfect Tense.

Singular.

Coptic.		Sahidic.		Bash.	
ⲉ̀ⲧⲁⲓ,		ⲛ̅ⲧⲁⲓ,		ⲉⲧⲁⲓ, *I have.*	
ⲉ̀ⲧⲁⲕ,		ⲛ̅ⲧⲁⲕ,		ⲉⲧⲁⲕ, *thou hast,* m.	
ⲉ̀ⲧⲁⲣⲉ,		ⲛ̅ⲧⲁⲣ,		ⲉⲧⲁⲣⲉ, *thou hast,* f.	
ⲉ̀ⲧⲁϥ,} ⲉⲧⲁ̀,		ⲛ̅ⲧⲁϥ,} ⲛ̅ⲧⲁ,		ⲉⲧⲁϥ,}	*he hath.*
ⲉ̀ⲧⲁⲥ,}		ⲛ̅ⲧⲁⲥ,}		ⲉⲧⲁⲥ,} ⲉ̀ⲧⲁ, *he a. she. hath.*	

Plural.

Coptic.		Sahidic.		Bash.
ⲉ̀ⲧⲁⲛ,		ⲛ̅ⲧⲁⲛ,		ⲉⲧⲁⲛ, *we have.*
ⲉ̀ⲧⲁⲡⲉⲧⲉⲛ,		ⲛ̅ⲧⲁⲧⲉⲧⲛ̅,		ⲉⲧⲁⲡⲉⲧⲉⲛ, *ye have.*
ⲉ̀ⲧⲁⲩ, ⲉⲧⲁ,		ⲛ̅ⲧⲁⲩ, ⲛ̅ⲧⲁ,		ⲉⲧⲁⲩ, ⲉⲧⲁ, *they have.*

The Pluperfect Tense.

Singular.

Coptic.	Sahidic and Bash.	
ⲛⲉ ⲁⲓ ⲡⲉ,	ⲛⲉ ⲁⲓ ⲡⲉ, *I had.*	
ⲛⲉ ⲁⲕ ⲡⲉ,	ⲛⲉ ⲁⲕ ⲡⲉ, *thou,* m.	
ⲛⲉ ⲁⲣⲉ ⲡⲉ,	ⲛⲉ ⲁⲣⲉ ⲡⲉ, *thou,* f.	
ⲛⲉ ⲁϥ ⲡⲉ,}	ⲛⲉ ⲁϥ ⲡⲉ,}	*he.*
ⲛⲉ ⲁ̀ ⲡⲉ,}	ⲛⲉ ⲁ̀ ⲡⲉ,}	
ⲛⲉ ⲁⲥ ⲡⲉ,	ⲛⲉ ⲁⲥ ⲡⲉ, *she.*	
ⲛⲉ ⲁ̀ ⲡⲉ,}	ⲛⲉ ⲁ̀ ⲡⲉ,}	*he and she.*
ⲛⲉ ⲁⲡⲉ ⲡⲉ,}	ⲛⲉ ⲁⲡⲉ ⲡⲉ,}	

Plural.

Coptic.	Sahidic and Bash.
ⲚⲈ ⲀⲚ ⲠⲈ,	ⲚⲈ ⲀⲚ ⲠⲈ, *we.*
ⲚⲈ ⲀⲢⲈⲦⲈⲚ ⲠⲈ,	ⲚⲈ ⲀⲦⲈⲦⲚ̄ ⲠⲈ, *ye.*
ⲚⲈ ⲀⲨ ⲠⲈ,	ⲚⲈ ⲀⲨ ⲠⲈ, *they.*

The Present Tense Indefinite.

Singular.

Coptic.	Sahidic.	Bash.
ⲱⲀⲒ,	ⲱⲀⲒ,	ⲱⲀⲒ, *I am.*
ⲱⲀⲔ,	ⲱⲀⲔ,	ⲱⲀⲔ, *thou,* m.
ⲱⲀⲢⲈ,	ⲱⲀⲢⲈ,	ⲱⲀⲖⲈ, *thou,* f.
ⲱⲀϥ,} ⲱⲀⲢⲈ,	ⲱⲀϥ,} ⲱⲀⲢⲈ,	ⲱⲀϥ,}ⲱⲀⲖⲈ, *he & she.* *he.* *she.*
ⲱⲀⲤ,}	ⲱⲀⲤ,}	ⲱⲀⲤ,}

Plural.

ⲱⲀⲚ,	ⲱⲀⲚ,	ⲱⲀⲚ, *we.*
ⲱⲀⲢⲈⲦⲈⲚ,	ⲱⲀⲦⲈⲦⲚ̄,	ⲱⲀⲦⲈⲦⲈⲚ, *ye.*
ⲱⲀⲨ, ⲱⲀⲢⲈ,	ⲱⲀⲨ, ⲱⲀⲢⲈ,	ⲱⲀⲨ, ⲱⲀⲖⲈ, *they.*

The Imperfect Tense Indefinite.

Singular.

Coptic.	Sahidic.
ⲚⲈ ⲱⲀⲒ ⲠⲈ,	ⲚⲈ ⲱⲀⲒ ⲠⲈ, *I was.*
ⲚⲈ ⲱⲀⲔ ⲠⲈ,	ⲚⲈ ⲱⲀⲔ ⲠⲈ, *thou,* m.
ⲚⲈ ⲱⲀⲢⲈ ⲠⲈ,	ⲚⲈ ⲱⲀⲢⲈ ⲠⲈ, *thou,* f.
ⲚⲈ ⲱⲀϥ ⲠⲈ,} ⲚⲈ ⲱⲀⲢⲈ ⲠⲈ,	ⲚⲈ ⲱⲀϥ ⲠⲈ,}ⲚⲈ ⲱⲀⲢⲈ ⲠⲈ, *he.* *he & she.* *she.*
ⲚⲈ ⲱⲀⲤ ⲠⲈ,}	ⲚⲈ ⲱⲀⲤ ⲠⲈ,}

7

Plural.

Coptic.	Sahidic.
ⲛⲉ ϣⲁⲛ ⲡⲉ,	ⲛⲉ ϣⲁⲛ ⲡⲉ, *we.*
ⲛⲉ ϣⲁⲣⲉⲧⲉⲛ ⲡⲉ,	ⲛⲉ ϣⲁⲧⲉⲧⲛ̅ ⲡⲉ, *ye.*

ⲛⲉ ϣⲁⲩ ⲡⲉ, ⲛⲉ ϣⲁⲣⲉ ⲡⲉ, ⲛⲉ ϣⲁⲩ ⲡⲉ, ⲛⲉ ϣⲁⲣⲉ ⲡⲉ, *they.*

Singular.

Bash.

ⲛⲉ ϣⲁⲓ ⲡⲉ, *I was.*

ⲛⲉ ϣⲁⲕ ⲡⲉ, *thou,* m.

ⲛⲉ ϣⲁⲗⲉ ⲡⲉ, *thou,* f.

ⲛⲉ ϣⲁϥ ⲡⲉ, ⎰ *he.*
ⲛⲉ ϣⲁⲥ ⲡⲉ, ⎱ ⲛⲉ ϣⲁⲗⲉ ⲡⲉ, *he* and *she.* *she.*

Plural.

ⲛⲉ ϣⲁⲛ ⲡⲉ, *we.*

ⲛⲉ ϣⲁⲧⲉⲧⲉⲛ ⲡⲉ, *ye.*

ⲛⲉ ϣⲁⲩ ⲡⲉ, ⎰
ⲛⲉ ϣⲁⲗⲉ ⲡⲉ, ⎱ *they.*

The 1st Future Tense.

Coptic.	Sahidic.	Bash.
ϯⲛⲁ,	ϯⲛⲁ,	ϯⲛⲉ, vel ⲁ, *I shall.*
ⲭⲛⲁ,	ⲕⲛⲁ,	ⲕⲛⲉ, *thou,* m.
ⲧⲉⲛⲁ,	ⲧⲉⲛⲁ,	*thou,* f.
ϥⲛⲁ,	ϥⲛⲁ,	ϥⲛⲉ, *he.*
ⲥⲛⲁ,	ⲥⲛⲁ,	ⲥⲛⲉ, *she.*

Plural.

ⲧⲉⲛⲛⲁ,	ⲧⲉⲛⲛⲁ, ⲧⲉⲛⲁ, ⲧⲉⲛⲛⲉ, vel ⲁ, *we.*	
ⲧⲉⲧⲉⲛⲛⲁ,	ⲧⲉⲧⲛ̅ⲛⲁ, ⲧⲉⲧⲛ̅ⲁ,	*ye.*
ⲥⲉⲛⲁ,	ⲥⲉⲛⲁ,	ⲥⲉⲛⲉ, *they.*

The 2nd Future Tense.

Singular.

Coptic.	Sahidic.	Bash.
ⲉⲓⲛⲁ,	ⲉⲓⲛⲁ,	ⲁⲓⲛⲁ vel ⲛⲉ, *I shall.*
ⲉⲕⲛⲁ,	ⲉⲕⲛⲁ,	ⲁⲕⲛⲁ, *thou,* m.
ⲉⲣⲉⲛⲁ,	ⲉⲣⲉⲛⲁ,	ⲁⲣⲉⲛⲁ, *thou,* f.

ⲉϥⲛⲁ,｝ ⲉⲣⲉ..ⲛⲁ, ⲉϥⲛⲁ,｝ ⲉⲣⲉ..ⲛⲁ, ⲁϥⲛⲁ,｝ⲁⲣⲉ..ⲛⲁ,*he &she.*
ⲉⲥⲛⲁ,｝ ⲉⲥⲛⲁ,｝ ⲁⲥⲛⲁ,｝ *he.* / *she.*

Plural.

ⲉⲛⲛⲁ,	ⲛ̄ⲛⲁ, ⲉⲛⲛⲁ,	ⲁⲛⲛⲁ, vel ⲛⲉ, *we.*
ⲉⲣⲉⲧⲉⲛⲛⲁ,	ⲉⲧⲉⲧⲛ̄ⲛⲁ, ⲉⲧⲉⲧⲛ̄ⲁ,	ⲁⲣⲉⲧⲉⲛⲛⲁ, *ye.*
ⲉⲩⲛⲁ, ⲟⲩⲛⲁ,	ⲉⲩⲛⲁ, ⲟⲩⲛⲁ,	ⲁⲩⲛⲁ, *they.*

The Prefixes Copt. are sometimes written ⲁⲓⲛⲁ, ⲁⲕⲛⲁ, ⲁⲣⲉⲛⲁ, etc.

The 3rd Future Tense.

Singular.

Coptic.	Sahidic.	Bash.
ⲉⲓⲉ̀,	ⲉⲓⲉ,	ⲉⲓⲉ, *I shall.*
ⲉⲕⲉ̀,	ⲉⲕⲉ,	ⲉⲕⲉ, *thou,* m.
ⲉⲣⲉ̀,	ⲉⲣⲉ,	ⲉⲣⲉ, *thou* f.

ⲉϥⲉ̀,｝ ⲉⲣⲉ̀, ⲉϥⲉ,｝ ⲉⲣⲉ, ⲉϥⲉ,｝ⲉⲣⲉ, *he* and *she.*
ⲉⲥⲉ̀,｝ ⲉⲥⲉ,｝ ⲉⲥⲉ,｝ *he.* / *she.*

Plural.

ⲉⲛⲉ̀,	ⲉⲛⲉ,	ⲉⲛⲉ, *we.*
ⲉⲣⲉⲧⲉⲛⲉ̀,	ⲉⲧⲉⲧⲛ̄ⲉ,	ⲉⲧⲉⲧⲛ̄ⲉ, *ye.*
ⲉⲩⲉ̀, ⲉⲣⲉ̀,	ⲉⲩⲉ, ⲉⲣⲉ,	ⲉⲩⲉ, ⲉⲣⲉ, *they.*

The 4th Future Tense.

Singular.

Coptic.	Sahidic.	Bash.
ⲧⲁ,	ⲧⲁ, ⲧⲁⲡⲓ,	ⲧⲁ, *I shall.*
	ⲧⲁⲡⲉⲕ,	*thou,* m.
ⲧⲉⲣⲁ,	ⲧⲉⲣⲁ,	ⲧⲉⲣⲁ, *thou,* f.
	ⲧⲁⲣⲉϥ,	*he.*
	ⲧⲁⲣⲉⲥ,	*she.*

Plural.

	ⲧⲁⲡⲛ̄,	*we.*
	ⲧⲁⲣⲉⲧⲛ̄,	ⲧⲁⲗⲉⲧⲉⲛ, *ye.*
	ⲧⲁⲣⲟⲩ,	*they.*

The Imperfect Tense.

Singular.

Coptic.	Sahidic.
ⲛⲁⲓⲛⲁ,	ⲛⲉⲓⲛⲁ, *I should.*
ⲛⲁⲕⲛⲁ,	ⲛⲉⲕⲛⲁ, *thou,* m.
ⲛⲁⲣⲉⲛⲁ,	ⲛⲉⲣⲉⲛⲁ, *thou,* f.
ⲛⲁϥⲛⲁ,⎱ ⲛⲁⲡⲉ..ⲛⲁ,	ⲛⲉϥⲛⲁ,⎱ ⲛⲉⲡⲉ..ⲛⲁ,*he&she.* *he.*
ⲛⲁⲥⲛⲁ,⎰	ⲛⲉⲥⲛⲁ,⎰ *she.*

Bash.

ⲛⲁⲓⲛⲉ vel ⲛⲁ, *I should.*

ⲛⲁⲕⲛⲉ, *thou,* m.

ⲛⲁⲣⲉⲛⲉ, *thou,* f.

ⲛⲁϥⲛⲉ,⎱ ⲛⲁⲡⲉ   *he.*
ⲛⲁⲥⲛⲉ,⎰ ..ⲛⲉ, *he & she.* *she.*

Plural.

Coptic.	Sahidic.
ⲚⲀⲚⲚⲀ ⲠⲈ,	ⲚⲈⲚⲚⲀ ⲠⲈ, *we.*
ⲚⲀⲢⲈⲦⲈⲚⲚⲀ ⲠⲈ,	ⲚⲈⲦⲈⲦⲚ̄Ⲁ ⲠⲈ, *ye.*

ⲚⲀⲨⲚⲀ, ⲚⲀⲢⲈ..ⲚⲀ ⲠⲈ, ⲚⲈⲨⲚⲀ, ⲚⲈⲢⲈ..ⲚⲀ ⲠⲈ, *they.*

Bash.

ⲚⲀⲚⲚⲈ ⲠⲈ, *we.*

ⲚⲀⲢⲈⲦⲈⲚⲚⲈ ⲠⲈ, *ye.*

ⲚⲈⲨⲚⲈ, ⲚⲀⲢⲈⲚⲈ ⲠⲈ, *they.*

The Subjunctive Mood.

Singular.

Coptic.	Sahidic.	Bash.
Ⲛ̄ⲦⲀ,	Ⲛ̄ⲦⲀ,	Ⲛ̄ⲦⲀ, *that I.*
Ⲛ̄ⲦⲈⲔ,	Ⲛ̄Ⲅ,	Ⲛ̄Ⲅ, *thou,* m.
Ⲛ̄ⲦⲈ,	Ⲛ̄ⲦⲈ,	Ⲛ̄ⲦⲈ, *thou,* f.
Ⲛ̄ⲦⲈϥ,} Ⲛ̄ⲦⲈ,	ⲚⲈϥ, Ⲛ̄ϥ,} Ⲛ̄ⲦⲈ,	ⲚⲈϥ, Ⲛ̄ϥ, }Ⲛ̄ⲦⲈ,*he & she.*
Ⲛ̄ⲦⲈⳅ,}	Ⲛ̄ⳅ, }	ⲚⲈⳅ, Ⲛ̄ⳅ,} *she.*

he.

Plural.

Ⲛ̄ⲦⲈⲚ,	Ⲛ̄ⲦⲚ̄,	Ⲛ̄ⲦⲚ̄, *we.*
Ⲛ̄ⲦⲈⲦⲈⲚ,	Ⲛ̄ⲦⲈⲦⲚ̄,	Ⲛ̄ⲦⲈⲦⲚ̄, *ye.*
Ⲛ̄ⲦⲞⲨ, Ⲛ̄ⲦⲈ,	Ⲛ̄ⳅⲈ, Ⲛ̄ⲦⲈ,	Ⲛ̄ⳅⲈ, ⲚⲦⲈ, *they.*

The Optative Mood.

Singular.

Coptic.	Sahidic.	Bash.
ⲙⲁⲣⲓ,	ⲙⲁⲣⲓ,	ⲙⲁⲗⲓ, *I may,*
ⲙⲁⲣⲉⲕ,	ⲙⲁⲣⲉⲕ,	ⲙⲁⲗⲉⲕ, *thou,* m.
ⲙⲁⲣⲉ,	ⲙⲁⲣⲉ,	ⲙⲁⲗⲉ, *thou,* f.

ⲙⲁⲣⲉϥ,
ⲙⲁⲣⲉⲥ, } ⲙⲁⲣⲉ,   ⲙⲁⲣⲉϥ,
ⲙⲁⲣⲉⲥ, } ⲙⲁⲣⲉ,   ⲙⲁⲗⲉϥ,
ⲙⲁⲗⲉⲥ, } ⲙⲁⲗⲉ, *he &she.*   *he.* *she.*

Plural.

ⲙⲁⲣⲉⲛ,	ⲙⲁⲣⲛ̄,	ⲙⲁⲗⲉⲛ, *we.*
ⲙⲁⲣⲉⲧⲉⲛ,	ⲙⲁⲣⲉⲧⲛ̄,	ⲙⲁⲗⲉⲧⲉⲛ, *ye.*
ⲙⲁⲣⲟⲩ, ⲙⲁⲣⲉ,	ⲙⲁⲣⲟⲩ, ⲙⲁⲣⲉ,	ⲙⲁⲗⲟⲩ, ⲙⲁⲗⲉ, *they.*

The Imperative Mood.

Singular and Plural.

ⲁ; ⲁⲣⲓ, or ⲙⲁ, or the root itself.

The Infinitive Mood.

ⲉ̀ or ⲛ̀ or the root itself.

Participles.

ⲡⲁϫⲓⲛ, ⲡⲉⲕϫⲓⲛ, ⲡⲉϥϫⲛ &c. or ⲡϫⲓⲛⲧⲁ, ⲡϫⲓⲛⲧⲉⲕ, ⲡϫⲓⲛⲧϥ &c.

The verb ⲧⲁⲕⲟ, *to destroy,* is given with the augments, to convey a more clear idea of their position.

Indicative Mood.
The 1st Present Tense.
Singular.

Coptic.   Sahidic.

ϯ-ⲧⲁⲕⲟ,   ϯ-ⲧⲁⲕⲟ, *I am destroying.*

ⲕ-ⲧⲁⲕⲟ, ⎱
           ⲕ-ⲧⲁⲕⲟ, *thou art destroying,* m.
ⲭ-ⲧⲁⲕⲟ, ⎰

ⲧⲉ-ⲧⲁⲕⲟ,   ⲧⲉ-ⲧⲁⲕⲟ, *thou art destroying,* f.

ϥ-ⲧⲁⲕⲟ,   ϥ-ⲧⲁⲕⲟ, *he is destroying:*

ⲥ-ⲧⲁⲕⲟ,   ⲥ-ⲧⲁⲕⲟ, *she is destroying.*

Plural.

Coptic.   Sahidic.

ⲧⲉⲛ-ⲧⲁⲕⲟ,   ⲧⲛ̄, or ⲧⲉⲛ-ⲧⲁⲕⲟ, *we are destroying.*

ⲧⲉⲧⲉⲛ-ⲧⲁⲕⲟ,   ⲧⲉⲧⲛ̄, or ⲧⲉⲧⲉⲛ-ⲧⲁⲕⲟ, *ye are destroying.*

ⲥⲉ-ⲧⲁⲕⲟ,   ⲥⲉ-ⲧⲁⲕⲟ, *they are destroying.*

The 2nd Present Tense.
Singular.

Coptic.   Sahidic.   Bashmuric.

ⲉⲓ-ⲧⲁⲕⲟ,   ⲉⲓ-ⲧⲁⲕⲟ,   ⲉⲓ-ⲧⲁⲕⲟ, *I am destroying,* ὤν.

ⲉⲕ-ⲧⲁⲕⲟ,   ⲉⲕ-ⲧⲁⲕⲟ,   ⲉⲕ-ⲧⲁⲕⲟ, *thou,* m.

ⲉⲣⲉ-ⲧⲁⲕⲟ,   ⲉⲣⲉ-ⲧⲁⲕⲟ,   ⲉⲗⲉ-ⲧⲁⲕⲟ, *thou,* f.

ⲉϥ- ⎱   ⲉϥ- ⎱   ⲉϥ- ⎱
    ⎰ ⲧⲁⲕⲟ,   ⎰ ⲧⲁⲕⲟ,   ⎰ ⲧⲁⲕⲟ, *he.*
ⲉⲣⲉ- ⎰   ⲉⲣⲉ- ⎰   ⲉⲗⲉ- ⎰

ⲉⲥ- ⎱   ⲉⲥ- ⎱   ⲉⲥ- ⎱
    ⎰ ⲧⲁⲕⲟ,   ⎰ ⲧⲁⲕⲟ,   ⎰ ⲧⲁⲕⲟ, *she.*
ⲉⲣⲉ- ⎰   ⲉⲣⲉ- ⎰   ⲉⲗⲉ- ⎰

Plural.

ⲉⲛ-ⲧⲁⲕⲟ,   ⲛ̄, or ⲉⲛ-ⲧⲁⲕⲟ, ⲉⲛ-ⲧⲁⲕⲟ, *we.*

ⲉⲧⲉⲧⲉⲛ-ⲧⲁⲕⲟ, ⲉⲧⲉⲧⲛ̄-ⲧⲁⲕⲟ, ⲉⲧⲉⲧⲉⲛ-ⲧⲁⲕⲟ, *ye.*

ⲉⲩ- ⎱   ⲉⲩ- ⎱   ⲉⲩ- ⎱
ⲟⲩ- ⎰ ⲧⲁⲕⲟ, ⲟⲩ- ⎰ ⲧⲁⲕⲟ, ⲟⲩ- ⎰ ⲧⲁⲕⲟ, *they.*
ⲉⲣⲉ- ⎰   ⲉⲣⲉ- ⎰   ⲉⲗⲉ- ⎰

The Imperfect Tense.

Singular.

Coptic.	Sahidic.	Bashmuric.
ⲚⲀⲒ-ⲦⲀⲔⲞ ⲠⲈ,	ⲚⲈⲒ-ⲦⲀⲔⲞ ⲠⲈ,	ⲚⲀⲒ-ⲦⲀⲔⲞ ⲠⲈ, *I was.*
ⲚⲀⲔ-ⲦⲀⲔⲞ ⲠⲈ,	ⲚⲈⲔ-ⲦⲀⲔⲞ ⲠⲈ,	ⲚⲀⲔ-ⲦⲀⲔⲞ ⲠⲈ, *thou,* m.
ⲚⲀⲢⲈ-ⲦⲀⲔⲞ ⲠⲈ,	ⲚⲈⲢⲈ-ⲦⲀⲔⲞ ⲠⲈ,	ⲚⲀⲢⲈ-ⲦⲀⲔⲞ ⲠⲈ, *thou,* f.

ⲚⲀϤ- } ⲦⲀⲔⲞ ⲠⲈ, ⲚⲈϤ- } ⲦⲀⲔⲞ ⲠⲈ, ⲚⲀϤ- } ⲦⲀⲔⲞ ⲠⲈ, *he.*
ⲚⲀⲢⲈ-}   ⲚⲈⲢⲈ-}   ⲚⲀⲢⲈ-}

ⲚⲀⲤ- } ⲦⲀⲔⲞ ⲠⲈ, ⲚⲈⲤ- } ⲦⲀⲔⲞ ⲠⲈ, ⲚⲀⲤ- } ⲦⲀⲔⲞ ⲠⲈ, *she.*
ⲚⲀⲢⲈ-}   ⲚⲈⲢⲈ-}   ⲚⲀⲢⲈ-}

Plural.

ⲚⲀⲚ-ⲦⲀⲔⲞ ⲠⲈ,	ⲚⲈⲚ-ⲦⲀⲔⲞ ⲠⲈ,	ⲚⲀⲚ-ⲦⲀⲔⲞ ⲠⲈ, *we.*
ⲚⲀⲢⲈⲦⲈⲚ-ⲦⲀⲔⲞ ⲠⲈ,	ⲚⲈⲦⲈⲦⲚ̄-ⲦⲀⲔⲞ ⲠⲈ,	ⲚⲀⲢⲈⲦⲈⲚ-ⲦⲀⲔⲞ ⲠⲈ, *ye.*

ⲚⲀⲨ- } ⲦⲀⲔⲞ ⲠⲈ, ⲚⲈⲨ- } ⲦⲀⲔⲞ ⲠⲈ, ⲚⲀⲨ- } ⲦⲀⲔⲞ ⲠⲈ, *they.*
ⲚⲀⲢⲈ-}   ⲚⲈⲢⲈ-}   ⲚⲀⲢⲈ-}

The 1st Perfect Tense.

Singular.

Coptic.	Sahidic.	Bashmuric.
ⲀⲒ-ⲦⲀⲔⲞ,	ⲀⲒ-ⲦⲀⲔⲞ,	ⲀⲒ-ⲦⲀⲔⲞ, *I have.*
ⲀⲔ-ⲦⲀⲔⲞ,	ⲀⲔ-ⲦⲀⲔⲞ,	ⲀⲔ-ⲦⲀⲔⲞ, *thou,* m.
ⲀⲢⲈ-ⲦⲀⲔⲞ,	ⲀⲢⲈ-ⲦⲀⲔⲞ,	ⲀⲢⲈ-ⲦⲀⲔⲞ, *thou,* f.

ⲀϤ- } ⲦⲀⲔⲞ, ⲀϤ- } ⲦⲀⲔⲞ, ⲀϤ- } ⲦⲀⲔⲞ, *he.*
Ⲁ̀- }   Ⲁ- }   Ⲁ- }

ⲀⲤ- } ⲦⲀⲔⲞ, ⲀⲤ- } ⲦⲀⲔⲞ, ⲀⲤ- } ⲦⲀⲔⲞ, *she.*
Ⲁ̀- }   Ⲁ- }   Ⲁ- }

Plural.

Coptic.	Sahidic.	Bashmuric.
ⲀⲚ-ⲦⲀⲔⲞ,	ⲀⲚ-ⲦⲀⲔⲞ,	ⲀⲚ-ⲦⲀⲔⲞ, *we.*
ⲀⲢⲈⲦⲈⲚ-ⲦⲀⲔⲞ,	ⲀⲦⲈⲦⲚ̄-ⲦⲀⲔⲞ,	ⲀⲦⲈⲦⲚ̄-ⲦⲀⲔⲞ, *ye.*

ⲀⲨ-) Ⲁ̀- } ⲦⲀⲔⲞ, ⲀⲨ-) Ⲁ- } ⲦⲀⲔⲞ, ⲀⲨ-) Ⲁ- } ⲦⲀⲔⲞ, *they.*

The 2nd Perfect Tense.

Singular.

Coptic.	Sahidic.	Bashmuric.
Ⲉ̀ⲦⲀⲒ-ⲦⲀⲔⲞ,	Ⲛ̄ⲦⲀⲒ-ⲦⲀⲔⲞ,	ⲈⲦⲀⲒ-ⲦⲀⲔⲞ, *I have.*
Ⲉ̀ⲦⲀⲔ-ⲦⲀⲔⲞ,	Ⲛ̄ⲦⲀⲔ-ⲦⲀⲔⲞ,	ⲈⲦⲀⲔ-ⲦⲀⲔⲞ, *thou,* m.
Ⲉ̀ⲦⲀⲢⲈ-ⲦⲀⲔⲞ,	Ⲛ̄ⲦⲀⲢ-ⲦⲀⲔⲞ,	ⲈⲦⲀⲢⲈ-ⲦⲀⲔⲞ, *thou,* f.

Ⲉ̀ⲦⲀϥ-) Ⲉ̀ⲦⲀ̀- } ⲦⲀⲔⲞ, Ⲛ̄ⲦⲀϥ-) Ⲛ̄ⲦⲀ- } ⲦⲀⲔⲞ, ⲈⲦⲀϥ-) ⲈⲦⲀ- } ⲦⲀⲔⲞ, *he.*

Ⲉ̀ⲦⲀⲤ-) Ⲉ̀ⲦⲀ̀- } ⲦⲀⲔⲞ, Ⲛ̄ⲦⲀⲤ-) Ⲛ̄ⲦⲀ- } ⲦⲀⲔⲞ, ⲈⲦⲀⲤ-) ⲈⲦⲀ- } ⲦⲀⲔⲞ, *she.*

Plural.

Ⲉ̀ⲦⲀⲚ-ⲦⲀⲔⲞ,	Ⲛ̄ⲦⲀⲚ-ⲦⲀⲔⲞ,	ⲈⲦⲀⲚ-ⲦⲀⲔⲞ, *we.*
Ⲉ̀ⲦⲀⲢⲈⲦⲈⲚ-ⲦⲀⲔⲞ,	Ⲛ̄ⲦⲀⲦⲈⲦⲚ̄-ⲦⲀⲔⲞ,	ⲈⲦⲀⲢⲈⲦⲈⲚ-ⲦⲀⲔⲞ, *ye.*

Ⲉ̀ⲦⲀⲨ-) Ⲉ̀ⲦⲀ̀- } ⲦⲀⲔⲞ, Ⲛ̄ⲦⲀⲨ-) Ⲛ̄ⲦⲀ- } ⲦⲀⲔⲞ, ⲈⲦⲀⲨ-) ⲈⲦⲀ- } ⲦⲀⲔⲞ, *they.*

The Pluperfect Tense.

Singular.

Coptic.	Sahidic.
ⲚⲈ ⲀⲒ-ⲦⲀⲔⲞ ⲠⲈ,	ⲚⲈ ⲀⲒ-ⲦⲀⲔⲞ ⲠⲈ, *I had.*
ⲚⲈ ⲀⲔ-ⲦⲀⲔⲞ ⲠⲈ,	ⲚⲈ ⲀⲔ-ⲦⲀⲔⲞ ⲠⲈ, *thou,* m.
ⲚⲈ ⲀⲢⲈ-ⲦⲀⲔⲞ ⲠⲈ,	ⲚⲈ ⲀⲢⲈ-ⲦⲀⲔⲞ ⲠⲈ, *thou,* f.

8

<table>
<tr><td colspan="2">Coptic.</td><td colspan="2">Sahidic.</td></tr>
</table>

Ⲛⲉ Ⲁϥ- ⎫
Ⲛⲉ ⲁ̀- ⎬ ⲧⲁⲕⲟ ⲡⲉ,   Ⲛⲉ Ⲁϥ- ⎫
     Ⲛⲉ ⲁ- ⎬ ⲧⲁⲕⲟ ⲡⲉ, *he.*

Ⲛⲉ Ⲁⲥ- ⎫
Ⲛⲉ ⲁ̀- ⎬ ⲧⲁⲕⲟ ⲡⲉ,   Ⲛⲉ Ⲁⲥ- ⎫
Ⲛⲉ ⲁⲣⲉ- ⎭   Ⲛⲉ ⲁ- ⎬ ⲧⲁⲕⲟ ⲡⲉ, *she.*
   Ⲛⲉ ⲁⲣⲉ- ⎭

Plural.

<table>
<tr><td>Coptic.</td><td>Sahidic.</td></tr>
<tr><td>Ⲛⲉ Ⲁⲛ-ⲧⲁⲕⲟ ⲡⲉ,</td><td>Ⲛⲉ Ⲁⲛ-ⲧⲁⲕⲟ ⲡⲉ, we.</td></tr>
<tr><td>Ⲛⲉ Ⲁⲣⲉⲧⲉⲛ-ⲧⲁⲕⲟ ⲡⲉ,</td><td>Ⲛⲉ Ⲁⲧⲉⲧⲛ̄-ⲧⲁⲕⲟ ⲡⲉ, ye.</td></tr>
<tr><td>Ⲛⲉ Ⲁⲩ-ⲧⲁⲕⲟ ⲡⲉ,</td><td>Ⲛⲉ Ⲁⲩ-ⲧⲁⲕⲟ ⲡⲉ, they.</td></tr>
</table>

The Present Tense Indefinite.

Singular.

<table>
<tr><td>Coptic.</td><td>Sahidic.</td><td>Bashmuric.</td></tr>
<tr><td>ϣⲁⲓ-ⲧⲁⲕⲟ,</td><td>ϣⲁⲓ-ⲧⲁⲕⲟ,</td><td>ϣⲁⲓ-ⲧⲁⲕⲟ, I am.</td></tr>
<tr><td>ϣⲁⲕ-ⲧⲁⲕⲟ,</td><td>ϣⲁⲕ-ⲧⲁⲕⲟ,</td><td>ϣⲁⲕ-ⲧⲁⲕⲟ, thou, m.</td></tr>
<tr><td>ϣⲁⲣⲉ-ⲧⲁⲕⲟ,</td><td>ϣⲁⲣⲉ-ⲧⲁⲕⲟ,</td><td>ϣⲁⲗⲉ-ⲧⲁⲕⲟ, thou, f.</td></tr>
</table>

ϣⲁϥ- ⎫   ϣⲁϥ- ⎫   ϣⲁϥ- ⎫
ϣⲁⲣⲉ- ⎭ ⲧⲁⲕⲟ,   ϣⲁⲣⲉ- ⎭ ⲧⲁⲕⲟ,   ϣⲁⲗⲉ- ⎭ ⲧⲁⲕⲟ, *he.*

ϣⲁⲥ- ⎫   ϣⲁⲥ- ⎫   ϣⲁⲥ- ⎫
ϣⲁⲣⲉ- ⎭ ⲧⲁⲕⲟ,   ϣⲁⲣⲉ- ⎭ ⲧⲁⲕⲟ,   ϣⲁⲗⲉ- ⎭ ⲧⲁⲕⲟ, *she.*

Plural.

<table>
<tr><td>ϣⲁⲛ-ⲧⲁⲕⲟ,</td><td>ϣⲁⲛ-ⲧⲁⲕⲟ,</td><td>ϣⲁⲛ-ⲧⲁⲕⲟ, we.</td></tr>
<tr><td>ϣⲁⲣⲉⲧⲉⲛ-ⲧⲁⲕⲟ,</td><td>ϣⲁⲧⲉⲧⲛ̄-ⲧⲁⲕⲟ,</td><td>ϣⲁⲧⲉⲧⲉⲛ-ⲧⲁⲕⲟ, ye.</td></tr>
</table>

ϣⲁⲩ- ⎫   ϣⲁⲩ- ⎫   ϣⲁⲩ- ⎫
ϣⲁⲣⲉ- ⎭ ⲧⲁⲕⲟ,   ϣⲁⲣⲉ- ⎭ ⲧⲁⲕⲟ,   ϣⲁⲗⲉ- ⎭ ⲧⲁⲕⲟ, *they.*

The Imperfect Tense Indefinite.
Singular.

Coptic.   Sahidic.

ⲚⲈ ϢⲀⲒ-ⲦⲀⲔⲞ ⲠⲈ,   ⲚⲈ ϢⲀⲒ-ⲦⲀⲔⲞ ⲠⲈ, *I was.*

ⲚⲈ ϢⲀⲔ-ⲦⲀⲔⲞ ⲠⲈ,   ⲚⲈ ϢⲀⲔ-ⲦⲀⲔⲞ ⲠⲈ, *thou,* m.

ⲚⲈ ϢⲀⲢⲈ-ⲦⲀⲔⲞ ⲠⲈ,   ⲚⲈ ϢⲀⲢⲈ-ⲦⲀⲔⲞ ⲠⲈ, *thou,* f.

ⲚⲈ ϢⲀϤ- ⎫   ⲚⲈ ϢⲀϤ- ⎫
         ⎬ ⲦⲀⲔⲞ ⲠⲈ,   ⎬ ⲦⲀⲔⲞ ⲠⲈ, *he.*
ⲚⲈ ϢⲀⲢⲈ-⎭   ⲚⲈ ϢⲀⲢⲈ-⎭

ⲚⲈ ϢⲀⳓ- ⎫   ⲚⲈ ϢⲀⳓ- ⎫
         ⎬ ⲦⲀⲔⲞ ⲠⲈ,   ⎬ ⲦⲀⲔⲞ ⲠⲈ, *she.*
ⲚⲈ ϢⲀⲢⲈ-⎭   ⲚⲈ ϢⲀⲢⲈ-⎭

Plural.

ⲚⲈ ϢⲀⲚ-ⲦⲀⲔⲞ ⲠⲈ,   ⲚⲈ ϢⲀⲚ-ⲦⲀⲔⲞ ⲠⲈ, *we.*

ⲚⲈ ϢⲀⲢⲈⲦⲈⲚ-ⲦⲀⲔⲞ ⲠⲈ,   ⲚⲈ ϢⲀⲦⲈⲦⲚ̄-ⲦⲀⲔⲞ ⲠⲈ, *ye.*

ⲚⲈ ϢⲀⲨ- ⎫   ⲚⲈ ϢⲀⲨ- ⎫
         ⎬ ⲦⲀⲔⲞ ⲠⲈ,   ⎬ ⲦⲀⲔⲞ ⲠⲈ, *they.*
ⲚⲈ ϢⲀⲢⲈ-⎭   ⲚⲈ ϢⲀⲢⲈ-⎭

Singular.

Bashmuric.

ⲚⲈ ϢⲀⲒ-ⲦⲀⲔⲞ ⲠⲈ, *I was.*

ⲚⲈ ϢⲀⲔ-ⲦⲀⲔⲞ ⲠⲈ, *thou,* m.

ⲚⲈ ϢⲀⲖⲈ-ⲦⲀⲔⲞ ⲠⲈ, *thou,* f.

ⲚⲈ ϢⲀϤ- ⎫
         ⎬ ⲦⲀⲔⲞ ⲠⲈ, *he.*
ⲚⲈ ϢⲀⲖⲈ-⎭

ⲚⲈ ϢⲀⳓ- ⎫
         ⎬ ⲦⲀⲔⲞ ⲠⲈ, *she.*
ⲚⲈ ϢⲀⲖⲈ-⎭

Plural.

ⲚⲈ ϢⲀⲚ-ⲦⲀⲔⲞ ⲠⲈ, *we.*

ⲚⲈ ϢⲀⲦⲈⲦⲈⲚ-ⲦⲀⲔⲞ ⲠⲈ, *ye.*

ⲚⲈ ϢⲀⲨ- ⎫
         ⎬ ⲦⲀⲔⲞ ⲠⲈ, *they.*
ⲚⲈ ϢⲀⲢⲈ-⎭

8*

The 1st Future Tense.

Singular.

Coptic.	Sahidic.	Bashmuric.	
ϮNA-TAKO,	ϮNA-TAKO,	ϮNA, ϮNE-TAKO,	*I shall.*
ⲬNA-TAKO,	KNA-TAKO,	KNE-TAKO,	*thou,* m.
TENA-TAKO,	TENA-TAKO,		*thou,* f.
ϥNA-TAKO,	ϥNA-TAKO,	ϥNE-TAKO,	*he.*
CNA-TAKO,	CNA-TAKO,	CNE-TAKO,	*she.*

Plural.

	Coptic.	Sahidic.	Bashmuric.	
	TENNA-TAKO,	TENNA- / TENA- } TAKO,	TENNA- or TENNE- } TAKO,	*we.*
	TETENNA-TAKO,	TETN̄NA- / TETN̄A- } TAKO,		*ye.*
	CENA-TAKO,	CENA-TAKO,.	CENE-TAKO,	*they.*

The 2nd Future Tense.

Singular.

Coptic.	Sahidic.	Bashmuric.	
EINA-TAKO,	EINA-TAKO,	AINA- or AINE- } TAKO,	*I shall.*
EKNA-TAKO,	EKNA-TAKO,	AKNA-TAKO,	*thou,* m.
EPENA-TAKO,	EPENA-TAKO,·	APENA-TAKO,	*thou,* f.
EϥNA- / EPENA- } TAKO,	EϥNA- / EPENA- } TAKO,	AϥNA- / APENA- } TAKO,	*he.*
ECNA- / EPENA } TAKO,	ECNA- / EPENA- } TAKO,	ACNA- / APENA- } TAKO,	*she.*

Plural.

Coptic.	Sahidic.	Bashmuric.
ⲈⲚⲚⲀ-ⲦⲀⲔⲞ,	ⲈⲚⲚⲀ-⎫ ⟩ ⲦⲀⲔⲞ, ⲚⲚⲀ-⎭	ⲀⲚⲚⲀ-⎫ or ⟩ ⲦⲀⲔⲞ, *we.* ⲀⲚⲚⲈ-⎭
ⲈⲠⲈⲦⲈⲚⲚⲀ-ⲦⲀⲔⲞ,	ⲈⲦⲈⲦⲚⲚⲀ-⎫ ⟩ⲦⲀⲔⲞ, ⲈⲦⲈⲦⲚⲀ-⎭	ⲀⲠⲈⲦⲈⲚⲚⲀ-ⲦⲀⲔⲞ, *ye.*
ⲈⲨⲚⲀ-⎫ ⟩ ⲦⲀⲔⲞ, ⲞⲨⲚⲀ-⎭	ⲈⲨⲚⲀ-⎫ ⟩ ⲦⲀⲔⲞ, ⲞⲨⲚⲀ-⎭	ⲈⲨⲚⲀ-ⲦⲀⲔⲞ, *they.*

The 3rd Future Tense.

Singular.

Coptic.	Sahidic.	Bashmuric.
ⲈⲒⲈ-ⲦⲀⲔⲞ,	ⲈⲒⲈ-ⲦⲀⲔⲞ,	ⲈⲒⲈ-ⲦⲀⲔⲞ, *I shall.*
ⲈⲔⲈ-ⲦⲀⲔⲞ,	ⲈⲔⲈ-ⲦⲀⲔⲞ,	ⲈⲔⲈ-ⲦⲀⲔⲞ, *thou,* m.
ⲈⲠⲈ-ⲦⲀⲔⲞ,	ⲈⲠⲈ-ⲦⲀⲔⲞ,	ⲈⲠⲈ-ⲦⲀⲔⲞ, *thou,* f.
ⲈϤⲈ-⎫ ⟩ ⲦⲀⲔⲞ, ⲈⲠⲈ-⎭	ⲈϤⲈ-⎫ ⟩ ⲦⲀⲔⲞ, ⲈⲠⲈ-⎭	ⲈϤⲈ-⎫ ⟩ ⲦⲀⲔⲞ, *he.* ⲈⲠⲈ-⎭
ⲈⲤⲈ-⎫ ⟩ ⲦⲀⲔⲞ, ⲈⲠⲈ-⎭	ⲈⲤⲈ-⎫ ⟩ ⲦⲀⲔⲞ, ⲈⲠⲈ-⎭	ⲈⲤⲈ-⎫ ⟩ ⲦⲀⲔⲞ, *she.* ⲈⲠⲈ-⎭

Plural.

ⲈⲚⲈ-ⲦⲀⲔⲞ,	ⲈⲚⲈ-ⲦⲀⲔⲞ,	ⲈⲚⲈ-ⲦⲀⲔⲞ, *we.*
ⲈⲠⲈⲦⲈⲚⲈ-ⲦⲀⲔⲞ,	ⲈⲦⲈⲦⲚⲈ-ⲦⲀⲔⲞ,	ⲈⲦⲈⲦⲚⲈ-ⲦⲀⲔⲞ, *ye.*
ⲈⲨⲈ-⎫ ⟩ ⲦⲀⲔⲞ, ⲈⲠⲈ-⎭	ⲈⲨⲈ-⎫ ⟩ ⲦⲀⲔⲞ, ⲈⲠⲈ-⎭	ⲈⲨⲈ-⎫ ⟩ ⲦⲀⲔⲞ, *they.* ⲈⲠⲈ-⎭

The 4th Future Tense.

Singular.

Coptic.	Sahidic.	Bashmuric.	
ⲦⲀ-ⲦⲀⲔⲞ,	ⲦⲀ- ⲦⲀⲢⲒ- } ⲦⲀⲔⲞ,	ⲦⲀ-ⲦⲀⲔⲞ,	*I shall.*
	ⲦⲀⲢⲈⲔ-ⲦⲀⲔⲞ,		*thou*, m.
ⲦⲈⲢⲀ-ⲦⲀⲔⲞ,	ⲦⲈⲢⲀ-ⲦⲀⲔⲞ,	ⲦⲈⲢⲀ-ⲦⲀⲔⲞ,	*thou*, f.
	ⲦⲀⲢⲈϥ-ⲦⲀⲔⲞ,		*he.*
	ⲦⲀⲢⲈⲤ-ⲦⲀⲔⲞ,		*she.*

Plural.

ⲦⲀⲢⲚ̄-ⲦⲀⲔⲞ,		*we.*
ⲦⲀⲢⲈⲦⲚ̄-ⲦⲀⲔⲞ,	ⲦⲀⲖⲈⲦⲈⲚ-ⲦⲀⲔⲞ,	*ye.*
ⲦⲀⲢⲞⲨ-ⲦⲀⲔⲞ,		*they.*

The Imperfect Future.

Singular.

Coptic.	Sahidic.	Bashmuric.	
ⲚⲀⲒⲚⲀ·ⲦⲀⲔⲞ,	ⲚⲈⲒⲚⲀ-ⲦⲀⲔⲞ,	ⲚⲀⲒⲚⲈ- or ⲚⲀⲒⲚⲀ- } ⲦⲀⲔⲞ,	*I should.*
ⲚⲀⲔⲚⲀ-ⲦⲀⲔⲞ,	ⲚⲈⲔⲚⲀ-ⲦⲀⲔⲞ,	ⲚⲀⲔⲚⲈ-ⲦⲀⲔⲞ,	*thou*, m.
ⲚⲀⲢⲈⲚⲀ-ⲦⲀⲔⲞ,	ⲚⲈⲢⲈⲚⲀ-ⲦⲀⲔⲞ,	ⲚⲀⲢⲈⲚⲈ-ⲦⲀⲔⲞ,	*thou*, f.
ⲚⲀϥⲚⲀ- ⲚⲀⲢⲈⲚⲀ- } ⲦⲀⲔⲞ,	ⲚⲈϥⲚⲀ- ⲚⲈⲢⲈⲚⲀ- } ⲦⲀⲔⲞ,	ⲚⲀϥⲚⲈ- ⲚⲀⲢⲈⲚⲈ- } ⲦⲀⲔⲞ,	*he.*
ⲚⲀⲤⲚⲀ- ⲚⲀⲢⲈⲚⲀ- } ⲦⲀⲔⲞ,	ⲚⲈⲤⲚⲀ- ⲚⲈⲢⲈⲚⲀ- } ⲦⲀⲔⲞ,	ⲚⲀⲤⲚⲈ- ⲚⲀⲢⲈⲚⲈ, } ⲦⲀⲔⲞ,	*she.*

Plural.

Coptic.	Sahidic.	Bashmuric.
ⲚⲀⲚⲚⲀ-ⲦⲀⲔⲞ,	ⲚⲈⲚⲚⲀ-ⲦⲀⲔⲞ,	ⲚⲀⲚⲚⲈ-ⲦⲀⲔⲞ, *we.*
ⲚⲀⲠⲈⲦⲈⲚⲚⲀ-ⲦⲀⲔⲞ,	ⲚⲈⲦⲈⲦⲚ̅Ⲁ-ⲦⲀⲔⲞ,	ⲚⲀⲠⲈⲦⲈⲚⲚⲈ-ⲦⲀⲔⲞ,*ye.*

ⲚⲀⲨⲚⲀ-	} ⲦⲀⲔⲞ,	ⲚⲈⲨⲚⲀ-	}ⲦⲀⲔⲞ,	ⲚⲈⲨⲚⲈ-	}ⲦⲀⲔⲞ, *they.*
ⲚⲀⲠⲈⲚⲀ-		ⲚⲈⲠⲈⲚⲀ-		ⲚⲀⲠⲈⲚⲈ-	

The Subjunctive Mood.

Singular.

Coptic.	Sahidic.	Bashmuric.
Ⲛ̅ⲦⲀ-ⲦⲀⲔⲞ,	Ⲛ̅ⲦⲀ-ⲦⲀⲔⲞ,	Ⲛ̅ⲦⲀ-ⲦⲀⲔⲞ, *that I.*
Ⲛ̅ⲦⲈⲔ-ⲦⲀⲔⲞ,	Ⲛ̅Ⲅ-ⲦⲀⲔⲞ,	Ⲛ̅Ⲅ-ⲦⲀⲔⲞ, *thou,* m.
Ⲛ̅ⲦⲈ-ⲦⲀⲔⲞ,	Ⲛ̅ⲦⲈ-ⲦⲀⲔⲞ,	Ⲛ̅ⲦⲈ-ⲦⲀⲔⲞ, *thou,* f.

Ⲛ̅ⲦⲈϥ-̇	}ⲦⲀⲔⲞ,	Ⲛ̅Ⲉϥ, Ⲛ̅ϥ̅-	}ⲦⲀⲔⲞ,	Ⲛ̅Ⲉϥ, Ⲛ̅ϥ̅-̇	}ⲦⲀⲔⲞ, *he.*
Ⲛ̅ⲦⲈ-		Ⲛ̅ⲦⲈ-		Ⲛ̅ⲦⲈ-	
Ⲛ̅ⲦⲈⲤ-	}ⲦⲀⲔⲞ,	Ⲛ̅Ⲥ-	}ⲦⲀⲔⲞ,	Ⲛ̅ⲈⲤ- Ⲛ̅Ⲥ̅-̇	}ⲦⲀⲔⲞ, *she.*
Ⲛ̅ⲦⲈ-		Ⲛ̅ⲦⲈ-		Ⲛ̅ⲦⲈ-	

Plural.

Ⲛ̅ⲦⲈⲚ-ⲦⲀⲔⲞ,	Ⲛ̅ⲦⲚ̅-ⲦⲀⲔⲞ,	Ⲛ̅ⲦⲚ̅-ⲦⲀⲔⲞ, *we.*
Ⲛ̅ⲦⲈⲦⲈⲚ-ⲦⲀⲔⲞ,	Ⲛ̅ⲦⲈⲦⲚ̅-ⲦⲀⲔⲞ,	Ⲛ̅ⲦⲈⲦⲚ̅-ⲦⲀⲔⲞ, *ye.*

Ⲛ̅ⲦⲞⲨ-̇	}ⲦⲀⲔⲞ,	Ⲛ̅ⲤⲈ-	}ⲦⲀⲔⲞ,	Ⲛ̅ⲤⲈ-̇	}ⲦⲀⲔⲞ, *they.*
Ⲛ̅ⲦⲈ-		Ⲛ̅ⲦⲈ-		Ⲛ̅ⲦⲈ-	

The Optative Mood.

Singular.

Coptic.	Sahidic.	Bashmuric.
ⲙⲁⲣⲓ-ⲧⲁⲕⲟ,	ⲙⲁⲣⲓ-ⲧⲁⲕⲟ,	ⲙⲁⲗⲓ-ⲧⲁⲕⲟ, *I may.*
ⲙⲁⲣⲉⲕ-ⲧⲁⲕⲟ,	ⲙⲁⲣⲃⲕ-ⲧⲁⲕⲟ,	ⲙⲁⲗⲉⲕ-ⲧⲁⲕⲟ, *thou,* m.
ⲙⲁⲣⲉ-ⲧⲁⲕⲟ,	ⲙⲁⲣⲉ-ⲧⲁⲕⲟ,	ⲙⲁⲗⲉ-ⲧⲁⲕⲟ, *thou,* f.
ⲙⲁⲣⲉϥ-⎫ ⲧⲁⲕⲟ, ⲙⲁⲣⲉ- ⎭	ⲙⲁⲣⲉϥ-⎫ ⲧⲁⲕⲟ, ⲙⲁⲣⲉ- ⎭	ⲙⲁⲗⲉϥ-⎫ ⲧⲁⲕⲟ, *he.* ⲙⲁⲗⲉ- ⎭
ⲙⲁⲣⲉⲥ-⎫ ⲧⲁⲕⲟ, ⲙⲁⲣⲉ- ⎭	ⲙⲁⲣⲉⲥ-⎫ ⲧⲁⲕⲟ, ⲙⲁⲣⲉ- ⎭	ⲙⲁⲗⲉⲥ-⎫ ⲧⲁⲕⲟ, *she.* ⲙⲁⲗⲉ- ⎭

Plural.

ⲙⲁⲣⲉⲛ-ⲧⲁⲕⲟ,	ⲙⲁⲣⲛ̅-ⲧⲁⲕⲟ,	ⲙⲁⲗⲉⲛ-ⲧⲁⲕⲟ, *we.*
ⲙⲁⲣⲉⲧⲉⲛ-ⲧⲁⲕⲟ,	ⲙⲁⲣⲉⲧⲛ̅-ⲧⲁⲕⲟ,	ⲙⲁⲗⲉⲧⲉⲛ-ⲧⲁⲕⲟ, *ye.*
ⲙⲁⲣⲟⲩ-⎫ ⲧⲁⲕⲟ, ⲙⲁⲣⲉ- ⎭	ⲙⲁⲣⲟⲩ-⎫ ⲧⲁⲕⲟ, ⲙⲁⲣⲉ- ⎭	ⲙⲁⲗⲟⲩ-⎫ ⲧⲁⲕⲟ, *they.* ⲙⲁⲗⲉ- ⎭

The Imperative Mood.

Singular and Plural.

ⲁ-ⲧⲁⲕⲟ, ⎫
ⲁⲣⲓ-ⲧⲁⲕⲟ, ⎪ *destroy.*
ⲙⲁ-ⲧⲁⲕⲟ, ⎬
ⲧⲁⲕⲟ, ⎭

The Infinitive Mood.

ⲉ̀-ⲧⲁⲕⲟ, ⎫
ⲛ̀-ⲧⲁⲕⲟ, ⎬ *to destroy.*
ⲧⲁⲕⲟ, ⎭

Participles.

Coptic.	Sahidic.	Bashmuric.
ϫιν,	ϭιν,	ϫιν,
ⲡⲁϫιν or ⲡϫιⲛⲧⲁ,	ⲡⲁϭιⲛ,	ⲡⲁϫιⲛ,
ⲡⲉⲕϫιⲛ,	ⲡⲉⲕϭιⲛ,	ⲡⲉⲕϫιⲛ,
ⲡⲉϥϫιⲛ, &c.	ⲡⲉϥϭιⲛ, &c.	ⲡⲉϥϫιⲛ, &c.

That these are participles is evident from the Arabic, with which they correspond.

Participles.

26. The participles are formed by ⲉ, ⲉⲧ or ⲉⲑ, before the prefixes to the verbs. There are also some peculiar forms of participles, which end in ⲛⲟⲩⲧ, Copt. ⲏⲩⲧ, Sah. ⲱⲟⲩⲧ, Copt. ⲟⲟⲩⲧ, Sah. and ⲗⲟⲩⲧ, Bash. as ⲧⲟⲩⲃⲏⲟⲩⲧ, Copt. ⲙⲱⲟⲩⲧ, Copt. and ⲙⲁⲟⲩⲧ, Bash.

Verbs united with particles expressive of time.

The particles ⲉⲧⲉ, Copt. ⲛ̅ⲧⲉⲣⲉ, Sah. *when.*

Singular.

Coptic.	Sahidic.	Bashmuric.
ⲉ̀ⲧⲁι,	ⲛ̅ⲧⲉⲣι, ⲛ̅ⲧⲉⲣⲉι,	ⲉⲧⲁι, ⲛ̀ⲧⲉⲗⲉι,
ⲉ̀ⲧⲁⲕ,	ⲛ̅ⲧⲉⲣⲉⲕ,	
ⲉ̀ⲧⲁⲣⲉ,	ⲛ̅ⲧⲉⲣⲉ,	ⲉⲧⲁϥ, ⲛ̀ⲧⲉⲗⲉϥ,
ⲉ̀ⲧⲁϥ⎱ ⲉ̀ⲧⲁⲣⲉ,	ⲛ̅ⲧⲉⲣⲉϥ, ⎱ ⲛ̅ⲧⲉⲣⲉ,	
ⲉ̀ⲧⲁⲥ⎰	ⲛ̅ⲧⲉⲣⲉⲥ, ⎰	

Plural.

Coptic.	Sahidic.	Bashmuric.
ⲉ̀ⲧⲁⲛ,	ⲛ̄ⲧⲉⲣⲉⲛ,	ⲉ̀ⲧⲁⲛ, ⲛ̀ⲧⲉⲗⲉⲛ,
ⲉ̀ⲧⲁⲣⲉⲧⲉⲛ,	ⲛ̄ⲧⲉⲣⲉⲧⲛ̄,	ⲉ̀ⲧⲁⲧⲉⲧⲉⲛ, ⲛ̀ⲧⲉⲗⲉⲧⲉⲛ,
ⲉ̀ⲧⲁⲩ, ⲉ̀ⲧⲁⲣⲉ,	ⲛ̄ⲧⲉⲣⲟⲩ,	ⲛ̀ⲧⲉⲗⲟⲩ, ⲛ̀ⲧⲉⲗⲉⲩ.

Verbs with the particles ⳛⲁⲧⲉ, Copt. ⳛⲁⲛⲧⲉ, Sah. until.

Singular.

Coptic.	Sahidic.	Bashmuric.
ⳛⲁϯ,	ⳛⲁⲛⲧⲉⲓ, ⳛⲁⲛϯ,	ⳛⲁⲛⲧⲉⲓ,
ⳛⲁⲧⲉⲕ,	ⳛⲁⲛⲧⲕ̄,	
ⳛⲁⲧⲉ,	ⳛⲁⲛⲧⲉ,	
ⳛⲁⲧⲉϥ,⎱ ⳛⲁⲧⲉ,	ⳛⲁⲛⲧϥ,⎱ ⳛⲁⲛⲧⲉ,	ⳛⲁⲛⲧⲉϥ,
ⳛⲁⲧⲉⲥ,⎰	ⳛⲁⲛⲧⲥ̄,⎰	

Plural.

Coptic.	Sahidic.	
ⳛⲁⲧⲉⲛ,	ⳛⲁⲛⲧⲛ̄,	
ⳛⲁⲧⲉⲧⲉⲛ,	ⳛⲁⲛⲧⲉⲧⲛ̄,	
ⳛⲁⲧⲟⲩ, ⳛⲁⲧⲉ,	ⳛⲁⲛⲧⲟⲩ, ⳛⲁⲛⲧⲉ,	ⳛⲁⲛⲧⲟⲩ.

Verbs with the particle ⲉ̀ⲛⲉ or ⲉ̀ⲛ, if.

Singular.

Coptic.	Sahidic.
ⲉ̀ⲛⲁⲓ, ⲉ̀ⲛⲉⲁⲓ ⲡⲉ,	ⲉⲛⲉⲓ ⲡⲉ,
ⲉ̀ⲛⲁⲕ, ⲉ̀ⲛⲉⲁⲕ ⲡⲉ,	ⲉⲛⲉⲕ ⲡⲉ,
ⲉ̀ⲛⲁⲣⲉ ⲡⲉ,	ⲉⲛⲉⲣⲉ ⲡⲉ,
ⲉ̀ⲛⲁϥ, ⲉ̀ⲛⲁⲣⲉ ⲡⲉ,	ⲉⲛⲉϥ,⎱ ⲉⲛⲉⲣⲉ ⲡⲉ,
ⲉ̀ⲛⲁⲥ, ⲉ̀ⲛⲉ ⲁ ⲡⲉ,	ⲉⲛⲉⲥ,⎰

Plural.

Coptic.	Sahidic.
ⲉ̀ⲛⲁⲛ ⲡⲉ,	ⲉⲛⲉⲛ ⲡⲉ,
ⲉ̀ⲛⲁⲣⲉⲧⲉⲛ ⲡⲉ,	ⲉⲛⲉⲧⲉⲧⲛ̄ ⲡⲉ,
ⲉ̀ⲛⲁⲩ, ⲉ̀ⲛⲁⲣⲉ ⲡⲉ,	ⲉⲛⲉⲩ, ⲉⲛⲉⲣⲉ ⲡⲉ.

Verbs with the particle ⲰⲀⲚ, if, when.

Singular.

Coptic.	Sahidic.	Bashmuric.
ⲀⲒⲰⲀⲚ,	ⲈⲒⲰⲀⲚ,	
ⲀⲔⲰⲀⲚ,	ⲈⲔⲰⲀⲚ,	
ⲀⲢⲈⲰⲀⲚ,	ⲈⲢⲰⲀⲚ,	ⲀⲖⲈⲰⲀⲚ,
ⲀϥⲰⲀⲚ,⎫ ⲀⲢⲈⲰⲀⲚ,	ⲈϥⲰⲀⲚ,⎫ ⲈⲢⲰⲀⲚ,	
ⲀⲤⲰⲀⲚ,⎭	ⲈⲤⲰⲀⲚ,⎭	

Plural.

ⲀⲚⲰⲀⲚ,   ⲈⲚⲰⲀⲚ,

ⲀⲢⲈⲦⲈⲚⲰⲀⲚ,   ⲈⲦⲈⲦⲚⲰⲀⲚ,

ⲀⲨⲰⲀⲚ, ⲀⲢⲈⲰⲀⲚ, ⲈⲨⲰⲀⲚ, ⲈⲢⲰⲀⲚ.

Verbs with the particle ⲘⲠⲀⲦⲈ, before.

Singular.

Coptic.	Sahidic.
ⲘⲠⲀϮ,	ⲘⲠⲀϮ,
ⲘⲠⲀⲦⲈⲔ,	ⲘⲠⲀⲦⲔ,
ⲘⲠⲀⲦⲈ,	ⲘⲠⲀⲦⲈ,
ⲘⲠⲀⲦⲈϥ,⎫ ⲘⲠⲀⲦⲈ,	ⲘⲠⲀⲧϥ,⎫ ⲘⲠⲀⲦⲈ,
ⲘⲠⲀⲦⲈⲤ,⎭	ⲘⲠⲀⲦⲤ,⎭

Plural.

ⲘⲠⲀⲦⲈⲚ,   ⲘⲠⲀⲦⲚ,

ⲘⲠⲀⲦⲈⲦⲈⲚ,   ⲘⲠⲀⲦⲈⲦⲚ,

ⲘⲠⲀⲦⲞⲨ, ⲘⲠⲀⲦⲈ,   ⲘⲠⲀⲦⲞⲨ, ⲘⲠⲀⲦⲈ.

9*

The Tenses.

The 1st Present Tense.

27. The 1st Present Tense is formed by adding the following prefixes to the root, ϯ *I am*, ⲕ, or ⲭ Copt. before ⲗ, ⲙ, ⲛ, ⲟⲩ, or ⲣ, *thou art*, m.: ⲧⲉ *thou art*, f.: ϥ, *he is;* ⲥ, *she is;* ⲧⲉⲛ, C. ⲧⲉⲛ, ⲧⲛ̅, S. *we are;* ⲧⲉⲧⲉⲛ, C. ⲧⲉⲧⲉⲛ, or ⲧⲉⲧⲛ̅, S. *ye are;* ⲥⲉ, *they are.* Thus, ϯⲥⲱⲟⲩⲛ ⲙ̅ⲡⲉⲕⲑⲟⲝϩⲉⲝ, *I know thy tribulation,* Rev. II, 9. ϥⲟ ⲛ̅ⲛⲟⲉⲓⲕ, *is an adulterer,* Luke XVI, 18. Sah. ⲝⲉ ϥ ⲙ̅ⲙⲁⲩ *that he is there.* John XII, 9. Sah.

The 2nd Present Tense.

28. The 2nd Present Tense has the following prefixes, as, ⲉⲓ, *I am;* ⲉⲕ, *thou art,* m. ⲉⲣⲉ, *thou art,* f.; ⲉϥ or ⲉⲣⲉ, *he is;* ⲉⲥ or ⲉⲣⲉ, *she is;* ⲉⲛ, Copt. ⲉⲛ or ⲛ̅, Sah. *we are;* ⲉⲧⲉⲧⲉⲛ, ⲉⲧⲉⲧⲛ̅, *ye are;* ⲉⲩ, ⲟⲩ or ⲉⲣⲉ, *they are.*

29. The second person f. is ⲉⲣⲉ, (Bash. ⲉⲗⲉ,) but before vowels it is written ⲉⲣ, and occasionally, ⲉⲣⲁ, as ⲉⲣⲉⲓⲣⲉ, *thou doest;* S. Ming. 258. ⲉⲣⲟⲩⲉϣ, *thou wilt;* S. Zoeg. p. 509. Sometimes it is written ⲡ̅ ⲡ̅ⲗⲟⲃⲉ, *thou art mad;* S. Acts XII, 15. The Bash. corresponds as ⲉⲗⲥⲟⲟⲩⲛ, *thou knowest,* Zoeg. 151. ⲉⲣⲉ the prefix of the third persons sing. and plur. is always separated from the verb, by the noun or some other word, as ⲉⲣⲉ ⲡⲟⲩϩⲏⲧ ⲙⲟⲕϩ, *their heart was afflicted,* Matt. XXVI, 22. ⲉ̀ⲣⲉ ⲟⲩⲛⲓϣϯ ⲅⲁⲣ ⲛ̀ϩⲟⲝϩⲉⲝ ϣⲱⲡⲓ, *for great tribulation shall be.* Matt. XXIV, 21.

30. The Prefix ⲉⲣⲉ appears to be almost indefinite as to time.

31. The third person plural is ⲉⲩ, but after ⲧ it is written ⲟⲩ, as ϥⲏⲉⲧ ⲟⲩⲙⲟⲩⳁ ⲉ̀ⲡⲟϥ, *when they call.* Matt. XXVII, 22.

ⲉ̀ is the sign of the participle present as ⲉ̀ⲥⲱ ⲉ̀ ⲁ̀ⲛⲟⲕ ⲟⲩⲥ̀ⳅⲓⲙⲓ ⲛ̀ⲥⲁⲙⲁⲣⲓⲧⲏⲥ, *to drink, I being* (οὖσα) *a woman of Samaria,* John IV, 9. ⲉ ⲁⲛⲟⲛ ⳅⲉⲛⲣⲱⲙⲉ ⲛ̄ⳅⲣⲱⲙⲁⲓⲟⲥ, ⲉ ⲙⲛ̄ ⲛⲟⲃⲉ ⲉⲣⲟⲛ, *we being men Romans, not being a fault in us.* Sah. Acts XVI, 37.

32. The following examples will serve to show the prefixes of the 2nd present tense, as, ⲁⲛⲟⲕ ⲇⲉ ⲉⲓ ⳅⲛ̄ ⲧⲉⲧⲛ̄ⲙⲏⲧⲉ, *but I am among you,* Luke XXII, 27. Sah. ⲉⲕ ⳅⲓ ⲧⲉⳅⲓⲏ ⲛ̄ⲏⲙⲁϥ, *thou art in the way with him.* Matt. V, 25. Sah. ⲉϥ ⳅⲛ̄ ⲧⲡⲉ, *is in heaven.* Matt. VI, 10. Sahidic.

33. The prefixes of this tense also express the present participle, as, ⲁϥⲛⲁⲩ ⲉ̀ⲟⲩⲣⲱⲙⲓ ⲉϥⳅⲉⲙⲥⲓ, *he saw a man sitting,* Matt. IX, 9. ⲛⲓⲃ ⲇⲉ ⲛⲁⲩⳁⳅⲟ ⲉ̀ⲡⲟϥ ⲡⲉ ⲉⲩⳈⲱⲙ̀ⲙⲟⲥ, *and the devils besought him saying,* Matt. VIII, 31.

Imperfect Tense.

34. The Imperfect Tense is formed by prefixing the following particles to the root, ⲛⲁⲓ. *I was;* ⲛⲁⲕ, *thou wast,* m. ⲛⲁⲣⲉ, *thou wast,* f. ⲛⲁϥ or ⲛⲁⲣⲉ, *he was;* ⲛⲁⲥ or ⲛⲁⲣⲉ, *she was.* Plur. ⲛⲁⲛ, *we were;* ⲛⲁⲡⲉⲧⲉⲛ, *ye were;* ⲛⲁⲩ or ⲛⲁⲣⲉ, *they were.* The Sahidic is ⲛⲉⲓ, ⲛⲉⲕ, ⲛⲉⲣⲉ, ⲛⲉϥ or ⲛⲉⲣⲉ, ⲛⲉⲥ or ⲛⲉⲣⲉ. Plur. ⲛⲉⲛ, ⲛⲉⲧⲉⲧⲛ̄, ⲛⲉⲩ or ⲛⲉⲣⲉ. Sometimes the Sahidic is written without the ⲉ, as, ⲛϥ, ⲛⲥ̄, ⲛⲛ̄, etc.

35. The Imperfect Tense has ⲡⲉ frequently following the verb, as, ⲟⲩⲟⲋ ⲛⲁϥⲧⲥⲃⲱ ⲡⲉ, *and taught,* John VII, 14. ⲛⲉϥϣⲟⲟⲡ ⲡⲉ ⲛϭⲓ ⲡⲗⲟⲅⲟⲥ, *the word was,* John I, 1. Sah. ⲛⲁϥⲃⲱⲛⲧ ⲇⲉ ⲡⲉ ⲡⲓⲡⲁⲥⲭⲁ, *and the Passover was near,* John XI, 55. ⲇⲉ ⲛⲉϥⲁⲋϥⲣⲁⲧϥ̄ ⲡⲉ ⲛ̄ⲃⲟⲗ, *but he stood without,* John XVII, 16. Sah.

ⲛⲁⲣⲉ or ⲛⲉⲣⲉ Sah. is generally separated from the verb, and usually occurs before the nominative preceding it, as ⲛⲁⲣⲉ ⲛⲓⲙⲁⲑⲏⲧⲏⲥ ⲑⲟⲩⲏⲧ, *the disciples were assembled,* John XX, 19. S. ⲛⲉⲣⲉ ⲡⲉϥⲛⲟϭ ⲇⲉ ⲛ̄ϣⲏⲣⲉ ϩⲛ̄ ⲧⲥⲱϣⲉ, *and his greater son was in the field,* Luke XXII, 25. Sah. The Bashmuric will probably be written occasionally ⲛⲁⲗⲉ.

The 1st Perfect Tense.

36. The Prefixes to the 1st Perfect Tense are ⲁⲓ, *I;* ⲁⲕ, *thou,* m. ⲁⲣⲉ or ⲁⲣ, *thou,* f. ⲁϥ or ⲁ̀, *he;* ⲁⲥ or ⲁ̀, *she;* Plur. ⲁⲛ, *we;* ⲁⲣⲉⲧⲉⲛ, ⲁⲧⲉⲧⲛ̄, Sahidic, *ye;* ⲁⲩ or ⲁ̀, *they.*

37. When ⲁ occurs in composition it is usually found before the nominative to the verb, as ⲓⲏⲥ ⲁ̀ ⲡⲓⲡⲛ̄ⲁ̄ ⲟⲗϥ, *the spirit took Jesus,* Matt. IV, 1. ⲁ ⲓⲥ̄ ⲭⲟⲟⲥ ⲛⲁϥ, *Jesus said to him.* Sah. Mark XIV, 72. ⲁ ⲛⲓⲟⲩⲇⲁⲓ ⲧⲱⲟⲩⲛ, *the Jews rose,* Acts XVIII, 12. Sah. ⲛⲏⲉ̀ⲧ ⲁ̀ ⲛⲓⲡⲣⲟⲫⲏⲧⲏⲥ ⲭⲟⲧⲟⲩ, *those things which the Prophets said,* Acts XXVI, 22.

38. Although ⲁ̀ is used instead of the Prefixes ⲁϥ, ⲁⲥ and ⲁⲩ, yet it occurs also with them; as, ⲁ̀ ⲧⲁϣⲉⲣⲉ ⲁⲥⲃⲱⲛⲧ ⲉ̀ⲫⲙⲟⲩ, *my daughter hath approached to death,*

Mark. V, 23. ⲁ ⲡⲥⲁⲧⲁⲛⲁⲥ ⲁϥϣⲉⲛⲁϥ ⲉⲃⲟⲩⲛ ⲉⲡⲍⲏⲧ
ⲛ̅ⲓⲟⲩⲁⲁⲥ, *Satan entered into the heart of Judas.* Luke
XXII, 3. ⲝⲉ ⲁ ⲍⲏⲗⲓⲁⲥ ⲟⲩⲱ ⲁϥⲉⲓ, *that Elias hath now*
come. Matt. XVII, 12. Sah.

The 2nd Perfect Tense.

39. The 2nd Perfect Tense is distinguished by ⲉⲧ
Copt. and ⲛ̅ⲧ Sah. being added to the first perfect, in
all the persons, except that the 2 pers. fem. is ⲛ̅ⲧⲁⲣ,
instead of ⲛ̅ⲧⲁⲣⲉ.

40. The ⲛ̅ⲧⲁ, is found in the same position in composition as the ⲁ in the first perfect, thus; ⲛ̅ⲧ ⲁ ⲓ̅ⲥ̅
ⲁⲉ ⲝⲟⲟⲥ ⲉⲧⲃⲉ, *but Jesus spoke concerning,* John XI, 13.
Sah. ⲉⲛⲉⲙⲓ ⲝⲉ ⲡⲭ̅ⲥ̅ ⲉⲧⲁϥⲧⲱⲛϥ ⲉⲃⲟⲗⲃⲉⲛ ⲛⲏⲉⲧⲙⲱⲟⲩⲧ,
we know that Christ hath risen from the dead. Rom. VI, 9.

41. The Prefixes are often found after the particle
ⲝⲉ, *that,* and sometimes after ⲉⲛⲉ, *if;* and ⲁⲗⲗⲁ, *but.*
But the ⲛ̅ⲧ must not be confounded with ⲛ̅ⲧ, *who, which.*

The Pluperfect Tense.

42. The Pluperfect Tense is formed by adding the
auxiliary verb ⲛⲉ ⲡⲉ to the prefixes of the perfect, as
ⲛⲉ ⲁⲓ ⲡⲉ, *I;* ⲛⲉ ⲁⲕ ⲡⲉ, *thou,* m.; ⲛⲉ ⲁⲣⲉ ⲡⲉ, *thou,* f.;
ⲛⲉ ⲁϥ or ⲁ ⲡⲉ, *he;* ⲛⲉ ⲁⲥ or ⲁ ⲡⲉ, *she;* Plur. ⲛⲉ ⲁⲛ
ⲡⲉ, *we;* ⲛⲉ ⲁⲣⲉⲧⲉⲛ or ⲁⲧⲉⲧⲛ̅, ⲡⲉ, *ye.* S. ⲛⲉ ⲁⲩ or ⲁ
ⲡⲉ, *they;* as, ⲛⲉ ⲁϥⲉⲣⲍⲏⲧⲥ ⲛ̅ⲣⲓⲕⲓ ⲡⲉ, *had begun to de-*
cline, Luke IX, 12. ⲛ̅ⲓⲟⲩⲁⲁⲓ ⲛⲉ ⲁⲩⲉⲓ ⲡⲉ ϣⲁ ⲙⲁⲣⲑⲁ,
the Jews had come to Martha, John XI, 19 Sah. ⲛⲉ ⲁⲩ-
ⲛⲁⲩ ⲅⲁⲣ ⲉⲣⲟϥ ⲧⲏⲣⲟⲩ ⲡⲉ, *for all had seen him,* Mark

VI, 50. This Tense is also found without the ⲡⲉ, as, ⲓⲏⲥ ⲇⲉ ⲁϥⲓ ⲉⲃⲟⲗ, *Jesus had gone out,* John V, 13. ⲧⲁⲓ ⲇⲉ ⲛⲉ ⲁⲥⲟⲩⲁϩⲧ̄ ⲛ̄ⲥⲁ ⲡⲁⲩⲗⲟⲥ, *and this had followed Paul.* Acts XVI, 17. Sah.

The Present Tense Indefinite.

43. This Tense is formed by adding ⲱ, and sometimes ⲉⲱ in the Sahidic to the Perfect Tense, as ⲱⲁⲓ, *I;* ⲱⲁⲕ, *thou,* m.; ⲱⲁⲣⲉ or ⲱⲁⲣ, *thou,* f. ⲱⲁⲗⲉ, B. ⲱⲁϥ or ⲱⲁⲣⲉ, ⲱⲁⲗⲉ, B. *he;* ⲱⲁⲥ or ⲱⲁⲣⲉ, ⲱⲁⲗⲉ, B. *she;* Plur. ⲱⲁⲛ, *we;* ⲱⲁⲣⲉⲧⲉⲛ, ⲱⲁⲧⲉⲧⲛ̄, S. *ye;* ⲱⲁⲩ or ⲱⲁⲣⲉ, ⲱⲁⲗⲉ, Bash. *they.*

This Tense sometimes expresses the present, and sometimes the perfect.

The Imperfect Tense Indefinite.

44. The Imperfect Tense Indefinite is formed from the preceding by adding ⲛⲉ to it, as ⲟⲩⲟϩ ⲛⲉ ⲱⲁⲩⲥⲟⲛϩϥ ⲡⲉ, *and they had bound him,* or *he was bound.* Luke VIII, 29. ⲛⲉ ⲱⲁϥⲟⲩⲱⲙ ⲡⲉ ⲛⲉⲙ ⲛⲓⲉⲑⲙⲟⲥ, *he did eat with the gentiles.* Galat. II, 12.

The 1st Future Tense.

45. The Prefixes to the first Future are ⲛⲁ or ⲛⲉ Bash. with the Prefixes of the first Present Tense, as, ϯⲛⲁ, *I;* ⲕ or ⲭⲛⲁ, *thou,* m.; ⲧⲉⲛⲁ, *thou,* f.; ϥⲛⲁ, *he;* ⲥⲛⲁ, *she;* Plur. ⲧⲉⲛⲛⲁ, ⲧⲉⲛⲁ, Sah. *we;* ⲧⲉⲧⲉⲛⲛⲁ, ⲧⲉⲧⲛ̄ⲛⲁ, Sah. *ye;* ⲥⲉⲛⲁ, *they;* thus: ⲉⲥⲉ ⲡⲓⲁⲫⲟⲧ ⲉ̀ⲧⲛⲁⲥⲟϥ, *to drink the cup which I shall drink?* Matt. XX, 22.

ⲦⲈⲦⲚⲀⲊⲘⲞⲞⳜ ⲊⲰⲦⲦⲎⲨⲦⲚ̄, *ye also shall sit.* Matt. XIX, 28. Sahidic.

The 2nd Future Tense.

46. The ·characteristics of the second Future are ⲚⲀ or ⲚⲈ Bash. united with the Prefixes of the second Present Tense, ⲈⲓⲚⲀ, *I;* ⲈⲔⲚⲀ, *thou,* m.; ⲈⲢⲈⲚⲀ, *thou,* f.; ⲈⳊⲚⲀ or ⲈⲢⲈ̣ⲚⲀ, *he;* ⲈⳜⲚⲀ or ⲈⲢⲈⲚⲀ, *she;* Plur. ⲈⲚⲚⲀ or Ⲛ̄ⲚⲀ, Sah. *we;* ⲈⲢⲈⲦⲈⲚⲚⲀ or ⲈⲦⲈⲦⲚ̄ⲚⲀ, ⲈⲦⲈⲦⲚ̄Ⲁ, Sah.*ye;* ⲈⲨⲚⲀ or ⲞⲨⲚⲀ, *they;* thus: ⲈⳊⲚⲀⲘⲞⲞⳜⲈ Ⲛ̄ⲦⲞⲦⳊ Ⲛ̄ⲢⲀⲦⳊ, *he will go on foot.* Acts XX, 13. Sah. ⲬⲈⲔⲀⳜ ⲊⲰⲦⲦⲎⲨⲦⲚ̄ ⲈⲦⲈⲦⲚⲀⲠⲓⳜⲦⲈⲨⲈ, *that ye might believe.* John XIX, 35. Sah. ⲞⲨⲞⲊ ⲠⲓⳝⲖⲞⲖ ⲈⲦ ⲞⲨⲚⲀⲈⲢⲂⲰⲔ, *and the nation that they shall serve,* Acts VII, 7.

47. The second person fem. sing. Sah. occurs thus, ⲈⲢⲚⲀ. These Prefixes do not always express the Future, for instance they express the present participle, ⲠⲈⲦⲢⲞⳜ ⲘⲚ̄ ⲓⲰⲊⲀⲚⲚⲎⳜ ⲈⲨⲚⲀⲂⲰⲔ ⲈⲊⲞⲨⲚ Ⲉ ⲠⲈⲢⲠⳐ, *Peter and John entering into the Temple,* Acts III, 3. Sah. and with ⲊⲓⲚⲀ they express the Subjunctive Mood.

The Coptic has sometimes ⲀⲓⲚⲀ, ⲀⲔⲚⲀ, ⲀⲢⲈⲚⲀ etc. as, ⲊⲀⲢⲀ ⲀⳊⲚⲀⲬⲈⲘ Ⲋ̄Ⲗⲓ ⲊⲓⲰⲦⳜ, *if he might find any thing upon it,* Mark XI, 13.

The 3rd Future Tense.

48. The Prefixes of the third Future.

The Prefixes of this Tense are ⲈⲓⲈ̀, *I;* ⲈⲔⲈ̀, *thou,* m.; ⲈⲢⲈ̀, *thou,* f.; ⲈⳊⲈ̀ or ⲈⲢⲈ̀, *he;* ⲈⳜⲈ̀ or ⲈⲢⲈ̀, *she;* Plur. ⲈⲚⲈ̀, *we;* ⲈⲢⲈⲦⲈⲚⲈ̀, ⲈⲦⲈⲦⲚ̄Ⲉ, Sah. *ye;* ⲈⲨⲈ̀, ⲈⲢⲈ̀, *they;* thus:

10

ⲉⲥⲉ̀ⲙⲓⲥⲓ ⲛ̀ⲟⲩϣⲏⲣⲓ ⲉⲩⲉ̀ⲙⲟⲩ† ⲉ̀ⲡⲉϥⲣⲁⲛ, *she shall bring forth a son and they shall call his name.* Matt. I, 23. ⲉⲣⲉ̀ ⲡⲓⲣⲱⲙⲓ ⲭⲁ ⲡⲉϥⲓⲱⲧ ⲛⲉⲙ ⲧⲉϥⲙⲁⲩ ⲛ̀ⲥⲱϥ ⲟⲩⲟϩ ⲉϥⲉ̀- ⲧⲟⲙϥ ⲉ̀ⲧⲉϥⲥϩⲓⲙⲓ, *a man shall leave his father and his mother, and shall cleave to his wife.* Matt. XIX, 5.

This Tense sometimes expresses the Optative Mood, as, ⲧⲉⲭⲁⲣⲓⲥ ⲉⲥⲉϣⲱⲡⲉ ⲛⲙ̄ⲙⲁⲛ, *grace be with us,* 2. John 5. Sah. ϫⲉⲕⲁⲥ ⲉⲣⲉ̀ ⲟⲩⲣⲱⲙⲓ ⲛ̀ⲟⲩⲱⲧ ⲙⲟⲩ, *that one man should die,* John XI, 50.

The 4th Future Tense.

49. The Prefixes to this Tense are very seldom met with, but we may note a few examples, as, ⲡⲥⲁϩ ⲧⲁⲟⲩⲁϩⲧ̄ ⲛ̀ⲥⲱⲕ, *Master, I will follow thee.* Matt. VIII, 19. Sah. ⲟⲩⲟϩ ϩⲏⲡⲡⲉ ⲧⲉⲣⲁⲉⲣⲃⲟⲕⲓ, *and behold thou shalt conceive,* Luke I, 31. ⲧⲉⲣⲁⲛⲁⲩ ⲉ̀ⲡⲱⲟⲩ ⲙ̀ⲫ†, *thou shalt see the glory of God.* John XI, 40. ⲧⲁⲣⲛ̄ⲣ̄ⲛⲟⲃⲉ ϫⲉ ⲛ̄ⲧ- ⲛ̄ϣⲟⲟⲡ ⲁⲛ ϩⲁ ⲡⲛⲟⲙⲟⲥ, *shall we sin because we are not under the law?* Rom. VI, 15. Sah. ϣⲓⲛⲉ ⲧⲁⲣⲉⲧⲛ̄ϭⲓⲛⲉ. ⲧⲱϩⲙ̄ ⲧⲁⲣⲟⲩⲟⲩⲱⲛ ⲛⲏⲧⲛ̄, *seek, ye shall find; knock, they shall open to you.* Luke XI, 9. Sah.

The Imperfect Future Tense.

50. This Tense contains the Prefixes to the imperfect, and ⲛⲁ the characteristic of the future, as, ⲛⲁⲓⲛⲁ, ⲛⲉⲓⲛⲁ, *I;* ⲛⲁⲕⲛⲁ, ⲛⲉⲕⲛⲁ, Sah. *thou,* m.; ⲛⲁⲣⲉⲛⲁ, ⲛⲉⲣⲉⲛⲁ, Sah. *thou,* f.; etc. often with ⲡⲉ. ⲟⲩⲟϩ ⲑⲁⲓ ⲛⲁⲥ- ⲛⲁⲙⲟⲩ ⲡⲉ, *and she was about to die,* Luke VIII, 42. ⲛⲁⲣⲉ ⲡⲓϫⲟⲓ ⲅⲁⲣ ⲛⲁϩⲓⲟⲩⲓ̀ ⲙ̀ⲡⲉϥⲁ̀ⲟⲩⲓⲛ ⲉ̀ⲙⲙⲁⲩ, *for*

the ship was to cast out her burden there. Acts XXI, 3.
ⲚⲀⲡⲈⲦⲈⲚⲚⲀⲦⲎⲒⲦⲞⲨ ⲚⲎⲒ ⲡⲈ, *ye would have given them to
me.* Galat. IV, 15. ⲚⲈⲨⲚⲀⲘⲒϢⲈ ⲡⲈ ⲚϬⲒ ⲚⲀⲍⲨⲡⲈⲣⲎⲦⲦⲎⲤ,
my servants would fight, John XVIII, 36. Sah.

The Subjunctive Mood.

51. The Prefixes to this Mood are ⲚⲦⲀ, *I;* ⲚⲦⲈⲔ,
Ⲛⲅ, Sah. *thou,* m.; ⲚⲦⲈ. *thou,* f.; ⲚⲦⲈϥ, ⲚⲦⲈ. Ⲛϥ, ⲚⲈϥ,
ⲚⲦⲈ, Sah. *he;* ⲚⲦⲈⲤ, ⲚⲦⲈ. ⲚⲤ̄, ⲚⲦⲈ. Sah. *she;* Plur. ⲚⲦⲈⲚ,
ⲚⲦⲚ̄, Sah. *we;* ⲚⲦⲈⲦⲈⲚ, ⲚⲦⲈⲦⲚ̄. Sah. *ye;* ⲚⲦⲞⲨ, ⲚⲦⲈ, ⲚⲤⲈ,
ⲚⲦⲈ, Sah. *they.*

This Mood follows the tense of the verb that precedes it, whether of the present Tense, the Imperfect,
the Perfect, or the Future, as, ⲚⲈⲨⲤⲰⲦⲘ̄ ⲘⲚ̄ · ⲈⲦⲈⲤⲘⲎ
ⲚⲤⲈⲚⲞⲒ ⲀⲚ, *they heard a voice, but they understood not,*
Sah. Acts IX, 7. ⲤⲈⲚⲀⲡⲀⲣⲀⲆⲒⲆⲞⲨ Ⲙ̄ⲘⲞϥ Ⲉ ⲦⲞⲞⲦⲞⲨ ⲚⲚ̄-
ⲣⲰⲘⲈ ⲚⲤⲈⲘⲞⲞⲨⲦϥ. *they shall deliver him into the hands
of men, they shall kill him.* Matt. XVII, 22. Sah.

Also ⲈⲦⲣⲈϥⲀⲗⲈ ⲚϥⲍⲘⲞⲞⲤ ⲍⲒⲦⲞⲨⲰⲦϥ, *that he would
ascend and sit with him.* Sah. Acts VIII, 31. ⲈⲐⲢⲞⲨϢⲈ
ⲈⲂⲟⲨⲚ, *that they went in,* Acts XIV, 1. ⲍⲘ̄ ⲡⲦⲈⲨⲤⲰⲦⲘ̄
Ⲉⲣⲟϥ ⲀⲨⲰ ⲚⲤⲈⲚⲀⲨ Ⲙ̄ⲘⲀⲈⲒⲚ ⲈⲚⲈϥⲈⲒⲣⲈ Ⲙ̄ⲙⲟⲟⲨ, *when
they heard and saw the miracles which he did.* Acts IX, 6.
Sah. ⲍⲘ̄ ⲡⲦⲣⲀⲰϣ, *when I cry.* Ps. IV, 3. Sah.

After the Particles ⲍⲒⲚⲀ, ϢⲀⲚ, ⲍⲰⲤⲦⲈ, ⲬⲈ, ⲬⲈⲔⲀⲤ,
ⲘⲎⲡⲞⲦⲈ etc., it is the Subjunctive; as, ⲍⲒⲚⲀ ⲚⲦⲈⲦⲈⲚ
ⲈⲘⲒ, *that ye may know.* Matt. IX, 6.

The Optative Mood.

52. This Mood has ⲙⲁⲡ added to the Prefixes of the second Present Tense, as, ⲙⲁⲣⲓ, *I;* ⲙⲁⲣⲉⲕ, *thou,* m.; ⲙⲁⲣⲉ, *thou,* f.; ⲙⲁⲣⲉϥ, ⲙⲁⲣⲉ, *he;* ⲙⲁⲣⲉⲥ, ⲙⲁⲣⲉ, *she;* Plur. ⲙⲁⲣⲉⲛ, ⲙⲁⲣⲛ̄, Sah. *we;* ⲙⲁⲣⲉⲧⲉⲛ, ⲙⲁⲣⲉⲧⲛ̄, Sah.*ye;* ⲙⲁⲣⲟⲩ, ⲙⲁⲣⲉ, *they;* thus, ⲙⲁⲣⲉ ⲡⲁⲓ ⲁ̀ϥⲟⲧ ⲥⲉⲛⲧ, *this cup pass from me.* Matt. XXVI, 39. ⲙⲁⲣⲉϥⲛⲁⲍⲙⲉϥ ⲙⲁ-ⲣⲉϥⲧⲟⲩⲝⲟϥ, *let him deliver him, let him save him,* Psalm XXII, 8. The Bashmuric has ⲙⲁⲗⲉϥ, ⲙⲁⲗⲉⲛ, etc.

The Imperative Mood.

53. The Imperative Mood is expressed by the root itself without any Prefix, as, ⲥⲱⲧⲉⲙ, *hear thou, hear ye;* ⲥⲙⲟⲩ, *praise thou, praise ye;* or it takes ⲁ, ⲁⲣⲓ, or ⲙⲁ before the root, as, ⲁ̀ⲛⲁⲩ ⲟⲩⲟⲍ ⲁ̀ⲣⲉⲍ ⲉ̀ⲣⲱⲧⲉⲛ, *see, and keep you,* Luke XII, 15. ⲛⲏⲉⲧϣⲱⲛⲓ ⲁ̀ⲣⲓⲫⲁⲃⲣⲓ ⲉ̀ⲣⲱⲟⲩ, *heel the sick,* Matt. X, 8. ⲁⲣⲓⲙⲛ̄ⲧⲣⲉ ⲍⲁ ⲡⲁⲡⲉⲑⲟⲟⲩ, *bear witness of the evil,* John XVIII, 23. Sah. ⲁ̀ⲣⲓⲫⲙⲉⲩⲓ̀ ⲙ̀ⲫⲣⲏϯ ⲉ̀ⲧⲁϥⲥⲁⲝⲓ ⲛⲉⲙⲱⲧⲉⲛ, *remember, as he spoke with you,* Luke XXIV, 6. ϥⲁⲓ ⲁⲉ ⲁ̀ⲣⲓⲉ̀ⲙⲓ, *and know this,* Luke XII, 39. ⲁ̀ⲝⲟⲥ, Copt. ⲁⲝⲓⲥ, Sah. *say, say ye;* ⲁ̀ⲙⲟⲩ, *come;* ⲁ̀ⲗⲓ, *take,* from ⲉⲗ; ⲁⲗⲟⲕ, Zoeg. p. 520. ⲁⲗⲱⲧⲛ̄, *suffer ye her,* John XII, 7. Sah. from ⲗⲟ. ⲁ̀ⲛⲓ, *bring,* from ⲉⲛ etc.

The Infinitive Mood.

54. The Infinitive Mood is sometimes expressed by the root itself, but more frequently it has ⲉ̀ or ⲛ̀ pre-fixed, as, ⲉⲩⲕⲱϯⲛⲥⲁ ⲥⲁⲝⲓ ⲛⲉⲙⲁϥ, *seeking to speak*

with him, Luke XII, 46. thus, ⲁⳅⲧⲁⲟⲅⲟⳅ ⲉ̀ⲥⲙⲟⲩ ⲉ̀ⲣⲱⲧⲉⲛ, *he sent him to bless you*, Acts III, 26. ⲟⲩⲟⳅ ⲁⲓ̀ⲓ ⲉ̀ⲡⲉⲥⲏⲧ ⲉ̀ⲛⲁⳅⲙⲟⲩ, *and I have come down to deliver them*, Acts VII, 34. ⲁⳅⲉⲣⲡⳅⲏⲧⲥ ⲛ̀ⳅⲓⲟⲩⲓ̀ ⲉ̀ⲃⲟⲗ, *he began to cast out*, Luke XIX, 45. ⲟⲩⲟⳅ ⲙ̅ⲡⲉ ⳅⲗⲓ ⳍⳃⲉⲙⳃⲟⲙ ⲛ̀ⲉⲣⲟⲩⲱ̀, *and no one could answer*, Matt. XXII, 46. ⲁⲩⲱ ⲁⲩⲁⲣⲭⲉⲓ ⲛⳍⲁ̅ⳃⲉ, *and began to speak*, Acts II, 4. Sahidic.

The Coptic takes ⲡ before the verb as a sign of the Infinitive, as ⲉ ⲡⲕⲟⲥⲧ, πρὸς τὸ ἐνταφιάσαι με, *to my burial*, Sah. Matt. XXVI, 12. ⲡⲥⲟⲩⲱⲛ̅, τὸ ἐπίστασθαί σε, Sap. 793.

ⲉ is also used to express the Infinitive with the verbs ⲑⲣⲉ, ⲧⲣⲉ, Sah. as, ⲁⲣⲉⲧⲉⲛⲉⲣⲡⲉ̀ⲧⲉⲛ ⲉⲑⲣⲟⲩⲭⲁ ⲟⲩ· ⲣⲱⲙⲓ ⲛⲱⲧⲉⲛ ⲉ̀ⲃⲟⲗ ⲛⲣⲉⳅⳃⲱⲧⲉⲃ, *ye have asked them to release a murderer to you*, or *that they would etc.*, Acts III, 14. ⲉⲧⲣⲉⲩⳅⲁⲣⳅ ⲉⲣⲟⳅ, *to keep him*, or *that they should keep etc.*, Acts XII, 4. ⲉⲑⲣⲉⲕⲁⲓⲧⲟⲩ, *to do them*, σοι ποιῆσαι, Acts XXII, 10. ⲉⲧⲣⲉⳅϯ ⲛ̅ⲟⲩⲙⲉⲧⲁⲛⲉⲁ ⲙ̅ⲡⲓⲏ̅ⲗ, *to give repentance to Israel*, Sah. Acts V, 31. ⲛⲁ·ⲛⲟⲩⲥ ⲛⲁⲛ ⲉⲧⲣⲉⲛⳍⲱ ⲙ̅ⲡⲓ ⲙⲁ, ὧδε εἶναι, *good for us to remain here*, or *that we should remain*, Mark. IX, 5. Sah. ⲉⲑⲣⲉ ⲛⲓⲉⲑⲛⲟⲥ ⲥⲱⲧⲉⲙ ⲉ̀ⲡⲓⲥⲁ̅ⳃⲓ, ἀκοῦσαι τὰ ἔθνη, *the gentiles to hear the word*, or *should hear the word*, Acts XV, 7.

We may here remark that ⳃⲓⲛ the sign of action and ⲑⲣⲉ are thus construed, ⲉ̀ⲡⳃⲓⲛⲧⲟⲩⲥⲱⲧⲉⲙ ⲛ̀ⲥⲱⲛ, πρὸς τὸ πείθεσθαι αὐτούς, Copt. ⲉⲧⲣⲉⲩⲥⲱⲧⲙ̅ ⲛⲁⲛ, *to obey us*, or *that they may obey us*, James III, 3. ⳍⲉⲛ ⲡⳃⲓⲛⲧⲟⲩⲧⲁⲥⲑⲟ, ἐν τῷ ὑποστρέφειν αὐτούς, *in their returning*, Luke II, 43.

The Participles.

55. The Participles of the Present Tense are expressed by the Prefixes of the 2nd Present Tense, as, ⲀϤⲦⲰⲂⲌ ⲈϤϪⲰⲘ̇ⲘⲞⲤ, *he prayed, saying*, Matt. XXVI, 39. ⲈⲨⲔⲒⲘ ⲚⲦⲞⲨⲀ̀ⲪⲈ ⲈⲨϪⲰⲘ̇ⲘⲞⲤ, *wagging their heads, saying*, Matt. XXVII, 39. ⲈϤⲘⲞⲞϢⲈ ⲀⲨⲰ ⲈϤϪⲒϤⲞϬⲤ ⲈϤⲤⲘⲞⲨ ⲈⲠⲚⲞⲨⲦⲈ, *walking and leaping, praising God*, Acts III, 8. S.

Participles are also expressed by the Prefixes of the Perfect and the Future with the relative pronoun prefixed, as, ⲚⲐⲰⲞⲨ ⲀⲈ ⲈⲦⲀⲨⲤⲰⲦⲈⲘ ⲀⲨⲦⲰ̀ⲞⲨ Ⲙ̀ⲪⲦ, οἱ δὲ ἀκήσαντες, ἐδόξαζον τὸν κύριον, *and they hearing*, or *(when they heard) glorified God*, Acts XXI, 20. ⲈⲦⲀϤϤⲀⲒ ⲀⲈ Ⲛ̀ⲚⲈϤⲂⲀⲖ ⲈⲠϢⲰⲒ, *and lifting up his eyes*, John VI, 5. ⲞⲨⲞⲌ ⲚⲎⲈⲐⲚⲀⲤⲰⲦⲈⲘ ⲈⲨⲈ̀ⲰⲚⳇ, *and those hearing* (οἱ ἀκούσαντες) *shall live*, John V, 25. ⲈⲐⲚⲀⲦⲀⲔⲞ, *perituram*, John VI, 27.

Participles are also formed by prefixing Ⲉ̀ to the signs of the Perfect Tense, as, ⲈⲀϤⲌⲞⲚⲌⲈⲚ, παραγγείλας, Matt. X, 5. ⲈⲀⲨⲦⲌⲀⲠ, κρίναντες, Acts XIII, 27. ⲈⲀⲦⲈⲦⲈⲚⲈⲢⲌ̇ⲎⲦⲤ ⲒⳤⲈⲚ Ⲓ̅Ⲗ̅ⲎⲘ̅, ἀρξάμενοι, *beginning from Jerusalem*, Luke XXIV, 47.

The Potential Mood.

56. The Letter ⲱ̀, (ⲈϢ Sahitic.) is often met with between the Prefixes and verbs, being the sign of the Potential Mood. It is found connected with the preformants of the Indicative Mood, and the Negative Prefixes, but is most frequently united with those of the

Future Tenses, thus: ⲚⲀⲨⲤⲞⳓⲚⲒ ϪⲈ ⲀⲢⲎⲞⲨ ⲤⲈⲚⲀⳤⲚⲞ-
ⲢⲈⲘ Ⲙ̄ⲠⲒϪⲞⲒ ⲈⲘⲀⲨ, *they took counsel whether they could
save the vessel there,* Acts XXVII, 39. ⲦⲈϤⲄⲈⲚⲈⲀ ⲚⲒⲘ
ⲠⲈⲦⲚⲀⲈⳤⲦⲀⲨⲞⲤ, *who can declare his generation,* Acts
VIII, 33. Sah. Ⲛ̄ⲚⲀⲈⳤⲞⲨϪⲀⲒ̈ Ⲛ̄ϨⲎⲦϤ, *δεῖ σωθῆναι, by
which we can be saved,* Acts IV, 12. Sah. ⲈⲨϪⲱⲘ̄ⲘⲞⲤ
ⲚⲀϤ ϪⲈ ⲚⲒⲘ ⲈⲐⲚⲀⳤⲚⲞϨⲈⲘ, *saying to him, who can be
saved?* Mark X, 26.

Of the Prefix ⳤⲞⲨ.

57. M. Quatremère says that ⳤⲞⲨ, when placed before verbs serves to indicate that a thing ought to be
done, — that it merits to be done; as "ⲀϤⲦⲞⲨⲦⲰⲚ ⲦⲈϤ-
ϪⲒϪ Ⲉⲃⲟⲗ Ⲛ̄ⳤⲞⲨⲤⲞⲗⲠⲤ, *It étendit sa main, qui eût mérité
d'être coupée."* In composition it appears to express di-
gnus, as, ϨⲰⲤ ϨⲀⲚⳤⲞⲨⲘⲈⲚⲢⲒⲦⲞⲨ ⲚⲈ ⲚⲈⲔⲘⲀⲚ̄ⳤⲰⲠⲒ,
how worthy to be loved (lovely) are thy tabernacles, Psalm
LXXXIII, 1. ⲆⲀⲨⲒⲆ ⲠⲒⲞⲨⲢⲟ Ⲛ̄ⲒⳤⲞⲨⲦⲀⲒⲟϥ, *David the king,
very worthy to be honoured.* Prec. Copt. MS. p. 277, 284 etc.
ϨⲰⲃ Ⲛ̄ⳤⲞⲨⲢ̄ⳤⲠⲎⲢⲈ Ⲙ̄Ⲙⲟϥ, *things worthy to be admired,*
Zoeg. 619. Sahidic.

The Negative Prefixes.

The Negative Prefix Ⲛ.

58. The negative Prefixes to verbs are ⲀⲚ, Ⲛ̄, with
ⲀⲚ, Ⲛ, Ⲙ, Ⲙ̄ⲠⲈ, Ⲙ̄ⲠⲀⲦⲈ, ⲦⲘ̄, ⳤⲦⲈⲘ, which are thus used.

The 1st Present Tense Negative.

Singular.

Coptic.	Sahidic.	Bashmuric.
ⲛ̀ϯ ⲁⲛ,	ⲛ̄ϯ ⲁⲛ,	ⲉⲛ or ⲛ̀ϯ ⲉⲛ, *I.*
ⲛ̀ⲕ ⲁⲛ,	ⲛ̄ⲣ ⲁⲛ,	*thou,* m.
ⲛ̀ⲧⲉ ⲁⲛ,	ⲛ̄ⲧⲉ ⲁⲛ,	*thou,* f.
ⲛ̀ϥ ⲁⲛ,	ⲛ̄ϥ ⲁⲛ,	ⲉⲛϥ ⲉⲛ, *he.*
ⲛ̀ⲥ ⲁⲛ,	ⲛ̄ⲥ ⲁⲛ,	*she.*

Plural.

ⲛ̀ⲧⲉⲛ ⲁⲛ, ·	ⲛ̄ⲧⲛ̄ ⲁⲛ,	*we.*
ⲛ̀ⲧⲉⲧⲉⲛ ⲁⲛ,	ⲛ̄ⲧⲉⲧⲛ̄ ⲁⲛ,	*ye.*
ⲛ̀ⲥⲉ ⲁⲛ, .	ⲛ̄ⲥⲉ ⲁⲛ,	ⲉⲛⲥⲉ ⲉⲛ, *they.*

The 2nd Present Tense Negative.

Singular.

Coptic.	Sahidic.
ⲛⲁⲓ ⲁⲛ,	ⲛⲉⲓ ⲁⲛ, *I.*
ⲛⲁⲕ ⲁⲛ,	ⲛⲉⲕ ⲁⲛ, *thou,* m.
ⲛⲁⲡⲉ ⲁⲛ,	*thou,* f.
ⲛⲁϥ ⲁⲛ, } ⲛⲁⲡⲉ ⲁⲛ,	ⲛⲉϥ ⲁⲛ, } ⲛⲁⲡⲉ ⲁⲛ, *he.* *he &she.*
ⲛⲁⲥ ⲁⲛ,	ⲛⲉⲧ ⲁⲛ, *she.*

Plural.

ⲛⲁⲛ ⲁⲛ,	ⲛⲉⲛ ⲁⲛ, *we.*
ⲛⲁⲡⲉⲧⲉⲛ ⲁⲛ,	ⲛⲉⲧⲉⲧⲛ̄ ⲁⲛ, *ye.*
ⲛⲁⲩⲁⲛ ⲁⲛ, ⲛⲁⲡⲉ ⲁⲛ,	ⲛⲉⲩ ⲁⲛ, *they.*

The Perfect Tense Negative.

Singular.

Coptic.

ⲚⲈⲦⲀⲓ ⲀⲚ, *I.*

ⲚⲈⲦⲀⲔ ⲀⲚ, *thou*, m.

ⲚⲈⲦⲀⲡⲉ ⲀⲚ, *thou*, f.

ⲚⲈⲦⲀϥ ⲀⲚ, *he.*

ⲚⲈⲦⲀⲤ ⲀⲚ, *she.*

Plural.

ⲚⲈⲦⲀⲚ ⲀⲚ, *we.*

ⲚⲈⲦⲀⲡⲉⲦⲈⲚ ⲀⲚ, *ye.*

ⲚⲈⲦⲀⲨ ⲀⲚ, ⲚⲈⲦⲀ ⲀⲚ, *they.*

The 1st Future Tense Negative.

Singular.

Coptic.	Sahidic.	Bashmuric.	
Ⲛ̀ϯⲚⲀ ⲀⲚ,	Ⲛ̄ϯⲚⲀ, ⲚⲈⲓⲚⲀ ⲀⲚ,	Ⲛ̀ϯⲚⲈ ⲈⲚ,	*I.*
Ⲛ̀ⲬⲚⲀ ⲀⲚ,	Ⲛ̄ⲅⲚⲀ ⲀⲚ,		*thou*, m.
Ⲛ̀ⲦⲈⲚⲀ ⲀⲚ,	Ⲛ̄ⲦⲈⲚⲀ ⲀⲚ,		*thou*, f.
Ⲛϥ̀ⲚⲀ ⲀⲚ, ⲚⲀⲡⲈⲚⲀ ⲀⲚ,	Ⲛ̄ϥⲚⲀ ⲀⲚ,	Ⲛϥ̀ⲚⲀ ⲈⲚ, *he.*	
Ⲛ̀ⲤⲚⲀ ⲀⲚ,	Ⲛ̄ⲤⲚⲀ ⲀⲚ,	*she.*	

Plural.

Ⲛ̀ⲦⲈⲚⲚⲀ ⲀⲚ,	Ⲛ̄ⲦⲚ̄ⲚⲀ ⲀⲚ,	*we.*	
Ⲛ̀ⲦⲈⲦⲈⲚⲚⲀ ⲀⲚ,	Ⲛ̄ⲦⲈⲦⲚ̄ⲚⲀ ⲀⲚ,	*ye.*	
Ⲛ̀ⲤⲈⲚⲀ ⲀⲚ,	Ⲛ̄ⲤⲈⲚⲀ ⲀⲚ,	*they.*	

11

The 2nd Future Tense Negative.
Singular.

Coptic.	Sahidic.
Ⲛ̀ⲚⲀ,	Ⲛ̄ⲚⲀ, *I*.
Ⲛ̀ⲚⲈⲔ,	Ⲛ̄ⲚⲈⲔ, *thou*, m.
Ⲛ̀ⲚⲈ,	Ⲛ̄ⲚⲈ, *thou*, f.
Ⲛ̀ⲚⲈϥ, Ⲛ̀ⲚⲈⳐ, } Ⲛ̀ⲚⲈ,	Ⲛ̄ⲚⲈϥ, Ⲛ̄ⲚⲈⳐ, } Ⲛ̄ⲚⲈ, *he and she*. *he. she.*

Plural.

Ⲛ̀ⲚⲈⲚ,	Ⲛ̄ⲚⲈⲚ, *we*.
Ⲛ̀ⲚⲈⲦⲈⲚ,	Ⲛ̄ⲚⲈⲦⲚ̄, *ye*.
Ⲛ̀ⲚⲞⲨ,	Ⲛ̄ⲚⲈⲨ, *they*.

The 1st Present Tense Negative.

59. The first Present Tense Negative and Participle
are thus expressed Ⲛ̀ϯⲤⲰⲞⲨⲚ Ⲙ̀ⲠⲒⲢⲰⲘⲒ ⲀⲚ, *I know not
the man*, Mat. XXVI, 72. ⲀⲨⲰ Ⲛ̄ⲦⲚ̄ⲈⲒⲢⲈ ⲀⲚ Ⲛ̄ⲦⲘⲈ, *and
we do not the truth*, 1 John I, 8. Sah. Ⲛ̄ϥⲤⲞⲞⲨⲚ ⲀⲚ,
knoweth not, 1 John II, 11. Sah.

The Prefixes of the present Tense also express the
Participle present, but the Coptic and Bashmuric often
add Ⲉ to the Prefixes, as ⲈⲚϥ̄ⲆⲒⲀⲔⲢⲒⲚⲈ ⲀⲚ Ⲙ̄ⲠⲤⲰⲘⲀ,
not discerning the body. 1 Cor. IX, 29. Sah. ⲈⲚⲄ̄ⲚⲀⲨ ⲀⲚ
ⲈⲂⲞⲖ Ⲉ ⲠⲢⲎ, *not seeing the sun*, Acts XII, 11. Sah. ⲈⲚ-
ϯⲈⲘⲠϢⲎ ⲈⲚ, *I am not worthy*, 1 Cor. XV, 9. Bash. ⲈⲚ-
ⲤⲈⲀⲢⲒⲤⲔⲈ ⲈⲚ Ⲙ̀Ⲫϯ, *they please not God*. 1 Thes. II, 15.
Bashmuric.

The 2nd Present Tense Negative.

60. The second Present Tense Negative is thus formed, naϥoɣнoɣ an ṁпιoɣaι пoɣaι ṅмon, *he is not far from each one of us*, Acts XVII, 27. neκбωϣτ гaр an eɡo ṅpωмe, *for thou regardest not the face of men.* Mat. XXII, 16. Sah. ṁпeтe neϥκpιne ṁмoϥ an, *who condemneth not himself*, Rom. XIV, 22. Sah.

The Perfect Tense Negative.

61. This Tense in the Coptic is thus presented to us. neтaιì гaр an èθaɡeм nιoмнι, *I came not to call the just*, Mark II, 17. oɣ гaр пϣнpι ṁɸpωмι neтaϥì an, *for the son of man hath not come*, Mark X, 45.

The 1st Future Tense Negative.

62. The following are specimens of the first Future Tense negative, ṅϥnaxa θннoɣ an, *he will not leave you*, 1 Cor. X, 13. epe пpωмe naωnɡ an e oeικ ṁмaтe, *man shall not live by bread alone*, Mat. III, 4. Sah. nape †метoɣpo ṅтe ɸ† naì an, *the kingdom of God will not come.* Luke XVII, 20. ṅceнaвoλϥ èвoλ an, *which shall not be thrown down.* Mat. XXIV, 2.

The 2nd Future Tense Negative.

63. This future occurs without the an, as пanaι ae ṅnaoλϥ èвoλ ɡapoϥ, *my mercy I will not take from him.* Ps. LXXXIX, 33. oɣaι èвoλ ṅbнтoɣ ṅneϥλoϥλeϥ, *one of them shall not be broken*, Ps. XXXIV, 20. ṅneтen-ɸoɡ èмeϣт nιвaκι ṅтe пicλ̄, *ye shall not have gone over*

11*

the cities of Israel, Mat. X, 23. When these Prefixes follow the Particles ϫⲉ, ϫⲉⲕⲁⲥ, ϩⲟⲡⲱⲥ, &c., they express the Subjunctive.

It may perhaps be hardly necessary to observe that the Prefix is sometimes written ⲉⲛ instead of ⲛ̄.

The Negative Prefix ⲙ.

64. The following form of this Prefix is only found in the Sahidic and Bashmuric Dialects. viz.

The Present Tense.

Singular.

Sahidic.

ⲙⲉⲓ, *I.*

ⲙⲉⲕ, *thou,* m.

ⲙⲉⲣⲉ, *thou,* f.

ⲙⲉϥ, ⎱   *he.*
      ⎰ ⲙⲉ́ⲣⲉ, *he* and *she.*
ⲙⲉⲥ, ⎰   *she.*

Plural.

ⲙⲉⲩ, ⲙⲉⲣⲉ, *they.*

The Imperfect Tense.

ⲛⲉⲙⲉϥ, *he.*

The Perfect Tense.

ⲙⲁⲕ, *thou,* m.

ⲙⲁϥ, *he.*

ⲉ is found prefixed to this form as the sign of the Participle, as ⲉⲙⲉϥ, ⲉⲙⲉⲥ, ⲉⲙⲉⲩ, &c.

The Negative Prefix ⲘⲡⲈ.

The Present Tense.

<table>
<tr><td colspan="2">Singular.</td><td colspan="2">Plural.</td></tr>
<tr><td colspan="2">Coptic.</td><td colspan="2">Coptic.</td></tr>
<tr><td>ⲘⲡⲀⲒ, I.</td><td></td><td>ⲘⲡⲀⲚ, we.</td><td></td></tr>
<tr><td>ⲘⲡⲀⲔ, thou, m.</td><td></td><td>ⲘⲡⲀⲦⲈⲦⲈⲚ, ye.</td><td></td></tr>
<tr><td>ⲘⲡⲀⲣⲈ, thou, f.</td><td></td><td>ⲘⲡⲀⲨ, ⲘⲡⲀⲣⲈ, they.</td><td></td></tr>
<tr><td>ⲘⲡⲀϥ,}
 ⲘⲡⲀⲤ,}</td><td>ⲘⲡⲀⲣⲈ,</td><td colspan="2">he.
 he and she.
 she.</td></tr>
</table>

The Perfect Tense.

Singular.

Coptic.	Sahidic.		Bashmuric.	
ⲘⲡⲒ,	ⲘⲡⲈⲒ, ⲘⲡⲒ,			<i>I.</i>
ⲘⲡⲈⲔ,	ⲘⲡⲈⲔ,		ⲈⲘⲡⲈⲔ, <i>thou,</i> m.	
ⲘⲡⲈ,	ⲘⲡⲈ,			<i>thou,</i> f.
ⲘⲡⲈϥ,	ⲘⲡⲈϥ,	}ⲘⲡⲈ, <i>he.</i>	ⲈⲘⲡⲈϥ, <i>he.</i>	
ⲘⲡⲈⲤ,	ⲘⲡⲈⲤ,	(<i>and she.</i>	ⲈⲘⲡⲈⲤ, <i>she.</i>	

Plural.

ⲘⲡⲈⲚ,	ⲘⲡⲚ, ⲘⲡⲈⲚ,			<i>we.</i>
ⲘⲡⲈⲦⲈⲚ,	ⲘⲡⲈⲦⲚ,			<i>ye.</i>
ⲘⲡⲟⲨ,	ⲘⲡⲟⲨ, ⲘⲡⲈ,		ⲈⲘⲡⲟⲨ, <i>they.</i>	

Ⲉ before the Ⲙ is a sign of the Participle.

The Subjunctive.

The Imperfect and Perfect Tenses.

Singular.

Coptic.

ⲉⲧⲉⲙ̀ⲡⲓ, *I.*

ⲉⲧⲉⲙ̀ⲡⲉⲕ, *thou,* m.

ⲉⲧⲉⲙ̀ⲡⲉ, *thou,* f.

ⲉⲧⲉⲙ̀ⲡⲉϥ,⎫   *he.*
⎬ ⲉⲧⲉⲙ̀ⲡⲉ, *he* and *she.*
ⲉⲧⲉⲙ̀ⲡⲉⲥ,⎭   *she.*

Plural.

ⲉⲧⲉⲙⲡⲉⲛ, *we.*

ⲉⲧⲉⲙ̀ⲡⲉⲧⲉⲛ, *ye.*

ⲉⲧⲉⲙ̀ⲡⲟⲩ, *they.*

These Prefixes in Coptic correspond with ⲛ̅ⲧⲉⲣⲓⲧ̅ⲙ̅ in Sahidic.

The Negative Prefix ⲙ̀ⲡⲁⲧⲉ.

The Indicative and Subjunctive.

Singular.

Coptic.	Sahidic.
ⲙ̀ⲡⲁϯ,	ⲙ̅ⲡⲁϯ, *I.*
ⲙ̀ⲡⲁⲧⲉⲕ,	ⲙ̅ⲡⲁⲧⲕ̅, *thou,* m.
ⲙ̀ⲡⲁⲧⲉ,	ⲙ̅ⲡⲁⲧⲉ, *thou,* f.

ⲙ̀ⲡⲁⲧⲉϥ, ⎫   ⲙ̅ⲡⲁⲧϥ̅,⎫   *he.*
⎬ ⲙ̀ⲡⲁⲧⲉ.   ⎬ ⲙ̅ⲡⲁⲧⲉ, *he & she.*
ⲙ̀ⲡⲁⲧⲉⲥ, ⎭   ⲙ̅ⲡⲁⲧⲥ̅,⎭   *she.*

Plural.

Coptic.	Sahidic.
ⲘⲠⲀⲦⲈⲚ,	ⲘⲠⲀⲦⲚ̄, *we.*
Ⲙ̀ⲠⲀⲦⲈⲦⲈⲚ,	Ⲙ̄ⲠⲀⲦⲈ́ⲦⲚ̄, *ye.*
Ⲙ̀ⲠⲀⲦⲞⲨ, Ⲙ̀ⲠⲀⲦⲈ,	Ⲙ̄ⲠⲀⲦⲞⲨ, Ⲙ̄ⲠⲀⲦⲈ, *they.*

The Imperfect and Pluperfect Tenses.

Singular.

Coptic.	Sahidic.
ⲚⲈ Ⲙ̀ⲠⲀϮ ⲠⲈ,	ⲚⲈ Ⲙ̄ⲠⲀϮ ⲠⲈ, *I.*
ⲚⲈ Ⲙ̀ⲠⲀⲦⲈⲔ ⲠⲈ,	ⲚⲈ Ⲙ̄ⲠⲀⲦⲔ̄ ⲠⲈ, *thou,* m.
ⲚⲈ Ⲙ̀ⲠⲀⲦⲈ ⲠⲈ,	ⲚⲈ Ⲙ̄ⲠⲀⲦⲈ ⲠⲈ, *thou,* f.
ⲚⲈ Ⲙ̀ⲠⲀⲦⲈϥ ⲠⲈ,	ⲚⲈ Ⲙ̄ⲠⲀⲦϥ̄ ⲠⲈ, *he.*
ⲚⲈ Ⲙ̀ⲠⲀⲦⲈⲤ ⲠⲈ,	ⲚⲈ Ⲙ̄ⲠⲀⲦⲤ̄ ⲠⲈ, *she.*

&c. &c.

The Negative Prefixes ϢⲦⲈⲘ Copt. and ⲦⲘ̄ Sah.

Singular.

Coptic.	Sahidic.
Ⲛ̀ⲦⲀϢⲦⲈⲘ,	ⲚⲦⲀⲦⲘ̄, *I.*
Ⲛ̀ⲦⲈⲔϢⲦⲈⲘ,	ⲚⲄ̄ⲦⲘ̄, *thou,* m.
Ⲛ̀ⲦⲈϢⲦⲈⲘ,	Ⲛ̄ⲦⲈⲦⲘ̄, *thou,* f.
Ⲛ̀ⲦⲈϥϢⲦⲈⲘ, Ⲛ̀ⲦⲈⲤϢⲦⲈⲘ, } Ⲛ̀ⲦⲈϢⲦⲈⲘ,	Ⲛϥ̄ⲦⲘ̄, ⲚⲤ̄ⲦⲘ̄, } ⲚⲦⲈⲦⲘ̄, *he. he & she. she.*

Plural.

Coptic.	Sahidic.
Ⲛ̀ⲦⲈⲚϢⲦⲈⲘ,	Ⲛ̄ⲦⲚ̄ⲦⲘ̄, *we.*
Ⲛ̀ⲦⲈⲦⲈⲚϢⲦⲈⲘ,	Ⲛ̄ⲦⲈⲦⲚ̄ⲦⲘ̄, *ye.*
Ⲛ̀ⲦⲞⲨϢⲦⲈⲘ, Ⲛ̀ⲤⲈϢⲦⲈⲘ,	Ⲛ̄ⲤⲈⲦⲘ̄, *they.*

The Subjunctive.

The Imperfect and Pluperfect Tenses.

Singular.

Sahidic.

ⲚⲦⲈⲢⲈⲓⲦⲘ̄, *I.*

ⲚⲦⲈⲢⲈⲕⲦⲘ̄, *thou,* m.

ⲚⲦⲈⲢⲈⲦⲘ̄, *thou,* f.

ⲚⲦⲈⲢⲈϥⲦⲘ̄, *he.*

ⲚⲦⲈⲢⲈⲥⲦⲘ̄, *she.*

Plural.

ⲚⲦⲈⲢⲟⲩⲦⲘ̄, *they.*

Conditional.

Singular.

Coptic.	Sahidic.	Bashmuric.
ⲀⲓϢⲦⲈⲘ, ˋ	ⲈⲓⲦⲘ̄,	*I.*
ⲀⲕϢⲦⲈⲘ,	ⲈⲕⲦⲘ̄,	*thou,* m.
ⲀⲣⲈϢⲦⲈⲘ,	ⲈⲣⲈⲦⲘ̄,	*thou,* f.
ⲀϥϢⲦⲈⲘ,	ⲈϥⲦⲘ̄,	*he.*
ⲀⲥϢⲦⲈⲘ, } ⲀⲣⲈϢⲦⲈⲘ,	ⲈⲥⲦⲘ̄, } ⲈⲣⲈⲦⲘ̄, ⲀⲗⲈϢⲦⲈⲘ,	*he & she.* / *she.*

Plural.

ⲀⲚϢⲦⲈⲘ,	ⲈⲚⲦⲘ̄,	*we.*
ⲀⲣⲈⲦⲈⲚϢⲦⲈⲘ,	ⲈⲦⲈⲦⲚ̄ⲦⲘ̄,	*ye.*
ⲀⲩϢⲦⲈⲘ,	ⲈⲩⲦⲘ̄,	*they.*

Another particle with this Prefix in the Sahidic is ϢⲀⲚ, *if,* as ⲈⲓϢⲀⲚⲦⲘ̄, ⲈⲕϢⲀⲚⲦⲘ̄, etc.

The Imperative.

Coptic.	Sahidic.	Bashmuric.
ⲙ̅ⲡⲉⲣ,	ⲙ̅ⲡⲣ̅,	ⲙ̅ⲡⲉⲗ,
ⲙ̅ⲡⲉⲛⲑⲣⲉ,	ⲙ̅ⲡⲣ̅ⲧⲣⲉ,	ⲙ̅ⲡⲉⲗⲧⲣⲉ.

These take the Pronoun Suffixes, as ⲙ̅ⲡⲉⲛⲑⲣⲓ, for which see the auxiliary verb ⲑⲣⲉ, Coptic. ⲧⲣⲉ, Sahidic which are below.

The Infinitive.

Coptic.	Sahidic.	Bashmuric.
ⲉ̀ϣⲧⲉⲙ,	ⲉⲧⲙ̅,	ⲉϣⲧⲙ̅,
and	and	
ⲉ̀ϣⲧⲉⲙⲑⲣⲉ,	ⲉⲧⲙ̅ⲧⲣⲉ,	
ⲉ̀ϣⲧⲉⲙⲉⲑⲣⲉ,	ⲉⲧⲙ̅ⲉⲧⲣⲉ.	

These like the above take the Pronoun Suffixes to the verb ⲑⲣⲉ, Coptic and ⲧⲣⲉ, Sahidic.

The Auxiliary verb ⲑⲣⲉ, ⲧⲣⲉ, Sah. to be, to do.

Singular.

Coptic.	Sahidic.	Bashmuric.
ⲑⲣⲓ,	ⲧⲣⲁ,	*I.*
ⲑⲣⲉⲕ,	ⲧⲣⲉⲕ,	*thou,* m.
ⲑⲣⲉ,	ⲧⲣⲉ,	*thou,* f.
ⲑⲣⲉϥ, } ⲑⲣⲉ,	ⲧⲣⲉϥ, } ⲧⲣⲉ,	*he.* *he* and *she.*
ⲑⲣⲉⲥ,	ⲧⲣⲉⲥ,	*she.*

Plural.

Coptic.	Sahidic.	Bashmuric.
ⲑⲣⲉⲛ,	ⲧⲣⲉⲛ,	*we.*
ⲑⲣⲉⲧⲉⲧⲉⲛ, ⲑⲣⲉⲧⲉⲛ,	ⲧⲣⲉⲧⲉⲧⲛ̅, ⲧⲣⲉⲧⲛ̅,	*ye.*
ⲑⲣⲟⲩ, ⲑⲣⲉ,	ⲧⲣⲉⲩ, ⲧⲣⲉ,	ⲧⲣⲟⲩ, *they.*

65. The Auxiliary is thus used ⲚⲎ ⲆⲈ ⲈⲦⲀⲨϬⲢ-ⲤⲰⲚⲦ, *and have made me angry*, or *have provoked me.* Num. XV, 23. ⲀϤϬⲢⲞ ⲘⲘⲞⲤ ⲈϪϤⲈ ⲚⲰⲒⲔ, *causeth her to commit adultery.* Matt. XIX, 9. ⲀⲨⲦⲢⲈ ⲠϪⲞⲒ ⲀⳤⲀⲒ, *they made the vessel that it should be lightened,* or *they lightened the vessel.* Acts XXVII, 38. Sahidic. ϮⲚⲀⲦⲢⲈⲦⲉⲦⲚ-ⲢⲠⲘⲈⲈⲨⲈ ⲚⲚⲈϥⲹⲂⲎⲨⲈ, *I will cause that you remember his works, I will remind you of his works,* 1 John 10. Sah. ⲘⲚⲚⲤⲀ ⲦⲢⲀⲂⲰⲔ, *after my departure.* Acts XX, 29. Sahidic. ⲠⲞⳞⲤ ⲪⲎⲦⲞⲢⲞ ⲚⲚⲀⲒ, *the Lord who doeth these things,* Acts XV, 17. ⲈⲐⲢⲞⲨⲚⲀⲨ ⲈⲢⲰⲞⲨ ⲚϪⲈ ⲚⲒⲢⲰⲘⲒ, *that men may see them,* Matt. XXIII, 5. ⲈⲐⲢⲈⲦⲈⲚⲰⳲ ⲈⲦⲀⲒ ⲈⲠⲒⲤⲦⲞⲖⲎ, *that ye read this epistle;* 1 Thes. V, 26.

66. ⲐⲢⲈ and ⲦⲢⲈ are signs of the Subjunctive with Ⲉ, or some sign of the Subjunctive before them, as ⲈⲐⲢⲈⲔⲀⲒⲦⲞⲨ, *that thou mayest do them,* or *to do them.* Acts XXII, 10. ⲈⲐⲢⲈϥⳲⲰⲠⲒ ⲚⲒⲰⲦ ⲚⲞⲨⲘⲎⳲ ⲚⲈⲐ-ⲚⲞⲤ, *that he might be the father of many nations,* Rom. IV, 18. ⲈⲐⲢⲞⲨⲤⲀϪⲒ ⲚⲀⳲⲢⲀⲔ, *that they might speak before thee,* Acts XXIII, 30. ⳲⲀⲠⲤ ⲞⲚ ⲈⲦⲢⲀⲚⲀⲨ ⲈⲦⲔⲈⳲ-ⲢⲰⲘⲎ, *it is necessary also that I should see Rome.* Acts XIX, 21. Sah. ⲚⲀⲚⲞⲨⲤ ⲚⲀⲚ ⲈⲦⲢⲈⲚϬⲰ ⲘⲠⲀⲒ ⲘⲀ, *it is good for us that we should remain here,* or *to remain here.* Mark IX, 5. Sah. ⲈⲐⲢⲈ ⲚⲒⲈⲐⲚⲞⲤ ⲤⲰⲦⲈⲘ ⲈⲠⲒⲤⲀϪⲒ, *that the gentiles should hear the word,* Acts XV, 7. ⲈⲦⲘⲦⲢⲈϥ-ⲂⲰⲔ ⲈⳲⲞⲨⲚ, *that he would not go in,* Acts XIX, 31. Sah. ⲘⲚⲚⲤⲀ ⲦⲢⲈ ⲠⲈⳲⲦⲞⲢⲦⲢ̄ Ⲗⲟ, *after the tumult ceased,* Acts XX, 1. Sah. ⲈⲦⲢⲈⲨⳲⲀⲢⲈⳲ ⲈⲢⲟϥ, *to keep him,* or *that they should keep him.* Acts XII, 4. Sah.

It will be seen that ⲉⲟⲡⲉ and ⲉⲧⲣⲉ with the suffixes express also the infinitive.

We may also observe that these auxiliaries, taking the Pronoun suffixes, often lose their distinctive signification, which is absorbed by the following verb.

The Auxiliary Verb ⲉⲣ, ⲡ̄, Sah. ⲉⲗ, Bash. to be, to do.

67. When the verb ⲉⲣ, ⲡ̄ or ⲉⲗ, is joined to a noun, it is a verb, as ⲟⲩⲱⲓⲛⲓ, *light;* ⲉⲣⲟⲩⲱⲓⲛⲓ, *to enlighten* or *to make light;* ⲙⲉⲟⲣⲉ, *a witness;* ⲉⲣⲙⲉⲟⲣⲉ, *to bear witness.*

ⲉⲣ is prefixed to verbs, and nouns used verbally, derived from the Greek, as ⲛⲁⲩⲉⲣⲁⲥⲡⲁⲍⲉⲥⲟⲉ ⲙ̇ⲙⲟϥ, *they saluted him,* Mark IX, 15. ⲉⲩⲉⲣⲅⲉⲗⲡⲓⲥ ⲉ̇ⲡⲉϥⲣⲁⲛ, *they shall hope in his name,* Mat. XII, 21. — But ⲡ̄ in Sah. is very seldom prefixed to words derived from the Greek.

ϯ, *to give,* is also an auxiliary, and is joined to ⲱⲟⲩ, Copt. ⲉⲟⲟⲩ, Sah. ⲉⲁⲩ, Bash. *glory.* ϯⲱⲟⲩ, ϯⲉⲟⲟⲩ, Sah. *to give glory, to glorify.* ⲧⲟⲧ, Copt. ⲧⲟⲟⲧ, Sahidic. ⲧⲁⲁⲧ, Bash., *the hand,* ϯⲧⲟⲧ, ϯⲧⲟⲟⲧ, *to give the hand, to help.* ⲙ̇ⲕⲁⲅ, *sorrow, grief,* ϯⲙ̇ⲕⲁⲅ, *to give sorrow, to afflict.*

Of Irregular and defective Verbs.

68. Of the verb ⲡⲉ, *to be,* which is generally accompanied with a personal Pronoun, as ⲁⲛⲟⲕ ⲡⲉ, *I am.* Psalm XLIX, 7. ⲛ̄ⲧⲟⲕ ⲡⲉ, *thou art,* Ezech. XXXVIII, 17. ⲛ̇ⲟⲟϥ ⲡⲉ, *he is,* John XIII, 26. ⲁⲛⲟⲛ ⲡⲉ, *we are,* 1. John III, 1. Sah. ⲛ̄ⲧⲱⲧⲛ̄ ⲡⲉ, *ye are,* Matt. V, 14. Sahidic.

12*

ⲍⲁⲛⲕⲟⲩϫⲓ ⲡⲉ, *few are,* Mat. XXII, 14. ⲛⲁⲓ ⲡⲉ, *these are,* John XX, 18. ⲧⲉ is construed with feminine nouns in the same way, as ⲧⲁⲥⲁⲣⲝ ⲧⲉ, John VI, 55.

The Present Tense.

Singular.

Masc.	Fem.
ⲡⲉ, *I am,* m.	ⲧⲉ, *I am,* f.
ⲡⲉ, *thou art,* f.	ⲧⲉ, *thou art,* f.
ⲡⲉ, *he* or *it is.*	ⲧⲉ, *she* or *it is.*

Plural.

ⲛⲉ, $\left.\begin{array}{l} we \\ ye \\ they \end{array}\right\}$ *are.*
ⲡⲉ,

The Imperfect Tense.

Sing. and Plural.

ⲛⲉ ⲡⲉ, *was* or *were,* m.

ⲛⲉ ⲧⲉ, *was* or *were,* f.

ⲛⲉⲩ, *were.*

The Irregular Verb ϫⲉ, ϫⲟ, ϫⲱ, or ϫⲟⲟ, Sah. ϫⲁ, Bash. to say.

The Present Tense.

Singular.

Coptic.

ϯϫⲱ ⲙ̇ⲙⲟⲥ, $\left.\right\}$ *I say.*
ϯϫⲟⲥ,

ⲕϫⲱ ⲙ̇ⲙⲟⲥ, *thou sayest,* m.

ⲉϥϫⲱ ⲙ̇ⲙⲟⲥ, $\left.\right\}$ ⲉⲣⲉϫⲱ ⲙ̇ⲙⲟⲥ, *he* or *she says.*
ϫⲱ ⲙ̇ⲙⲟⲥ,

ⲉⲥϫⲱ ⲙ̇ⲙⲟⲥ, *she says.*

Singular.

Sahidic.

ϯϫ⳿ⲟⲟⲥ, *I say.*

ⲉⲕϫⲱ, *thou sayest,* m.

ϫⲱ ⲙ̅ⲙⲟⲥ, ⎫
ϥ̅ϫⲱ ⲙ̅ⲙⲟⲥ, ⎭ ⲉⲣⲉϫⲱ ⲙ̅ⲙⲟⲥ, *he says.*
he or she says.

ⲉⲥϫⲱ ⲙ̅ⲙⲟⲥ, *she says.*

Plural.

Coptic and Sahidic.

ⲧⲉⲛϫⲱ ⲙ̀ⲙⲟⲥ, *we say.*

ⲧⲉⲧⲉⲛϫⲱ & ⲧⲉⲧⲛ̅ϫⲱ ⲙ̀ⲙⲟⲥ, *ye say.*

ⲉⲩϫⲱ ⲙ̀ⲙⲟⲥ, ⎫
ⲥⲉϫⲱ ⲙ̀ⲙⲟⲥ, ⎭ *they say.*

The Imperfect Tense.

Singular.

Coptic.	Sahidic.
ⲛⲁⲓϫⲱ ⲙ̀ⲙⲟⲥ,	ⲛⲉⲓϫⲱ ⲙ̅ⲙⲟⲥ, *I did say.*
ⲛⲁϥϫⲱ ⲙ̀ⲙⲟⲥ,	ⲛⲉϥϫⲱ ⲙ̅ⲙⲟⲥ, *he did say.*

Plural.

ⲛⲁⲩϫⲱ ⲙ̀ⲙⲟⲥ, ⲛⲉⲩϫⲱ ⲙ̅ⲙⲟⲥ, *they did say.*

The Perfect Tense.

Singular.

Coptic.	Sahidic.
ⲁⲓϫⲱⲧⲟⲩ,	ⲡⲉϫⲁⲓ, *I have said.*
ⲁⲕϫⲟⲥ,	ⲁⲓϫⲟⲧⲟⲩ, ⎫ *thou,* m.
ⲁϥϫⲟⲥ,	ⲁⲕϫⲟⲟⲥ, ⎭
	ⲁϥϫⲉ, *he.*
	ⲁϥϫⲟⲥ, ⎰ ⲁϥϫⲁⲥ, *he.*
ⲁⲥϫⲟⲥ,	ⲁϥϫⲟⲟⲥ, ⎱ ⲁϫⲟⲟⲥ, *he or she.*
	ⲁⲥϫⲟⲟⲥ, *he and she.*

Plural.

Coptic.		Sahidic.
ⲀⲢⲈⲦⲈⲚⲜⲰ Ⲙ̇ⲘⲞⲤ, *ye.*		
ⲠⲈⲜⲰⲞⲨ Ⲙ̇ⲘⲞⲤ, *they.*		ⲀⲨⲜⲞⲞⲤ, *they.*
ⲀⲨⲜⲞⲤ,		

The Future Tense.

Singular.

Coptic.	Sahidic.
ⲈⲔⲈ̀ⲜⲞⲤ,	ⲈⲔⲈⲜⲞⲞⲤ, *thou shalt,* etc.
ⲈϤⲚⲀⲜⲞⲤ,	ϤⲚⲀⲜⲟⲞⲤ, ⎱ *he.*
	ⲈϤⲚⲀⲜⲞⲞⲨ, ⎰

Plural.

Coptic.	Sahidic.
ⲦⲈⲚⲚⲀⲜⲈ, *we.*	ⲦⲈⲚⲀⲜⲞⲤ, *we.*
ⲈⲨⲈ̀ⲜⲰⲞⲨ, *they.*	ⲤⲈⲚⲀⲜⲞⲞⲨ, *they.*

The Imperative Mood.

Coptic.	Sahidic.
ⲀⲜⲞⲤ,	ⲀⲜⲒⲤ, *say.*

The Infinitive.

Coptic.	Sahidic.
ⲀⲜⲞϤ,	ⲀⲜⲒⲤ, *to say.*

The Perfect Tense.

Singular.

Coptic.		Sahidic.		Bashmuric.
ⲠⲈⲜⲎⲒ,		ⲠⲈⲜⲀⲒ, ⲠⲈⲜⲎⲒ,		*I said.*
ⲠⲈⲜⲀⲔ,		ⲠⲈⲜⲀⲔ,		*thou,* m.
ⲠⲈⲜⲀϤ, ⎱ ⲠⲈⲜⲈ,		ⲠⲈⲜⲀϤ, ⎱ ⲠⲈⲜⲈ,		ⲠⲈⲜⲈϤ, *he.*
ⲠⲈⲜⲀⲤ, ⎰		ⲠⲈⲜⲀⲤ, ⎰ *he and she.*		ⲠⲈⲜⲈⲤ, *she.*

Plural.

Coptic.	Sahidic.	Bashmuric.
ⲠⲈⲜⲀⲚ,		*we.*
ⲠⲈⲜⲰⲦⲈⲚ,		*ye.*
ⲠⲈⲜⲀⲨ, ⲠⲈⲜⲈ,	ⲠⲈⲜⲀⲨ, ⲠⲈⲜⲈ,	ⲠⲈⲜⲈⲨ, *they.*

69. ⲞⲨⲞⲚ, and ⲞⲨⲚ̄, Sah. ⲞⲨⲀⲚ, Bash. are used for the verb *to have* or *to be*, and Ⲙ̄ⲘⲞⲚ, Ⲙ̄Ⲛ̄ϯ, Sah. *not to have*, or *to be*. But when they take the Personal Suffixes after them, they always represent the verb *to have*, with Ⲙ̄ⲘⲀⲨ, which is very often added.

Singular.

Coptic.	Sahidic.
ⲞⲨⲞⲚⲐⲒ, ⲞⲨⲞⲚϯ,	ⲞⲨⲚ̄ⲦⲀⲒ, ⲞⲨⲚ̄ϯ, *I.*
ⲞⲨⲞⲚⲦⲀⲔ, ⲞⲨⲞⲚⲦⲈⲔ,	ⲞⲨⲚ̄ⲦⲀⲔ, ⲞⲨⲚ̄ⲦⲔ̄, *thou,* m.
ⲞⲨⲞⲚⲦⲈ,	ⲞⲨⲚ̄ⲦⲈ, *thou,* f.
ⲞⲨⲞⲚⲦⲀϥ, ⲞⲨⲞⲚⲦⲈϥ,	ⲞⲨⲚ̄ⲦⲀϥ, ⲞⲨⲚ̄Ⲧϥ, *he.*
ⲞⲨⲞⲚⲦⲀⲤ, ⲞⲨⲀⲚⲦⲈⲤ,	ⲞⲨⲚ̄ⲦⲀⲤ, ⲞⲨⲚ̄ⲦⲤ̄, *she.*

Plural.

ⲞⲨⲞⲚⲦⲀⲚ, ⲞⲨⲞⲚⲦⲈⲚ,	ⲞⲨⲚ̄ⲦⲀⲚ, *we.*
ⲞⲨⲞⲚⲦⲈⲦⲈⲚ, ⲞⲨⲞⲚⲦⲰⲦⲈⲚ,	ⲞⲨⲚ̄ⲦⲈⲦⲚ̄, ⲞⲨⲚ̄ⲦⲎⲦⲚ̄, *ye.*
ⲞⲨⲞⲚⲦⲞⲨ, ⲞⲨⲞⲚⲦⲰⲞⲨ,	ⲞⲨⲚ̄ⲦⲀⲨ, ⲞⲨⲚ̄ⲦⲈⲨ, *they.*

Singular.

Bashmuric.

ⲞⲨⲀⲚⲐⲒ, *I.*

ⲞⲨⲀⲚⲐⲎϥ, ⲞⲨⲀⲚⲦⲈϥ, *he.*

ⲞⲨⲀⲚⲐⲤ, *she.*

Plural.

ⲞⲨⲀⲚⲐⲎⲚ, *we.*

ⲞⲨⲀⲚⲐⲞⲨ, *they.*

The Participle is formed by adding ε, as ἐογοΝΤΕΚ, *thou having.* The above are also written ΟΥΟΝΝ̇ΤΗΙ, ΟΥΟΝΝ̇ΤΑΚ, ΟΥΟΝΝ̇ΤΑϥ, etc.

The Negative *not to have,* is thus expressed, and generally with ΠΜΑΥ.

The Present Tense.

Singular.

Coptic.	Sahidic.	Bashmuric.
Μ̇ΜΟΝΤΗΙ, Μ̇ΜΟΝΤ̇.	ΠΜΠΤ̇, ΜΠΤ̇,	ΜΕΝΤΗΙ, *I.*
Μ̇ΜΟΝΤΕΚ,	ΠΜΠ̅Τ̅Κ̅, ΜΠ̅Τ̅Κ̅,	*thou,* m.
Μ̇ΜΟΝΤΕ,	ΜΠ̅ΤΕ,	*thou,* f.
Μ̇ΜΟΝΤΕϥ, Μ̇ΜΟΝΤΑϥ,	ΠΜΠ̅ΤΑϥ, ΜΠ̅Τϥ̅,	ΜΕΝΤΗΙϥ, *he.*
Μ̇ΜΟΝΤΕϹ, Μ̇ΜΟΝΤΑϹ,	ΠΜΠ̅ΤΑϹ, ΜΠ̅ΤϹ̅,	*she,*

Plural.

Μ̇ΜΟΝΤΕΝ, Μ̇ΜΟΝΤΑΝ,	ΜΠ̅ΤΑΝ,	ΜΕΝΤΗΝ, *we.*
Μ̇ΜΟΝΤΕΤΕΝ, Μ̇ΜΟΝΤШΤΕΝ,	ΜΠ̅ΤΗΤΠ̅,	*ye.*
Μ̇ΜΟΝΤΟΥ, Μ̇ΜΟΝΤШΟΥ,	ΜΠ̅ΤΑΥ, ΜΠ̅ΤΟΥ,	ΜΕΝΤΕΥ, *they.*

The Imperfect Tense.

Coptic.	Sahidic.
ΝΕ Μ̇ΜΟΝΤΕϥ ΠΕ, *he.*	ΝΕ ΜΠ̅Τ̅Κ̅, *thou,* m.
ΝΕ Μ̇ΜΟΝΤΟΥ ΠΕ, *they.*	ΝΕ ΜΠ̅Τϥ̅, *he.*
	ΝΕ ΜΠ̅ΤϹ̅, *she.*

These are sometimes written ΜΜΟΝ Ν̇Τ̇ or Ν̇ΤΗΙ, Μ̇ΜΟΝΝ̇ΤΑΝ, Μ̇ΜΟΝΝ̇ΤШΤΕΝ, etc.

Of Verbs Passive.

70. To what has been said of verbs Passive under Chap. V, we may add the following.

Verbs active are made passive by changing the vowels of the root, as ⲕⲱ, *to put*, ⲕⲏ, *to be put*, Sah. ⲙⲟⲩⲣ, *to bind*, ⲙⲏⲣ, *to be bound*, ⲥⲁⲍ, *to write*, ⲥⲏⲍ. *to be written*, Sah. ⲧⲱⲍ, *to mix*, ⲧⲏⲍ, *to be mixed*, Sah. ϣⲱϥ, *to lay waste*, ϣⲏϥ, *to be laid waste*, Sah.

Verbs active ending in ⲟ and in the passive in ⲏⲟⲩⲧ, Copt. and in ⲏⲩ in Sah. as ⲧⲁⲗⲟ, *to put on*, ⲧⲁⲗⲏⲟⲩⲧ, Copt. ⲧⲁⲗⲏⲩ, Sah. *to be put on,* etc.

71. The Participles are formed by adding ⲉⲧ, as ⲉⲧⲧⲁⲕⲏⲟⲩⲧ, from ⲧⲁⲕⲟ, and ⲉⲧⲧⲁⲕⲧⲏⲟⲩⲧ. from ⲧⲁⲕⲧⲟ; and sometimes by suffixing ⲧ also to the end as ⲉⲧⲥⲍⲟⲩⲟⲣⲧ, from ⲥⲍⲟⲩⲣ, Sah.

Of Suffixes to Verbs.

The following are the Pronoun Suffixes to Verbs.

Singular.

Coptic.		Sahidic.
ⲓ or ⲧ,		ⲓ or ⲧ, *me*.
ⲕ,		ⲕ or ⲅ, *thee*, m.
ϯ, ⲓ,		ⲧⲉ or ⲉ, *thee*, f.
ϥ,		ϥ, *him*.
ⲥ,		ⲥ, *her*.

Plural.

Coptic.		Sahidic.
ⲛ, ⲧⲉⲛ,		ⲛ, ⲧⲛ̄, *us*.
ⲧⲉⲛ,		ⲧⲛ̄, *you*.
ⲟⲩ,		ⲟⲩ, *them*.

13

The first Person singular.

72. The ɪ is suffixed to verbs ending in o, as ΜΑ-
ΤΟΥΧΟΙ, *deliver me*, Ps. CXXXIX, 1. ϩΑ ϥΗΕΤΑϥΤΛΟΥΟΙ,
to him that sent me, John VII, 33. The ⲧ is suffixed to
other verbs as, ΟΥΟϩ ΤΕΤΕΝΝΑΧΕΜⲦ ΑΝ, *and ye shall
not find me*, John VII, 36. ΕΚΕΝΑϩΜΕⲦ, *thou shalt save
me*, Ps. XLII, 1.

The second Person singular.

73. ΠΕΧΕ ΙΗⲤ ΝΑϥ ΤⲰΝΚ, *Jesus said unto him rise,*
John V, 8. ΝΚΑΑΚ ΕΒΟΛ, *to release thee*, John XIX, 10.
Sah. ΤⲰΟΥΝϤ ΠΕΤΡΕ, *rise Peter*, Acts X, 13. Sah. Εϥ-
ΧⲰΜΜΟⲤ ΧΕ ΤⲰΟΥΝϤ, *saying arise*, Acts X, 26. Sahidic.
ΟΥΟϩ ⲤΕΝΑϥⲓ† ΕΒΟΛ, Copt. ΑΥⲰ ⲤΕΝΑϥⲓⲦϤ ΕΒΟΛ, Sah. *and
shall carry thee out*, f. Acts V, 9. ΠΕΚΝΑϩ† ΠΕΤΑϥΝΑϩΜⲒ,
thy faith hath saved thee, f. Mat. IX, 22. †ΑΛΟΥ ΤⲰΟΥΝⲒ,
maid arise, f. Luke VIII, 54.

The first Person plural.

74. ΑΛΛΑ ΝΑϩΜΕΝ ΕΒΟΛϩΑ ΠⲒΠΕΤϩⲰΟΥ, *but deliver
us from evil*, Mat. VI, 13. ϥΝΑΤΑΜΟΝ ΕϩⲰΒΝⲒΜ, *he will
show us all things*, John IV, 25. Sah. ΑΚϤΑⲤΤΕΝ ⲘϤΡΗ†
ⲘΠⲒϩΑⲦ, *thou hast tried us as silver*, Psalm LXVI, 10.
ΕⲰΧΕ Α ΠΝΟΥΤΕ ΜΕΝΡΕΤⲚ, *if God hath loved us*, 1. John
IV, 11. Sahidic.

The second Person plural.

75. ⲉϥⲉ̀ⲧⲁⲙⲱⲧⲉⲛ, *he shall make known unto you,* John XVI, 13. ⲁϥⲙⲉⲣⲓⲧⲛ̄, *hath loved us,* Rom VIII. 37. Sahidic.

The third Person plural.

76. ⲁϥⲧⲁⲙⲱⲟⲩ ⲉ̀ⲛⲉϥϫⲓϫ, *he showed them his hands,* John XX, 20. ⲉ̀ⲃⲟⲑⲃⲟⲩ, Copt. ⲉⲅⲟⲧⲃⲟⲩ, Sahidic. *to kill them,* Deut. IX, 28. ϫⲉⲕⲁⲥ ϥϥⲉϫⲓⲧⲟⲩ ⲉⲩⲙⲏⲣ, *that he might lead them bound,* Acts IX, 21. Sah.

Of Adverbs.

77. A few adverbs are formed from nouns by prefixing the letter ⲉ to them, with the article, as ⲉⲅⲟⲟⲩ, *a day,* Sah. ⲉⲡⲅⲟⲟⲩ, *daily,* ⲉ̀ϥⲗⲏⲟⲩ, *in vain.*

But most often adverbs are formed thus ϧⲉⲛ ⲟⲩⲥⲱⲟⲩⲧⲉⲛ, ὀρθῶς, *rightly,* Luke XX, 21. ϧⲉⲛ ⲟⲩⲙⲉⲑⲙⲏⲓ, *truly,* Luke XX, 21.

The other adverbs will be easily discovered in the course of reading.

Of the Conjunction ϫⲉ.

78. The conjunction ϫⲉ frequently answers to the word *quod,* and generally follows the verbs of seeing, hearing, saying, and declaring; as ⲟⲩⲟⲅ ⲁϥⲛⲁⲩ ⲉ̀ⲡⲟⲩ-ⲱⲓⲛⲓ ϫⲉ ⲛⲁⲛⲉϥ, *and he saw the light that it was good.* Gen. I, 4. ϫⲉ ⲑⲱⲟⲩ ⲧⲉ ⲧⲙⲉⲧⲟⲩⲣⲟ ·ⲛ̄ⲧⲉ ⲛⲓⲫⲛⲟⲩⲓ, *for theirs is the kingdom of heaven,* Mat. V, 3.

It is often united with prepositions, as ⲉⲑⲃⲉ ⳉⲉ, ⲉ̀ⲃⲏⲗ ⳉⲉ, ⲉ̀ⲫⲙⲁ ⳉⲉ, etc.

Of Prepositions.

79. 1) Prepositions abound in the Egyptian Language, two or more of them being frequently united in composition; as ⲉ̀ⲃⲟⲩⲛ ⲉ̀, ⲉⲅⲟⲩⲛ ⲉ, Sah. *in;* ⲉ̀ⲃ̇ⲣⲏⲓ ⲉⳉⲉⲛ, *above;* ⲉ̀ⲃⲟⲗⲃⲉⲛ, ⲉⲃⲟⲗ ⳉⲛ̄, Sah. *out of;* ⲛ̄ⲃ̇ⲣⲏⲓ ⲃ̇ⲉⲛ, *in;* ⲥⲁ ⲡⲉⲥⲏⲧ, ⳉⲓ ⲡⲉⲥⲏⲧ, and ⲉ̀ ⲡⲉⲥⲏⲧ, *beneath, under.* The Preposition ⲉ̀ is frequently ·found united with others: as ⲉ̀ⲃⲟⲩⲛ ⲉ̀, *in, into;* ⲉ̀ⳉⲣⲏⲓ ⲉ̀, *to, towards;* ϣⲁ ⲉ̀ⳉⲣⲏⲓ ⲉ̀, *to* etc.

2) Prepositions are sometimes prefixed to Substantives, which then have the force of Prepositions only, as has been already shown, as ⳉⲁⲣⲟ, *to;* ⳉⲁⲣⲟⲓ, *to me;* from ⳉⲁ, *to* and ⲣⲟ, *the mouth;* ⲉ̀ⳉⲣⲁ, *to, before;* from ⲉ̀ *to,* and ⳉⲣⲁ, *the face;* etc.

3) The Prepositions are also used in composition with verbs, to express the idea conveyed by the verb and preposition when separated; as ϣⲉ ⲉ̀ⲡϣⲱⲓ, *to ascend;* from ϣⲉ, *to go,* and ⲉ̀ⲡϣⲱⲓ, *above;* ⲓ̀ⲉⲡⲉⲥⲏⲧ, *to descend;* from ⲓ̀ *to go,* and ⲉ̀ⲡⲉⲥⲏⲧ, *beneath;* ϣⲉ ⲉ̀ⲃⲟⲩⲛ, *to enter;* from ϣⲉ, *to go,* and ⲉ̀ⲃⲟⲩⲛ, *in.*

4) The preposition ⲉ̀ⲃⲟⲗ, very often occurs in connection with verbs; as ϥⲓⲉ̀ⲃⲟⲗ, *to bear, to carry out;* ⲭⲁ ⲉ̀ⲃⲟⲗ, *to remit;* ⲥⲱⲣ ⲉ̀ⲃⲟⲗ, *to disperse;* ϭⲱⲣⲡ ⲉ̀ⲃⲟⲗ, *to reveal,* &c.

5) The Preposition ⲉ̀ⲃⲟⲗ is used with nouns in the same way, as ϣⲏⲗ·ⲉ̀ⲃⲟⲗ, *a paralytic;* ⳉⲟⲩϣⲧ ⲉ̀ⲃⲟⲗ, *expectation;* ⲭⲱⲣ ⲉ̀ⲃⲟⲗ, *a dispersion;* ⲃⲱⲗ ⲉ̀ⲃⲟⲗ, *a dissolu-*

tion; &c. It is also used with the same words when used verbally.

6) A considerable number of Prepositions take the Pronoun suffixes, as ⲁⲧⲟ̅ⲛⲉ, Copt. *without,* ⲁⲧⲟ̅ⲛⲟⲩⲓ, *without me,* ⲁⲧⲟ̅ⲛⲟⲩⲕ, *without thee,* m., ⲉⲑⲃⲉ, Copt., ⲉⲧⲃⲉ, Sah. *of* or *concerning,* ⲉⲑⲃⲏⲧ, Copt. ⲉⲧⲃⲏⲏⲧ, Sah. *concerning me;* ⲉⲑⲃⲏⲧϥ, Copt. ⲉⲧⲃⲏⲏⲧϥ. Sah. *concerning him;* &c. ⲛⲉⲙ, Copt. ⲛⲙ̅, Sah. *with,* ⲛⲉⲙⲏⲓ, Copt. ⲛⲙ̅ⲙⲁⲓ, Sah. *with me;* ⲛⲉⲙⲁⲕ, Coptic. ⲛⲙ̅ⲙⲁⲕ, Sah. *with thee;* m. ⲛⲁϩⲣⲉⲛ, Coptic. ⲛⲁϩⲣⲛ̅, Sahidic. *with, before.* ⲛⲁϩⲣⲁⲓ, *with me,* &c.

7) The following list of Prepositions is given, as they very frequently occur in Coptic, Sahidic and Bashmuric.

Coptic.	Sahidic.
ⲁⲧⲟ̅ⲛⲉ, *without.*	ⲁⳉⲛ̅, *without.*
ⲉ̀ⲃⲟⲗ, *from, out of.*	ⲉⲃⲟⲗ, *from, out of.*
ⲉ̀ⲃⲟⲗⲃⲉⲛ, *from, out of:*	ⲉⲃⲟⲗϩⲙ̅, *from, out of.*
ⲉ̀ⲃⲟⲗⲟⲩⲧⲉ, *before.*	ⲉⲃⲟⲗϩⲛ̅,
ⲉ̀ⲃⲟⲗϩⲁ, *from.*	ⲉⲃⲟⲗϩⲓⲧⲙ̅, *of, from.*
ⲉ̀ⲃⲟⲗϩⲓⲧⲉⲛ, *from, out of.*	ⲉⲃⲟⲗϩⲓⲧⲛ̅,
ⲉ̀ⲃⲟⲗϩⲓⲧⲟⲧ, *from.*	ⲉⲃⲟⲗϩⲓⲧⲟⲟⲧ, *from.*
ⲉ̀ⲃⲟⲗϩⲓⲱⲧ, *from.*	ⲉⲃⲟⲗϩⲓⳉⲙ̅, *of, from.*
ⲉ̀ⲃⲟⲗϩⲓⳉⲉⲛ, *of, from.*	ⲉⲃⲟⲗϩⲓⳉⲛ̅,
ⲉ̀ⲙⲏⲣ, *beyond, over.*	ⲉⲩ, *in, to.*
ⲉ̀ⲡⲉⲥⲏⲧ, *beneath, under.*	ⲉϩⲟⲩⲛ, *in, within.*
ⲉ̀ⲥⲕⲉⲛ, *by, near.*	ⲉϩⲣⲁⲓ, *in, to.*
ⲉⲩ, *in, to.*	ⲉϩⲣⲁⲓ ⲉⳉⲛ̅, *to.*
ⲉ̀ϧⲟⲩⲛ, *in, within.*	ⲉϩⲣⲁⲓ ϩⲙ̅, *of, from.*

Coptic.

Sahidic.

ⲉⲃⲣⲏⲓ, *in, to.*

ⲙ̄ⲛ̄ⲛ̄ⲥⲁ, *after.*

ⲉⲃⲣⲏⲓ,
ⲉⲅⲣⲏⲓ, } ⲉⲝⲉⲛ, *in, above, upon.*

ⲙ̄ⲡ̄ⲙ̄ⲧⲟ,
ⲙ̄ⲡ̄ⲙ̄ⲧⲟ ⲉⲃⲟⲗ, } *before.*

ⲉⲅⲣⲏⲓ ⲅⲁ, *upon.*

ⲙ̄ⲡⲕⲱⲧⲉ, *about.*

ⲉⲝⲉⲛ, *upon, above.*

ⲛⲁⲅⲣ̄ⲙ̄,
ⲛⲁⲅⲣ̄ⲛ̄, } *to.*

ⲓⲝⲱ, *above.*

ⲓⲥⲝⲉⲛ, *from.*

ⲛ̄ⲙ̄, *with.*

ⲙⲉⲛⲉⲛⲥⲁ, *after.*

ⲛ̄ⲅⲟⲩⲛ,
ⲥⲁⲅⲟⲩⲛ, } *within.*

ⲙ̄ⲡⲉⲙ̄ⲑⲟ, *before.*

ⲛⲁⲅⲣⲁ, *before.*

ⲛ̄ⲅⲏⲧ, *in.*

ⲛⲉⲙ, *with.*

ⲡⲁⲅⲟⲩ, *behind.*

ⲛⲟⲩⲉϣⲉⲛ, *without.*

ⲅⲁⲣⲟ, *of, from.*

ⲛ̄ⲥⲁ, *after.*

ⲅⲁⲧⲙ̄,
ⲅⲁⲧⲛ̄, } *nigh to.*

ⲛ̄ⲧⲉⲛ, *from.*

ⲛ̄ⲃⲏⲧ, *in.*

ⲅⲁⲑⲏ,
ⲅⲁⲧⲅⲏ, } *before.*

ⲛ̄ⲃⲟⲩⲛ, *within.*

ⲛ̄ⲃⲣⲏⲓ, *in.*

ⲅⲙ̄,
ⲅⲛ̄, } *in.*

ⲟⲩⲃⲉ, *against.*

ⲅⲓⲣⲛ̄, *before.*

ⲟⲩⲧⲉ, *between.*

ⲫⲁⲅⲟⲩ, *after, behind.*

ⲅⲓⲧⲙ̄,
ⲅⲓⲧⲛ̄, } *from.*

ϣⲁ, *to.*

ⲃⲁ, *towards.*

ⲅⲓⲝⲙ̄, *on, in.*

ⲃⲁⲑⲟⲩⲟ, *nigh to.*

ⲃⲁⲣⲁⲧ, *under.*

ⲃⲁⲣⲟ, *of, from.*

ⲃⲁⲧⲉⲛ, *nigh to.*

ⲃⲁⲧⲟⲧ, *nigh to, to.*

ⲃⲁⲧⲅⲏ, *before.*

Coptic.

ⲂⲀⲬⲈⲚ, ⲂⲀⲬⲰ, } *before.*

ⲂⲈⲚ, *in.*

ⲂⲈⲚⲦ, *near to.*

ⲌⲀ, *to.*

ⲌⲒ, *upon, in.*

ⲌⲒⲘⲎⲢ, *beyond.*

ⲌⲒⲠⲈⲚ, *before.*

ⲌⲒⲦⲈⲚ, *by, from.*

ⲌⲒⲰⲦ, *from, of.*

ⲌⲒⲬⲈⲚ, *upon, in.*

ⲌⲒⲬⲰ, *upon, in.*

Of Conjunctions.

80. 8) The conjunction ⲞⲨⲞⲌ, *and,* is frequently omitted in composition, as ⲞⲨⲞⲌ ⲀⲨⲞⲨⲰⲘ ⲦⲎⲢⲞⲨ ⲀⲨⳞⲒ, *and they all ate (and) were satisfied.* Mat. XV, 37. Copt. ⲞⲨⲞⲌ ⲒⳞ ⲌⲀⲚⲀⲄⲄⲈⲖⲞⳓ ⲀⳞⲒ ⲀⲨⳤⲈⲘⳤⲒ ⲘⲘⲟϥ, *and behold angels came, (and) ministered to him,* Mat. IV, 11. Copt.

9) The Conjunction ⲔⲈ, *and, also,* is placed between the article and the noun; as ⲚⲦⲈⲚⲌⲒⲞⳞⲒ ⲘⲠⲞⲨ ⲔⲈ ⲚⲀⲌⲂⲈϥ ⲈⲂⲞⲖ ⲌⲒⲬⲰⲚ, *that we may cast away also their yoke from us.* Ps. II, 2. ⲘⲠⲒ ⲔⲈ ⲒⲰⲦ ⲈⲦⲀϥⲦⲀⲞⲨⲟϥ, *the Father also, who hath sent him.*

Of Interjections.

81. The principal interjections in Egyptian are Ⲓⳓ, or ⲌⲎⲠⲠⲈ Ⲓⳓ, Copt. ⲌⲎⲎⲦⲈ Ⲓⳓ, Sah. *behold!* ⲞⲨⲞⲒ, *alas! woe to;* and Ⲱ, *oh!*

CHAP. VIII.

Of the Formation of words.

82. In treating of the formation of Egyptian words it is by no means intended to enter upon the controversy, whether nouns or verbs were the original words in language, but to give a simple statement of what the Egyptian presents to us.

83. Primitive words were no doubt short, and generally of one syllable, as ⲣⲏ, *the sun;* ⲫⲉ, *heaven;* ⲭⲱ, *the head;* ⳃⲣⲉ, *food;* &c.

84. Compound words are formed by uniting two or more words, as ϥⲧⲉⲫⲁⲧ, *a quadruped,* from ϥⲧⲉ, *four* and ⲫⲁⲧ, *a foot;* ⲟⲩⲱⲙⲛ̅ⳅⲏⲧ, *to repent,* from ⲟⲩⲱⲙ, *to consume,* and ⳅⲏⲧ, *the heart,* &c. ⲙⲁⲓ̈ⲛⲟⲩⲧⲉ, *religious,* from ⲙⲁⲓ̈, *loving,* ⲛⲟⲩⲧⲉ, *God,* Sah.

Some words are composed of ⲙⲁ, Copt., Sah. and Bash., *a place,* and ⲛ̅, the sign of the genitive, united with other words, as ⲙⲁⲛ̀ⲙⲟⲛⲓ, *a pasture, a place to feed;* from ⲙⲁ, and ⲙⲟⲛⲓ, *to feed,* ⲙⲁⲛⲫⲱⲧ, *a refuge, a place to flee to;* from ⲙⲁ, and ⲫⲱⲧ, *a flight.* ⲙⲁⲛ̀ϣⲱⲡⲓ, *a habitation;* from ⲙⲁ, and ϣⲱⲡⲓ, *to dwell.* ⲙⲁⲛ̀ⲧⳅⲁⲡ, *a tribunal;* from ⲙⲁ, and ⲧ, *to give,* and ⳅⲁⲡ, *judgment.*

Some words are composed of ⲙⲉ or ⲙⲁⲓ̈, *loving,* united with other words, as ⲙⲁⲓⳅⲁⲧ, *covetous;* from ⲙⲁⲓ, and ⳅⲁⲧ. *silver,* ⲙⲁⲓⲧⲁⲓⲟ, *ambitious;* from ⲙⲁⲓ, and ⲧⲁⲓⲟ, *honour.*

ⲙⲉⲧ or ⲙⲉⲑ, Copt. and ⲙⲛⲧ. Sah. are often prefixed to nouns and also to words derived from the Greek;
as ⲙⲉⲧⲟⲩⲣⲟ, *a kingdom;* from ⲙⲉⲧ and ⲟⲩⲣⲟ, *a king;*
ⲙⲉⲧⲙⲁⲧⲟⲓ, *an army;* from ⲙⲉⲧ and ⲙⲁⲧⲟⲓ, *a soldier;*
ⲙⲛⲧⲙⲛⲧⲣⲉ, *a testimony;* from ⲙⲛⲧ and ⲙⲛⲧⲣⲉ, *a witness;* Sah. &c.

The word ⲣⲉⲙ, Copt. and ⲣⲙ̄, Sah. ⲗⲉⲙ. Bash. *a
native, an inhabitant,* or *belonging to,* and the sign of the
genitive prefixed to nouns; as ⲣⲉⲙⲛ̀ϩⲓ, *a domestic;* from
ⲣⲉⲙ and ϩⲓ, *a house;* ⲣⲉⲙⲙ̀ⲫⲉ, *heavenly;* from ⲣⲉⲙ and
ⲫⲉ, *heaven;* ⲣⲉⲙⲛ̀ⲭⲏⲙⲓ, *an Egyptian;* ⲣⲉⲙⲧⲁⲣⲥⲟⲥ, *a
native of Tarsus.*

ⲣⲉϥ, Copt. and Sah. ⲗⲉϥ, Bash. added to verbs
form compound nouns, as ⲣⲉϥⲛⲁⲩ, *an inspector,* from
ⲛⲁⲩ, *to see.* ⲣⲉϥϣⲙ̄ϣⲉ, Sah. *a minister,* from ϣⲙ̄ϣⲉ,
to minister, ⲗⲉϥϯϩⲉⲡ, Bash. *a judge;* from ϯϩⲁⲡ, *to judge.*

ⲥⲁ, Copt. and Sah. *an artificer,* is used in the formation of some words, as ⲥⲁⲛ̀ϭⲏⲝⲓ, *a maker or seller
of purple;* from ϭⲓⲝⲓ, *purple.* ⲥⲁⲛ̀ⲱⲓⲕ, *a baker;* from
ⲱⲓⲕ, *bread.* ⲥⲁⲛ̄ϩⲟⲙⲛ̄ⲧ, Sah. *an artificer in brass;* from
ϩⲟⲙⲛ̄ⲧ, *brass.*

ⲝⲓⲛ, Copt. and Bash. ϭⲓⲛ, Sah. prefixed to verbs
often denote the presence of the action, so that they
then correspond with the infinite of the Greek, with the
article; as ⲝⲓⲛⲙⲟϣⲓ, Copt. ϭⲓⲛⲙⲟⲟϣⲉ, Sah. *the action of
going, to go.* With these prefixes verbs are frequently
used as nouns; as ⲝⲓⲛⲝⲫⲟ, *possession,* from ⲝⲫⲟ, *to possess.*
ⲝⲓⲛϭⲟⲃϯ, *a preparation,* from ϭⲟⲃϯ. *to prepare.*

ϣⲟⲩ. Copt. and Sah. when prefixed to verbs "serves
14

to indicate" Quatremère says, "that a thing merits to be done, — that it ought to be done." It consequently expresses *worthiness;* as ⲉⲱⲥ ⲉⲁⲛϣⲟⲩⲙⲉⲛⲡⲓⲧⲟⲩ ⲛⲉ· ⲛⲉⲕⲙⲁⲛ̀ϣⲱⲡⲓ, *How worthy to be loved are thy tabernacles.* Ps. LXXXIII, 1. from ⲙⲉⲛⲡⲓⲧ, *beloved.*

ⲉⲁ, Copt., Sah. and Bash. appears to express *a person, master* or *chief;* as ⲉⲁⲛϣⲉ, Sah. *a centurion,* or *chief of a hundred men,* from ϣⲉ, *a hundred.* ⲉⲁⲙ̅ϣⲉ, Sah. *a carpenter, an artificer in wood.* &c.

ⲁⲧ or ⲁⲑ, Copt., Sah. and Bash. which is a negative prefix to nouns.

ⲗⲁ, Copt. *much, greatly,* as ⲗⲁϫⲁⲗ, *very shady.*

Some nouns are formed from verbs by adding a Letter at the end, as ⲥⲉⲟⲩⲟⲣⲧ, *a curse,* from ⲥⲉⲟⲩⲟⲣ, *to curse.* ⲡⲁⲃⲧ, *a fuller;* from ⲡⲁⲃ, *to wash;* ⲭⲁⲣⲟϥ, *silence;* from ⲭⲁⲣⲱ, *to silence.*

Part IV.

Of the Dialects.

1. We know very little of the ancient Language of Egypt, and nearly all the remains of it we now possess, have been transmitted to us through the medium of the Coptic, Sahidic and Bashmuric Dialects. The Coptic Dialect was spoken in Lower Egypt, of which Memphis was the capital, hence it has been called with great propriety the Memphitic Dialect. The Sahidic derived its name from the Arabic word صعيد or الصعيد, *the Upper or Superior;* and was the Dialect of Upper Egypt,

of which Thebes was the capital; it has therefore been called the Thebaïc. It is impossible to say which of these two dialects was the more ancient. Georgius, Valperga, Munter, and others have decided in favour of the Coptic; and Macrizy, Renaudotius, Lacroze, and Jablonsky, with much more appearance of reason, have contended for the Sahidic. Still, however, the question must be very much left to conjecture, as we have not at present sufficient evidence to enable us to decide. Besides these two dialects, which have long been known, there is a third, which was spoken in Baschmour, a Province of the Delta.

The existence of three Dialects in Egypt has been so satisfactorily proved by Quatremère, Engelbreth and other writers, and so fully confirmed by the Bashmouric Fragments which have been discovered and published, that no more need be added to establish the fact. If however any doubt should remain on the mind of any one, the following quotation from a Manuscript work of Athanasius, a Prelate of the Coptic Church, who was Bishop of Kous, will entirely remove it.* "The Coptic Language," says he, "is divided into three dialects, the Coptic dialect of Misr, the Bahiric, and the Bashmuric: these different dialects are derived from the same language."

The introduction of Greek words into the Egyptian language commenced, no doubt, from the time of the

---

* Coptic MS. Royal Library Paris, quoted by Quatremère.

Macedonian conquest, which the introduction of Christianity tended to confirm and extend. The Christian Religion contained so many new ideas, that new words would be found necessary to express them. These words the Greek Language would readily supply, having been previously used by the Apostles of Christ, for a similar object: and it is probable that the Egyptians adopted the terms required, from the Greek writings of the Apostles. But we find in the Coptic and Sahidic Versions of the Scriptures, that the Translators often used Greek words in the Translation when they possessed Egyptian words, which fully expressed the same idea, which proves that the Greek and Egyptian Language were both extensively used at that period.

The Coptic Dialect.

2. The Coptic,*) or as it has been called the Bahiric, but more properly the Memphitic, was the Dialect of Lower Egypt, the מצור Mizur of the Scriptures. This Dialect is more free from Greek than the Sahidic.

Manuscripts exist in Coptic of nearly the whole of the Sacred Scriptures, of which the Pentateuch, the Book of Job, the Psalms, the Major and Minor Prophets, and the New Testament, with translations, have been published. Liturgies also of the Coptic Church exist in MSS. and the works of some of the early Fathers, the

---

*) The word Coptic was evidently derived from the word ⲄⲨⲠⲧⲟ as pronounced by the Egyptians.

Acts of the Council of Nice, and also the lives of a considerable number of Saints and Martyrs.

The Sahidic Dialect.

3. The Sahidic, or more correctly the Thebaic Dialect, was spoken in Upper Egypt. As has been hinted before, it has adopted a greater number of Greek words than the Coptic. The vowels in this dialect are more frequently expressed by lines above the consonants than in the Coptic or Bashmouric; as ⲙⲛ̄ⲛ̄ⲥⲁ, *after*, Sahidic. ⲙⲉⲛⲉⲛⲥⲁ, Copt. ⲡⲛ̄ⲡⲏ̄ⲧⲟ, Sah. *before*, ⲙⲡⲉⲙⲧⲟ, Copt.

Fragments of nearly every part of the Old and New Testament exist in Sahidic, but only fragments of the New Testament have as yet been published, and fragments of some of the Lives of Saints and Martyrs.

The Bashmouric Dialect.

4. The Bashmouric Dialect was spoken in Bashmour, a Province of the Delta, and agrees in some respects with the Coptic, and in others more nearly resembles the Sahidic.

The inhabitants of the Delta were described by ancient writers* as wild beasts, leading a wandering life, and living by robbery and plunder, whom the Persians, Greeks and Romans could hardly subdue. This will account in a great measure for the Bashmouric being more rude than the Sahidic.

A few Fragments only of this Dialect exist, and have been published.

---

* Thucydid. l. I. c. 110. and Diod. Sicul. l. II. c. 77.

Praxis.

Of the first Chapter of St. John's Gospel.

1. ϧⲉⲛ ⲧⲁⲣⲭⲏ ⲛⲉ ⲡⲓⲥⲁϫⲓ ⲡⲉ ⲟⲩⲟϩ ⲡⲓⲥⲁϫⲓ ⲛⲁϥⲭⲏ ϧⲁⲧⲉⲛ ⲫϯ ⲟⲩⲟϩ ⲛⲉ ⲟⲩⲛⲟⲩϯ ⲡⲉ ⲡⲓⲥⲁϫⲓ.

In the beginning was the Word, and the Word was with God, and God was the Word.

ϧⲉⲛ, prepos. ⲧⲁⲣⲭⲏ, noun f. with ⲧ the defin. art. f. prefixed ⲛⲉ....ⲡⲉ, verb. irreg. imper. 3 pers. sing. ⲡⲓⲥⲁϫⲓ, noun m. with ⲡ the defin. art. m. prefixed. ⲟⲩⲟϩ conjunct. ⲛⲁϥⲭⲏ verb indic. imper. 3. pers. sing. from ⲭⲏ. ϧⲁⲧⲉⲛ, prepos. ⲫϯ noun sing. m. ⲟⲩⲛⲟⲩϯ, noun masc. sing. with ⲟⲩ indef. art. prefixed.

2. ⲫⲁⲓ ⲉ̀ⲛⲁϥⲭⲏ ⲓⲥϫⲉⲛ ϩⲏ ϧⲁⲧⲉⲛ ⲫϯ.

This was from the beginning with God.

ⲫⲁⲓ, pron. demonstr. sing. m. ⲉ̀ⲛⲁϥⲭⲏ, verb. imperf. (see above) with ⲉ̀ pron. rel. ⲓⲥϫⲉⲛ, prepos. ϩⲏ, noun sing.

3. ϩⲱⲃⲛⲓⲃⲉⲛ ⲁⲩϣⲱⲡⲓ ⲉ̀ⲃⲟⲗϩⲓⲧⲟⲧϥ ⲟⲩⲟϩ ⲁⲧϭⲛⲟϥ ⲙ̀ⲡⲉ ϩⲗⲓ ϣⲱⲡⲓ ϧⲉⲛ ⲫⲏⲉ̀ⲧ ⲁϥϣⲱⲡⲓ.

All things were made by him, and without him was not anything made, among that which was made.

ϩⲱⲃⲛⲓⲃⲉⲛ, compound adject. from ϩⲱⲃ and ⲛⲓⲃⲉⲛ.. ⲁⲩϣⲱⲡⲓ, verb. perfect 3. pers. plur. from ϣⲱⲡⲓ. ⲉ̀ⲃⲟⲗϩⲓⲧⲟⲧϥ, prepos. with ϥ the pron. suff. 3. pers. sing. ⲁⲧϭⲛⲟϥ, prepos. with ϥ pron. suff. ⲙ̀ⲡⲉ, neg. pref. 3. pers. m. to verb. ϣⲱⲡⲓ, ϩⲗⲓ, adject. neut. ⲫⲏⲉ̀ⲧ, pron. demonst. and relat. sing. ⲁϥϣⲱⲡⲓ, verb. perf. 3. pers. sing. see above.

4. ne ⲡⲱⲛϧ ⲡⲉ ⲉ̀ⲧⲉ ⲛ̀ϧⲏⲧϥ ⲟⲩⲟϩ ⲡⲱⲛϧ ⲡⲉ ⲫⲟⲩⲱⲓⲛⲓ ⲛ̀ⲛⲓⲣⲱⲙⲓ ⲡⲉ.

In Him was life, and the life was the light of men.

. ⲡⲱⲛϧ, noun sing. with ⲡ, the defin. artic. m. pref.
ⲉ̀ⲧⲉ, pron. relat. sing. ⲛ̀ϧⲏⲧϥ, prep. with ϥ suff. ne...
ⲡⲉ, verb. irreg. imperf. 3. pers. sing. ⲫⲟⲩⲱⲓⲛⲓ, noun
sing. with ⲫ def. art. m. pref. ⲛ̀ⲛⲓⲣⲱⲙⲓ, noun pl. with
ⲛ̀ sign of gen. and ⲛⲓ def. art. plur. m. prefixed.

5. ⲟⲩⲟϩ ⲡⲓⲟⲩⲱⲓⲛⲓ ⲁϥⲉⲣⲟⲩⲱⲓⲛⲓ ϧⲉⲛ ⲡⲓⲭⲁⲕⲓ ⲟⲩⲟϩ
ⲙ̀ⲡⲉ ⲡⲓⲭⲁⲕⲓ ϣⲧⲁϩⲟϥ.

*And the light shined in the darkness, and the dark-
ness did not comprehend it.*

ⲁϥⲉⲣⲟⲩⲱⲓⲛⲓ, verb. perf. 3. pers. sing. from ⲟⲩⲱⲓⲛⲓ
with ⲉⲣ prefixed. ⲡⲓⲭⲁⲕⲓ, noun sing. with ⲡⲓ def. art.
m. sing. pref. ϣⲧⲁϩⲟϥ, verb perf. 3. pers. sing. with
ⲙ̀ⲡⲉ, (see above) and ϣ intensive prefixed, and ϥ suff.
from ⲧⲁϩⲟ.

6. ⲁϥϣⲱⲡⲓ ⲛ̀ϫⲉ ⲟⲩⲣⲱⲙⲓ ⲉ̀ⲁⲩⲟⲩⲟⲣⲡϥ ⲉ̀ⲃⲟⲗϩⲓⲧⲉⲛ
ⲫϯ ⲉ̀ⲡⲉϥⲣⲁⲛ ⲡⲉ ⲓⲱⲁⲛⲛⲏⲥ.

*There was a man who was sent by God, whose name
was John.*

ⲛ̀ϫⲉ, a sign of the nominative. ⲟⲩⲣⲱⲙⲓ, noun sing.
m. with ⲟⲩ indef. art. sing. prefixed. ⲉ̀, pron. relat. sing.
ⲁⲩⲟⲩⲟⲣⲡϥ, verb. perf. 3. pers. plur. for the pass. sing.
(see pass. v.) and ϥ 3. pers. sing. suff. ⲉ̀ⲃⲟⲗϩⲓⲧⲉⲛ, prep.
ⲉ̀ⲡⲉϥⲣⲁⲛ, ⲉ̀ rel. pron. ⲡⲉϥ, his m. ⲣⲁⲛ, noun sing. m.
ⲡⲉ, verb irreg. imperf.

7. ⲫⲁⲓ ⲁϥⲓ̀ ⲉⲩⲙⲉⲧⲙⲉⲑⲣⲉ ϩⲓⲛⲁ ⲛ̀ⲧⲉϥⲉⲣⲙⲉⲑⲣⲉ ϧⲁ
ⲡⲓⲟⲩⲱⲓⲛⲓ ϩⲓⲛⲁ ⲛ̀ⲧⲉ ⲟⲩⲟⲛ̀ⲛⲓⲃⲉⲛ ⲛⲁϩϯ ⲉ̀ⲃⲟⲗϩⲓⲧⲟⲧϥ.

*This (man) came for a witness, that he might witness
to the light, that every one might believe through him.*

ⲁϥ̀, verb perf. 3. pers. sing. from ⲓ̀ ⲉⲩⲙⲉⲧⲙⲉⲑⲣⲉ,
noun sing. with ⲉⲩ for ⲉⲟⲩ, ⲉ prepos. ⲟⲩ, indef. art.
contract. into ⲉⲩ. ⳅⲓⲛⲁ, conjunct. ⲛ̀ⲧⲉϥⲉⲣⲙⲉⲑⲣⲉ, verb.
subjunct. 3. pers. sing. from ⲙⲉⲑⲣⲉ with ⲉⲣ prefixed.
ⲃⲁ, prepos. ⲟⲩⲟⲛⲛⲓⲃⲉⲛ, adj. ⲛ̀ⲧⲉ ⲛⲁⳅ†, verb subjunct.
3. pers. sing.

8. ⲛⲉ ⲛ̀ⲑⲟϥ ⲁⲛ ⲡⲉ ⲡⲓⲟⲩⲱⲓⲛⲓ ⲁⲗⲗⲁ ⳅⲓⲛⲁ ⲛ̀ⲧⲉϥⲉⲣ-
ⲙⲉⲑⲣⲉ ⲃⲁ ⲡⲓⲟⲩⲱⲓⲛⲓ.

*He was not the light, but that he might witness to
the light.*

ⲛ̀ⲑⲟϥ, pron. 3. pers. m. ⲁⲛ, adv. ⲁⲗⲗⲁ, conj.

9. ⲛⲁϥϣⲟⲡ ⲛ̀ⲭⲉ ⲡⲓⲟⲩⲱⲓⲛⲓ ⲛ̀ⲧⲁⲫⲙⲏⲓ ⲫⲏⲉ̀ⲧ ⲉⲣⲟⲩⲱⲓⲛⲓ ⲉ̀ⲣⲱⲙⲓ ⲛⲓⲃⲉⲛ ⲉⲑⲛⲏⲟⲩ ⲉ̀ⲡⲓⲕⲟⲥⲙⲟⲥ.

*He was the true light, which enlighteneth every man
who cometh into the world.*

ⲛⲁϥϣⲟⲡ, verb imperf. 3. pers. sing. from ϣⲟⲡ.
ⲛ̀ⲧⲁⲫⲙⲏⲓ, adject. sing. with ⲛ̀, prefixed forming the
adjective. ⲉ̀ⲣⲟⲙⲓ, noun sing. with ⲉ̀ prep. ⲛⲓⲃⲉⲛ, adj.
ⲉⲑⲛⲏⲟⲩ, verb. pres. 3. pers. sing. with ⲉⲑ pron. relat.
from ⲛⲏⲟⲩ. ⲉ̀ⲡⲓⲕⲟⲥⲙⲟⲥ, noun sing. with ⲉ̀ prep. and
ⲡⲓ, defin. art. prefixed.

10. ⲛⲁϥⲭⲏ ⲃⲉⲛ ⲡⲓⲕⲟⲥⲙⲟⲥ ⲡⲉ ⲟⲩⲟⳅ ⲡⲓⲕⲟⲥⲙⲟⲥ
ⲁϥϣⲱⲡⲓ ⲉ̀ⲃⲟⲗⳅⲓⲧⲟⲧϥ ⲟⲩⲟⳅ ⲙ̀ⲡⲉ ⲡⲓⲕⲟⲥⲙⲟⲥ ⲥⲟⲩⲱⲛϥ.

*He was in the world, and the world was made by Him,
and the world knew Him not.*

ⲙ̀ⲡⲉ...ⲥⲟⲩⲱⲛϥ, verb. with neg. and ϥ suffix.

11. ⲁϥⲓ̀ ϩⲁ ⲛⲉⲧⲉⲛⲟⲩϥ ⲟⲩⲟϩ ⲛⲉⲧⲉⲛⲟⲩϥ ⲙ̀ⲡⲟⲩ-
ϣⲟⲡϥ ⲉ̀ⲣⲱⲟⲩ.

*He came to his own, and his own received him not
to them.*

ϩⲁ, prep. ⲛⲉⲧⲉⲛⲟⲩϥ, adj. plur. with ϥ suff. ⲙ̀ⲡⲟⲩ-
ϣⲟⲡϥ, verb. neg. with ϥ suff. 3. pers. plur. ⲉ̀ⲣⲱⲟⲩ, Dat.
proñ. plur.

12. ⲛⲏ ⲇⲉ ⲉ̀ⲧ ⲁⲩϣⲟⲡϥ ⲉ̀ⲣⲱⲟⲩ ⲁϥϯ ⲉⲣϣⲓϣⲓ ⲛⲱⲟⲩ
ⲉ̀ⲉⲣ ϣⲏⲣⲓ ⲛ̀ⲛⲟⲩϯ ⲛⲏⲉⲑ ⲛⲁϩϯ ⲉ̀ⲡⲉϥⲣⲁⲛ.

*But those who received him to them, he gave them
power to become sons of God, (to) those who believe in
his name.*

ⲛⲏ, pron. demon. plur· ⲇⲉ, conj. ⲉ̀ⲧ, pron. rel. pl.
ⲁⲩϣⲟⲡϥ, verb. perf. 3. pers. pl. ⲁϥϯ, verb. perf. 3. pers.
sing. from ϯ. ⲉⲣϣⲓϣⲓ, noun sing. masc. ⲛⲱⲟⲩ, pron.
dat. ⲉ̀ⲉⲣ, verb. infin. with ⲉ̀ pref. the sign of the infin.
ϣⲏⲣⲓ, noun plur.

13. ⲛⲏⲉ̀ⲧⲉ ⲉ̀ⲃⲟⲗⲃⲉⲛ ⲥⲛⲟϥ ⲁⲛ ⲛⲉ ⲟⲩⲇⲉ ⲉ̀ⲃⲟⲗⲃⲉⲛ
ⲫⲟⲩⲱϣ ⲛ̀ⲥⲁⲣⲝ̄ ⲁⲛ ⲛⲉ ⲟⲩⲇⲉ ⲉ̀ⲃⲟⲗⲃⲉⲛ ⲫⲟⲩⲱϣ ⲛ̀ⲣⲱⲙⲓ
ⲁⲛ ⲛⲉ ⲁⲗⲗⲁ ⲉ̀ⲧ ⲁⲩⲙⲁⲥⲟⲩ ⲉ̀ⲃⲟⲗⲃⲉⲛ ⲫϯ.

*Those who were not of blood, neither of the will of
flesh, nor of the will of man, but who were born of God.*

ⲥⲛⲟϥ, noun sing. m. ⲁⲛ, adv. negat. ⲟⲩⲇⲉ, conj.
ⲛ̀ⲥⲁⲣⲝ̄, noun sing. m. with ⲛ̀ sign of gen. ⲁⲩⲙⲁⲥⲟⲩ,
verb perf. 3. pers. plur. with ⲟⲩ, plur. suff. from ⲙⲁⲥ.

14. ⲟⲩⲟϩ ⲡⲓⲥⲁϫⲓ ⲁϥⲉⲣ ⲟⲩⲥⲁⲣⲝ̄ ⲟⲩⲟϩ ⲁϥϣⲱⲡⲓ
ⲛ̀ⲃ̀ⲣⲏⲓ ⲛ̀ⲃ̀ⲏⲧⲉⲛ ⲟⲩⲟϩ ⲁⲛⲛⲁⲩ ⲉ̀ⲡⲉϥⲱ̀ⲟⲩ ⲙ̀ⲫ̀ⲣⲏϯ ⲙ̀ⲡⲱ̀ⲟⲩ
ⲛ̀ⲟⲩϣⲏⲣⲓ ⲙ̀ⲙⲁⲩⲁⲧϥ ⲛ̀ⲧⲟⲧϥ ⲙ̀ⲡⲉϥⲓⲱⲧ ⲉϥⲙⲉϩ ⲛ̀ϩⲙⲟⲧ
ⲛⲉⲙ ⲙⲉⲑⲙⲏⲓ.

*And the word was made flesh, and dwelt among us,
and we saw his glory, as the glory of the only son of his
Father, full of grace and truth.*

ⲁϥⲉⲣ, verb perf. 3. pers. sing. from ⲉⲣ. ⲛ̀ⲃⲣⲏⲓ
ⲛ̀ⲃⲏⲧⲉⲛ, 2 prepos. the last ⲉⲛ suff. ⲁⲛⲛⲁⲩ, verb perf.
1. pers. plur. from ⲛⲁⲩ. ⲉ̀ⲡⲉϥⲱ̀ⲟⲩ, noun sing. m. with
ⲉ̀ sign of acc. and ⲡⲉϥ, pref. ⲙ̀ⲫⲣⲏϯ, adv. ⲛ̀ⲟⲩϣⲏⲣⲓ,
noun m. sing. with ⲛ̀ sign of gen. and ⲟⲩ indef. art.
prefixed. ⲙ̀ⲙⲁⲩⲁⲧϥ, adj. sing. ⲛ̀ⲧⲟⲧϥ, pron. partic. gen.
from ⲧⲟⲧ, see pronouns. ⲙ̀ⲡⲉϥⲓⲱⲧ, noun sing. with ⲙ̀
sign of gen. and ⲡⲉϥ prefixed. ⲉϥⲙⲉⲍ, verb present or
part. 3. pers. sing. ⲛ̀ⲍⲙⲟⲧ, noun sing. m. with ⲛ̀ sign
of gen. ⲛⲉⲙ, conj. ⲙⲉⲑⲙⲏⲓ, noun sing. f.

15. ⲓⲱⲁⲛⲛⲏⲥ ⲉϥⲉⲣⲙⲉⲑⲣⲉ ⲉ̀ⲑⲃⲏⲧϥ ⲟⲩⲟⲍ ⲉϥⲱϣ
ⲉ̀ⲃⲟⲗ ⲉϥⲭⲱⲙ̀ⲙⲟⲥ, ϫⲉ ⲫⲁⲓ ⲡⲉ ⲫⲏⲉ̀ⲧ ⲁⲓϫⲟϥ ϫⲉ ⲫⲏⲉⲑ
ⲛⲏⲟⲩ ⲙⲉⲛⲉⲛⲥⲱⲓ ⲁϥⲉⲣϣⲟⲣⲡ ⲉ̀ⲣⲟⲓ ϫⲉ ⲛⲉ ⲟⲩϣⲟⲣⲡ ⲉ̀ⲣⲟⲓ
ⲣⲱ ⲡⲉ.

*John witnesseth concerning him, and crieth out, say-
ing, that this is he of whom I spake, he who cometh after
me hath been before me, for he was before me.*

ⲉ̀ⲑⲃⲏⲧϥ, prepos. with ϥ suff. ⲉϥⲱϣ ⲉ̀ⲃⲟⲗ, verb
pres. 3. pers. sing. with ⲉ̀ⲃⲟⲗ, prepos. joined. ⲉϥⲭⲱⲙ̀ⲙⲟⲥ,
particip. from ⲭⲱ, and ⲙ̀ⲙⲟⲥ particle postfixed. ϫⲉ,
conjunct. but often expletive. ⲁⲓϫⲟϥ, verb perfect. 1. pers.
sing. with ϥ suffixed. ⲙⲉⲛⲉⲛⲥⲱⲓ, prepos. with 1. pers.
sing. suffixed. ⲁϥⲉⲣϣⲟⲣⲡ, verb perf. 3. pers. sing. from
ⲉⲣ and ϣⲟⲣⲡ, ⲉ̀ⲣⲟⲓ, particle used for pronoun. 1. pers.
sing. ⲣⲟ, *he, the same.*

16. ϫⲉ ⲁⲛⲟⲛ ⲧⲏⲣⲉⲛ ⲁⲛϭⲓ ⲉⲃⲟⲗϧⲉⲛ ⲡⲉϥⲙⲟϩ ⲛⲉⲙ ⲟⲩϩⲙⲟⲧ ⲛ̀ⲧϣⲉⲃⲓⲱ̀ ⲛ̀ⲟⲩϩⲙⲟⲧ.

Because we all have received out of his fulness, and grace for grace.

ⲁⲛⲟⲛ, pron. plur. 1. pers. ⲧⲏⲣⲉⲛ, adject. with ⲉⲛ, 1. pers. plur. suffixed. ⲁⲛϭⲓ, verb perf. 1. pers. plur. from ϭⲓ. ⲡⲉϥⲙⲟϩ, noun sing. m. with ⲡⲉϥ prefixed. ⲟⲩϩⲙⲟⲧ, noun sing. with ⲟⲩ indefin. artic. prefixed. ⲛ̀ⲧϣⲉⲃⲓⲱ̀, prepos.: from ϣⲉⲃⲓⲱ̀, with ⲧ the art. f. and ⲛ̀ prefixed.

17. ϫⲉ ⲡⲓⲛⲟⲙⲟⲥ ⲁⲩⲧⲏⲓϥ ⲉⲃⲟⲗϩⲓⲧⲉⲛ ⲙⲱⲩⲥⲏⲥ ⲡⲓϩⲙⲟⲧ ⲇⲉ ⲛⲉⲙ ϯⲙⲉⲑⲙⲏⲓ ⲁⲩϣⲱⲡⲓ ⲉⲃⲟⲗϩⲓⲧⲉⲛ ⲓⲏ̅ⲥ̅ ⲡⲭ̅ⲥ̅.

For the law was given by Moses, but the grace and the truth were by Jesus Christ.

ⲡⲓⲛⲟⲙⲟⲥ, noun sing. with ⲡⲓ defin. art. m. ⲁⲩⲧⲏⲓϥ, verb perf. 3. pers. plur. with ϥ suff. ϯⲙⲉⲑⲙⲏⲓ, noun sing. with ϯ, defin. art. f.

18. ⲫϯ ⲙ̀ⲡⲉ ϩⲗⲓ ⲛⲁⲩ ⲉⲣⲟϥ ⲉⲛⲉϩ ⲡⲓⲙⲟⲛⲟⲅⲉⲛⲏⲥ ⲛ̀ⲛⲟⲩϯ ⲫⲏⲉⲧ ⲭⲏ ϧⲉⲛ ⲕⲉⲛϥ ⲙ̀ⲡⲉϥⲓⲱⲧ ⲛ̀ⲑⲟϥ ⲡⲉⲧ ⲁϥⲥⲁϫⲓ.

Not any one hath ever seen God; the only begotten of God, he who is in the bosom of his Father, he hath declared him.

ⲙ̀ⲡⲉ..ⲛⲁⲩ, verb 3. pers. sing. negat. prefixed. ⲉⲛⲉϩ, adv. ⲕⲉⲛϥ, noun sing. with ϥ suffixed. ⲛ̀ⲑⲟϥ, pron. 3. pers. sing. ⲡⲉⲧ, pron. relat. ⲁϥⲥⲁϫⲓ, verb perf. 3. pers. sing.

19. ⲟⲩⲟϩ ⲑⲁⲓ ⲧⲉ ϯⲙⲉⲧⲙⲉⲑⲣⲉ ⲛ̀ⲧⲉ ⲓⲱⲁⲛⲛⲏⲥ ϩⲟⲧⲉ ⲉ̀ⲧ ⲁⲩⲟⲩⲱⲣⲡ ϩⲁⲣⲟϥ ⲛ̀ϫⲉ ⲛⲓⲟⲩⲇⲁⲓ ⲉ̀ⲃⲟⲗϧⲉⲛ

ⲡⲁⲏⲙ ⲛ̇ⲅⲁⲛⲟⲩⲏⲃ ⲛⲉⲙ ⲅⲁⲛⲗⲉⲅⲓⲧⲏⲥ ⲅⲓⲛⲁ ⲛ̇ⲧⲟⲩⲱϥⲛϥ
ⲭⲉ ⲛ̇ⲑⲟⲕ ⲛⲓⲙ.

*And this is the testimony of John, when the Jews, who
sent to him from Jerusalem Priests and Levites that they
might ask him, who art thou?*

ⲑⲁⲓ, pron. def. fem. sing. ⲧⲉ, verb. irreg. pres. 3. pers.
sing. fem. ⲛ̇ⲧⲉ, sign of gen. ⲅⲟⲧⲉ, adv. ⲅⲁⲣⲟϥ, prep.
joined with ⲣⲟϥ, a particle representing the pronoun.
ⲛⲓⲟⲩⳁⲁⲓ, noun with ⲛⲓ defin. art. plur. prefixed. ⲛ̇ⲅⲁⲛ-
ⲟⲩⲏⲃ, noun plur. with ⲛ̇ gen. and ⲅⲁⲛ, indef. art. pl.
prefixed. ⲛ̇ⲧⲟⲩⲱϥⲛϥ. verb subjunct. 3. pers. plur. with
ϥ suffixed. ⲛ̇ⲑⲟⲕ, pron. 2. pers. sing. ⲛⲓⲙ, pron. sing.

20. ⲟⲩⲟⲅ ⲁϥⲟⲩⲱⲛⲅ ⲙ̇ⲡⲉϥⲭⲱⲗ ⲉ̇ⲃⲟⲗ ⲟⲩⲟⲅ ⲁϥⲟⲩⲱⲛⲅ
ⲭⲉ ⲁ̇ⲛⲟⲕ ⲁⲛ ⲡⲉ ⲡⲭ̅ⲥ̅.

*And he confessed and denied not; and confessed that
I am not the Christ.*

ⲁϥⲟⲩⲱⲛⲅ, verb perf. 3. pers. sing. ⲙ̇ⲡⲉϥⲭⲱⲗ ⲉ̇ⲃⲟⲗ,
verb. negat. perf. 3. pers. sing. from ⲭⲱⲗ ⲉ̇ⲃⲟⲗ. ⲁ̇ⲛⲟⲕ,
pron. 1. pers. sing.

From the Hymns for the Principal Feasts.

ⲡⲁⲗⲓⲛ ⲟⲛ ⲁϥⲙⲟϣⲓ
Again he walked
ϣⲁ ϣⲙⲟⲩⲛ ⲥⲛⲁⲩ*)
To Shmoun the second;
ⲁϥⲭⲱⲣ ⲉ̇ⲃⲟⲗ ⲛ̇ⲛⲓⲭⲁⲭⲓ
He dispersed the enemies
ⲃⲉⲛ ⲡⲓⲙⲁ ⲉ̇ⲧⲉⲙⲙⲁⲩ.
In that place.

---

*) The name of a city of ancient Egypt.

ⲡⲓⲭⲱⲕ.

Index

of the

Prefixes, Suffixes, &c.

ⲉⲡⲉ, Pref. 3. Fut. 2. p. sing. f. and 3. p. sing. and plur. p. 51.

ⲉⲡⲉⲛⲁ, Pref. 2. Fut. 2. p. sing. f. p. 51.

ⲉⲡⲉⲧⲉⲛⲉ, Pref. 3. Fut. 2. p. plur. p. 51.

ⲉⲡⲉⲧⲉⲛⲛⲁ, Pref. 2. Fut. 2. p. plur. p. 51.

ⲉⲥ, Pref. 2. Pres. 3. p. sing. f. p. 47.

ⲉⲥⲉ, Pref. 3. Fut. 3. p. sing. f. p. 51.

ⲉⲥⲛⲁ, Pref. 2. Fut. 3. p. sing. f. p. 51.

ⲉⲧ, Forms Adjectives. p. 24.

ⲉⲧ, Forms Participles. p. 65.

ⲉⲧⲁ, Pref. 2. Perf. 3. p. sing. and plur. m. and f. p. 48.

ⲉⲧⲁⲓ, Pref. 2. Perf. 1. p. sing. p. 48, 65.

ⲉⲧⲁⲕ, Pref. 2. Perf. 2. p. sing. m. p. 48, 65.

ⲉⲧⲁⲛ, Pref. 2. Perf. 1. p. plur. p. 48, 66.

ⲉⲧⲁⲡⲉ, Pref. 2. Perf. 2. p. sing. f. p. 48, 65.

ⲉⲧⲁⲡⲉⲧⲉⲛ, Pref. 2. Pres. 2. p. plur. p. 48, 66.

ⲉⲧⲁⲥ, Pref. 2. Perf. 3. p. sing. f. p. 48, 65.

ⲉⲧⲁⲧⲉⲧⲉⲛ, Pref. p. 66.

ⲉⲧⲁⲩ, Pref. 2. Perf. 3. p. plur. p. 48, 66.

ⲉⲧⲁϥ, Pref. 2. Perf. 3. p. sing. m. p. 48, 65.

ⲉⲧⲉ, when, Prefixed to verbs. p. 65.

ⲉⲧⲉⲧⲉⲛ, Pref. 2. Pres. 2. p. plur. p. 47.

ⲉⲧⲉⲧⲛ̄, Pref. 2. Pres. 2. p. plur. p. 47.

ⲉⲧⲉⲧⲛⲁ, Pref. 2. Fut. 2. p. plur. p. 51.

ⲉⲧⲉⲧⲛⲉ, Pref. 3. Fut. 2. p. plur. p. 51.

ⲉⲧⲉⲧⲛⲛⲁ, Pref. 2. Fut. 2. p. plur. p. 51.

ⲉⲧⲡⲉ, Auxiliary verb. p. 90, 91.

ⲉⲩ, Pref. 2. Pres. 3. p. plur. p. 47.

ⲉⲩⲉ, Pref. 3. Fut. 3. p. plur. p. 51.

ⲉⲩⲛⲁ, Pref. 2. Fut. 3. p. plur. p. 51.

ⲉⲱ, Sign of the Potential Mood. p. 78.

ⲉϥ, Pref. 2. Pres. 3. p. sing. m. p. 47.

ⲉϥⲉ, Pref. 3. Fut. 3. p. sing. m. p. 51.

ⲉϥⲛⲁ, Pref. 2. Fut. 3. p. sing. m. p. 51.

ⲈⲀⲞⲦⲈ, Sign of the Comparative. p. 25.

ⲎⲞⲨⲦ, Participles. p. 65.

ⲎⲨ, Participles. p. 65.

ⲎⲨⲦ, Participles p. 65.

Ⲑ, Defin. Artic. p. 10.

ⲐⲀ, Posses. Article. p. 13.

ⲐⲠⲈ, Auxiliary Verb. p. 89.

Ⲓ, Suff. 1. pers. sing. and 2. pers. sing. f. p. 36, 45, 97.

Ⲕ, Pref. 1. Pres. 2. p. sing. m. p. 45, 46.

Ⲕ, Suff. 2. p. sing. m. p. 36, 45, 97.

ⲔⲈ, Between the Article and noun. p. 103.

ⲔⲚⲀ, Pref. 1. Fut. 2. p. sing. m. p. 50.

ⲔⲚⲈ, Pref. 1. Fut. 2. p. sing. m. p. 50.

ⲖⲀ, much. p. 106. Bash.

ⲖⲈⲘ, a native. p. 105. Bash.

ⲖⲈϭ, Forms compound nouns. p. 105. Bash.

Ⲙ̀, Pref. to Gen. Dat. Acc. Abl. p. 21, 22.

Ⲙ̀, Pref. Negat. p. 84.

ⲘⲀ, Pref. Imperat. p. 54.

ⲘⲀⲖⲈ, Pref. Optative. 2. p. sing. f. and 3. p. sing. and plur. p. 54. Bash.

ⲘⲀⲖⲈⲔ, Pref. Optat. 2. p. sing. m. p. 54. Bash.

ⲘⲀⲖⲈⲚ, Pref. Optat. 1. p. plur. p. 54. Bash.

ⲘⲀⲖⲈⲤ, Pref. Optat. 3. p. sing. f. p. 54. Bash.

ⲘⲀⲖⲈⲦⲈⲚ, Pref. Optat. 2. p. plur. p. 54. Bash.

ⲘⲀⲖⲈϭ, Pref. Optat. 3. p. sing. m. p. 54 Bash.

ⲘⲀⲖⲒ, Pref. Optat. 1. p. sing. p. 54. Bash.

ⲘⲀⲖⲞⲨ, Pref. Optat. 3. p. plur. p. 54. Bash.

ⲘⲀⲠⲈ, Pref. Optative 2. p. sing. f. and 3. p. sing. and plur. p. 54.

ⲘⲀⲠⲈⲔ, Pref. Optat. 2. p. sing. m. p. 54.

ⲘⲀⲠⲈⲚ, Pref. Optat. 1. p. plur. p. 54.

ⲘⲀⲠⲈⲤ, Pref. Optat. 3. p. sing. f. p. 54.

ⲘⲀⲠⲈⲦⲈⲚ, Pref. Optat. 2. p. plur. p. 54.

ⲘⲀⲠⲈⲦⲚ̄, Pref. Optat. 2. p. plur. p. 54.

ⲙⲁⲣⲉϥ, Pref. Optat. 3. p. sing. m. p. 54.

ⲙⲁⲣⲓ, Pref. Optat. 1. p. sing. p. 54.

ⲙⲁⲣⲛ, Pref. Optat. 2. p. plur. p. 54.

ⲙⲁⲣⲟⲩ, Pref. Optat. 3. p. plur. p. 54.

ⲙⲁⲍ, Forms the Ordinal numbers. Copt. p. 43.

ⲙⲉⲍ, Pref. to nouns, Copt. p. 105.

ⲙⲉⲧ, Pref. to nouns, Copt. p. 105.

ⲙⲛⲧ, Pref. to nouns, Sah. p. 105.

ⲙⲉⲍ, Forms the Ordinal numbers Sah. p. 43.

ⲙ̄ⲙⲁⲩ, Pref. Negat. p. 96.

ⲙ̀ⲡⲁⲧⲉ, Pref. Negat. p. 79, 86.

ⲙ̀ⲡⲉ, Pref. Negat. p. 79. 85.

ⲙ̀ⲡⲉⲗ, Pref. Negat. p. 89. Bash.

ⲙ̀ⲡⲉⲣ, Pref. Negat. p. 89.

ⲙ̀ⲡⲣ̄, Pref. Negat. p. 89.

ⲛ̀, Pref. Negat. p. 79.

ⲛ̀, Pref. to Gen., Dat., Acc., Abl. p. 21, 22.

ⲛ, Pref. 2. Pres. 2. p. plur. p. 47.

ⲛ̀, Pref. Infinit. p. 54.

ⲛ, Suff. 1. p. plur. p. 36, 46, 97.

ⲛ, Definite Artic. plur. p. 11.

ⲛⲁ, Possess. Article. plur. p. 13.

ⲛⲁ, *About.* p. 44.

ⲛⲁⲓ ⲡⲉ, Pref. Imperf. 1. p. sing. p. 47.

ⲛⲁⲓⲛⲁ, Pref. Imperf. Fut. 1. p. sing. p. 52.

ⲛⲁⲓⲛⲉ, Pref. Imperf. Fut. 1. p. sing. p. 52. Bash.

ⲛⲁⲕ ⲡⲉ, Pref. Imperf. 2. p. sing. m. p. 47.

ⲛⲁⲕⲛⲁ, Pref. Imperf. Fut. 2. p. sing. m. p. 52.

ⲛⲁⲕⲛⲉ, Pref. Imperf. Fut. 2. p. sing. m. p. 52. Bash.

ⲛⲁⲛ ⲡⲉ, Pref. Imper. 1. p. plur. p. 47.

ⲛⲁⲛⲛⲁ, Pref. Imper. Fut. 1. p. plur. p. 53.

ⲛⲁⲛⲛⲉ, Pref. Imperf. Fut. 1. p. plur. p. 53. Bash.

ⲛⲁⲣⲉ ⲡⲉ, Pref. Imperf. 2. p. sing. f. and 3. p. sing. and plur. p. 47.

16

ⲚⲀⲢⲈⲚⲀ, Pref. Imper. Fut. 2. p. sing. f. and 3. p. sing. and pl. p. 52, 53.

ⲚⲀⲢⲈⲚⲈ, Pref. Imperf. Fut. 2. p. sing, f. and 3. p. sing. and pl. p. 52, 53.

ⲚⲀⲢⲈⲦⲈⲚ ⲠⲈ, Pref. Imperf. 2. p. plur. p. 47.

ⲚⲀⲢⲈⲦⲈⲚⲚⲀ, Pref. Imperf. Fut. 2. p. plur. p. 53.

ⲚⲀⲢⲈⲦⲈⲚⲚⲈ, Pref. Imperf. Fut. 2. p. plur. p. 53.

ⲚⲀⲤ ⲠⲈ, Pref. Imperf. 3. p. sing. f. p. 47.

ⲚⲀⲤⲚⲀ, Pref. Imperf. Fut. 3. p. sing. p. 52.

ⲚⲀⲨ ⲠⲈ, Pref. Imperf. 3. p. plur. p. 47.

ⲚⲀⲨⲚⲀ, Pref. Imperf. Fut. 3. p. plur. p. 53.

ⲚⲀϥ ⲠⲈ, Pref. Imperf. 3. p. sing. m. p. 47.

ⲚⲀϥⲚⲀ, Pref. Imperf. Fut. 3. p. sing. m. p. 52.

ⲚⲢ, Pref. Subjunct. 2. p. sing. m. p. 53.

ⲚⲈ, Defin. Article plur. p. 11.

ⲚⲈ, Verb. p. 92.

ⲚⲈ ⲠⲈ,
ⲚⲈ ⲦⲈ, } Irreg. verb. p. 92.

ⲚⲈ Ⲁ ⲠⲈ, Pref. Pluperf. 3. p. sing. m. and f. p. 48.

ⲚⲈ Ⲁⲓ ⲠⲈ, Pref. Pluperf. 1. p. sing. p. 48.

ⲚⲈ Ⲁⲕ ⲠⲈ, Pref. Pluperf. 2. p. sing. m. p. 48.

ⲚⲈ ⲀⲚ ⲠⲈ, Pref. Pluperf. 1. p. plur. p. 49.

ⲚⲈ ⲀⲢⲈ ⲠⲈ, Pref. Pluperf. 2. p. sing. f. and 3. p. sing. m. and f. p. 48.

ⲚⲈ ⲀⲢⲈⲦⲈⲚ ⲠⲈ, Pref. Pluperf. 2. p. plur. p. 49.

ⲚⲈ ⲀⲤ ⲠⲈ, Pref. Pluperf. 3. p. sing. f. p. 48.

ⲚⲈ ⲀⲦⲈⲦⲚ ⲠⲈ, Pref. Pluperf. 2. p. plur. p. 49.

ⲚⲈ ⲀⲨ ⲠⲈ, Pref. Pluperf. 3. p. plur. p. 49.

ⲚⲈ Ⲁϥ ⲠⲈ, Pref. Pluperf. 3. p. sing. m. p. 48.

ⲚⲈ ϢⲀⲓ ⲠⲈ, Pref. Imperf. Indef. 1. p. sing. p. 49.

ⲚⲈ ϢⲀⲕ ⲠⲈ, Pref. Imperf. Indef. 2. p. sing. m. p. 49.

ⲚⲈ ϢⲀⲖⲈ ⲠⲈ, Pref. Imperf. Indef. 2. p. sing. f. and 3. p. sing. and pl. p. 49.

ⲚⲈ ϢⲀⲚ ⲠⲈ, Pref. Imperf. Indef. 1. p. plur. p. 49.

ⲚⲈ ϢⲀⲢⲈ ⲠⲈ, Pref. Imperf. Indef. 2. p. sing. f. and 3. p. sing. and pl. p. 49, 50.

ⲚⲈ ϢⲀⲢⲈⲦⲈⲚ ⲠⲈ, Pref. Imperf. Indef. 2. p. plur. p. 50.

ⲚⲈ ϢⲀⲤ ⲠⲈ, Pref. Imperf. Indef. 3. p. sing. f. p. 49, 50.

NE ⲰⲀⲦⲈⲦⲈⲚ ⲠⲈ, Pref. Imperf. Indef. 2. p. plur. p. 50.

NE ⲰⲀⲦⲈⲦⲚ̄ ⲠⲈ. Pref. Imperf. Indef. 2. p. plur. p. 50.

NE ⲰⲀⲨ ⲠⲈ, Pref. Imperf. Indef. 3. p. plur. p. 50.

NEⲒ ⲠⲈ, Pref. Imperf. 1. p. sing. p. 47.

NEⲒⲚⲀ ⲠⲈ, Pref. Imperf. Fut. 1. p. sing. p. 52.

NEⲔ ⲠⲈ, Pref. Imperf. 2. p. sing. m. p. 47.

NEⲔ̣ⲚⲀ, Pref. Imperf. Fut. 2. p. sing. m. p. 52.

NEⲚ, Defin. Artic. plur. p. 10.

NEⲚ ⲠⲈ, Pref. Imperf. 1. p. plur. p. 47.

NEⲚⲚⲀ ⲠⲈ, Pref. Imperf. Fut. 1. p. plur. p. 53.

NEC ⲠⲈ, Pref. Imperf. 3. p. sing. p. 47.

NECⲚⲀ, Pref. Imperf. Fut. 3. p. sing. p. 62.

NEⲦⲈⲦⲚ̄ ⲠⲈ, Pref. Imperf. 2. p. plur. p. 47.

NEⲦⲈⲦⲚ̄Ⲁ ⲠⲈ, Pref. Imperf. Fut. 2. p. plur. p. 53.

NEⲨ ⲠⲈ, Pref. Imperf. 3. p. plur. p. 47.

NEⲨⲚⲀ ⲠⲈ, Pref. Imperf. Fut. 3. p. plur. p. 53.

NEⲢⲈ ⲠⲈ, Pref. Imperf. 2. p. sing. f. 3. p. sing. and plur. p. 47.

NEⲢⲈⲚⲀ, Pref. Imperf. Fut. 2. p. sing. f. and 3. p. sing. and pl. p. 52, 53.

NEC, Pref. Subjunct. 3. p. sing. f. p. 53.

NEϤ, Pref. Subjunct. 3. p. sing. m. p. 53.

NEϤ ⲠⲈ, Pref. Imperf. 3. p. sing. p. 47.

NEϤⲚⲀ ⲠⲈ, Pref. Imperf. Fut. 3. p. sing. p. 52.

NⲒ, Defin. Artic. plur. p. 10, 11.

NⲚ̄, Defin. Artic. plur. p. 11.

Ⲛ̄ⲚⲀ, Pref. 2. Fut. 1. p. plur. p. 51.

Ⲛ̄C, Pref. Subjunct. 3. p. sing. f. p. 53.

Ⲛ̄CⲈ, Pref. Subjunct. 3. p. plur. p. 53.

Ⲛ̄ⲦⲀ, Pref. 2. Perf. 3. p. sing. m. and f. and 3. p. plur. p. 48.

Ⲛ̄ⲦⲀ. Pref. Subjunct. 1. p. sing. p. 53.

Ⲛ̄ⲦⲀⲒ, Pref. 2. Perf. 1. p. sing. p. 48.

Ⲛ̄ⲦⲀⲔ, Pref. 2. Perf. 2. p. sing. m. p. 48.

Ⲛ̄ⲦⲀⲚ, Pref. 2. Perf. 1. p. plur. p. 48.

Ⲛ̄ⲦⲀⲢ, Pref. 2. Perf. 2. p. sing. f. p. 48.

16*

ⲚⲦⲀⲤ, Pref. 2. Perf. 3. p. sing. f. p. 48.

ⲚⲦⲀⲦⲈⲦⲚ, Pref. 2. Perf. 2. p. plur. p. 48.

ⲚⲦⲀⲨ, Pref. 2. Perf. 3. p. plur. p. 48.

ⲚⲦⲀϥ, Pref. 2. Perf. 3. p. sing. m. p. 48.

ⲚⲦⲈ, Sign of the genitive, plur. p. 21.

ⲚⲦⲈ, Pref. Subjunctive, 2. p. sing. f. and 3. p. sing. and plur. p. 53.

ⲚⲦⲈⲔ, Pref. Subjunct. 2. p. sing. m. p. 53.

ⲚⲦⲈⲖⲈⲒ, Pref. Bash. 1. p. sing. p. 65.

ⲚⲦⲈⲖⲈϥ, Pref. Bash. 3. p. sing. p. 65.

ⲚⲦⲈⲚ, Pref. Subjunct. 1. p. plur. p. 53.

ⲚⲦⲈⲢⲈ, when, with prefixes to verbs. p. 65.

ⲚⲦⲈⲤ, Pref. Subjunct. 3. p. sing. f. p. 53.

ⲚⲦⲈⲦⲈⲚ, Pref. Subjunct. 2. p. plur. p. 53.

ⲚⲦⲈⲦⲚ, Pref. Subjunct. 2. p. plur. p. 53.

ⲚⲦⲚ, Pref. Subjunct. 1. p. plur. p. 53.

ⲚⲦⲈϥ, Pref. Subjunct. 3. p. sing. p. 53.

ⲚⲦⲞⲨ, Pref. Subjunct. 3. p. plur. p. 53.

Ⲛϥ, Pref. Subjunct. 3. p. sing. m. p. 53.

ⲚⲈⲞⲨⲞ, Comparative, p. 25.

ⲚⲬⲈ, Sign of the Nominative. Copt. p. 21. Prefix. to verbs. p. 105.

ⲚϬⲒ, Sign of the Nominative. Sahid. p. 21. Pref. to verbs. p. 105.

ⲞⲞⲨⲦ, Participle. p. 65.

ⲞⲨ, Indefin. Article sing. p. 12.

ⲞⲨ, Suff. 3. p. plur. p. 37, 47, 97.

ⲞⲨⲀⲚ, Used for the verb. *to be, to have*. p. 95.

ⲞⲨⲈⲚ, *a part*, p. 44.

ⲞⲨⲚ, *a part*, p. 44.

ⲞⲨⲚⲀ, Pref. 2. Fut. 3. p. plur. p. 51.

ⲞⲨⲚⲈ, *a part*, p. 44

ⲞⲨⲞⲚ, Used for the verb *to be, to have*, p. 95.

ⲞⲨⲰⲚ, *a part*, p. 44.

Ⲡ, Defin. Article. m. sing. p. 10, 11.

ⲠⲀ, Possess. Article. m. p. 13,

ΠⲀⲬⲒⲚ, Particip. pers. sing. p. 54.

ⲠⲈ, Definit. Article. m. sing. p. 11. vocat. p. 21.

ⲠⲈ, Verb *to be*, p. 91.

ⲠⲈⲔⲬⲒⲚ, Particip. 2. p. sing. p. 54.

ⲠⲈϤ, Signifies days. p. 44.

ⲠⲈϤⲬⲒⲚ, Particip. 3. p. sing. m. p. 54.

ⲠⲒ, Defin. Art. sing. m. p. 10, 11. vocat. p. 21.

ⲢⲈ, *a part*, p. 43.

ⲢⲈⲘ, *a native*, p. 105.

ⲢⲎ, *a native*, Sah. p. 105.

Ⲥ, Pref. 1. Pres. 3. p. sing. f. p. 46.

Ⲥ, Suff. 3. p. sing. f. p. 37, 46, 97.

ⲤⲀ, An artificer, p. 105.

ⲤⲈ, Pref. 1. Pres. 3. p. plur. p. 46.

ⲤⲈⲚⲀ, Pref. 1. Fut. 3. p. plur. p. 50.

ⲤⲈⲚⲈ, Pref. 1. Fut. 3. p. plur. p. 50.

ⲤⲚⲀ, Pref. 1. Fut. 3. p. sing. f. p. 50.

ⲤⲚⲈ, Pref. 1. Fut. 3. p. sing. f. p. 50.

ⲤⲞⲨ, Prefixed to days forms the Ordinal number. p. 43.

Ⲧ, Defin. Artic. sing. f. p. 10, 11.

Ⲧ, Suff. 1. p. sing. p. 36, 97.

ⲦⲀ, Pref. 4. Fut. 1. p. sing. p. 52,

ⲦⲀ, Possess. Article. f. sing. p. 13.

ⲦⲀⲖⲈⲦⲈⲚ, Pref. 4. Fut. 2. p. plur. p. 52.

ⲦⲀⲢⲈⲔ, Pref. 4. Fut. 2. p. sing. m. p. 52.

ⲦⲀⲢⲈⲤ, Pref. 4. Fut. 3. p. sing. f. p. 52.

ⲦⲀⲢⲈⲦⲚ, Pref. 4. Fut. 2. p. plur. p. 52.

ⲦⲀⲢⲈϤ, Pref. 4. Fut. 3. p. sing. m. p. 52.

ⲦⲀⲢⲚ, Pref. 4. Fut. 1. p. plur. p. 52.

ⲦⲀⲢⲒ, Pref. 4. Fut. 1. p. sing. p. 52.

ⲦⲀⲢⲞⲨ, Pref. 4. Fut. 3. p. plur. p. 52.

ⲦⲈ, Definit. Article. sing. f. p. 11.

ⲦⲈ, Pref. 1. Pres. 2. p. sing. f. p. 46.

ⲦⲈ, Suff. 2. p. sing. f. p. 97.

ⲦⲈⲚ, Pref. 1. Pres. 1. p. plur. p. 46.

ⲦⲈⲚ, Suff. 1. p. plur. p. 97.

ⲦⲈⲚⲀ, Pref. 1. Fut. 2. p. sing. f. p. 50 and 1. p. plur. p. 56.

ⲦⲈⲚⲚⲀ, Pref. 1. Fut. 1. p. plur. p. 50.

ⲦⲈⲚⲚⲈ, Pref. 1. Fut. 1. p. plur. p. 56.

ⲦⲈⲣⲀ, Pref. 4. Fut. 2. p. sing. f. p. 52.

ⲦⲈⲦⲈⲚ, Pref. 1. Pres. 2. p. plur. p. 46.

ⲦⲈⲦⲈⲚⲚⲀ, Pref. 1. Fut. 2. p. plur. p. 50.

ⲦⲈⲦⲚ̄, Pref. 1. Pres. 2. p. plur. p. 46.

ⲦⲈⲦⲚⲀ, Pref. 1. Fut. 2 p. plur. p. 50.

ⲦⲈⲦⲚ̄ⲚⲀ, Pref. 1. Fut. 2. p. plur. p. 50.

ⲦⲘ̄, Pref. negative. p. 87, 88.

ⲦⲚ̄, Pref. 1. Pres. 1. p. plur. p. 46.

ⲦⲚ̄, Suff. 3. p. plur. p. 36. 2. p. plur. and 1. p. plur. p. 97.

ⲦⲣⲈ, *a part,* p. 44.

ⲦⲣⲈ, The Auxiliary Verb. *to be, to do,* p. 89.

Ⲩ, Suff. 3. p. plur. p. 46.

Ⲫ, Defin. Article. sing. m. p. 10.

ⲪⲀ, Possess. Article. m. sing. p. 13.

Ⲭ, Pref. 1. Pres. 2. p. sing. m. p. 46.

ⲬⲚⲀ, Pref. 1. Fut. 2. p. sing. m. p. 50.

Ⲱ, Sign of the vocat. p. 21.

ⲰⲞⲨⲦ, Participle. p. 65.

Ⲱ, Sign of the Potential Mood. p. 78.

ⲰⲀⲓ, Pref. Pres. Indef. 1. p. sing. p. 49.

ⲰⲀⲕ, Pref. Pres. Indef. 2. p. sing. m. p. 49.

ⲰⲀⲗⲈ, Pref. Pres. Indef. 2. p. sing. and 3. p. sing. and pl. p. 49. Bash.

ⲰⲀⲚ, *If,* with the prefixes. p. 67, 88.

ⲰⲀⲚⲦⲈ, *Until,* with the prefixes. p. 66.

ⲰⲀⲣⲈ, Pref. Pres. Indef. 2. p. sing. f. and 3. p. sing. and plur. p. 49.

ⲰⲀⲣⲈⲦⲈⲚ, Pref. Pres. Indef. 2. p. plur. p. 49.

ⲰⲀⲤ, Pref. Pres. Indef. 3. p. sing. f. p. 49.

ⲱⲀⲦⲈ, *Until,* with the prefixes. p. 66.

ⲱⲀⲦⲈⲦⲈⲚ, Pref. Pres. Indef. 2. p. plur. p. 49.

ⲱⲀⲦⲈⲦⲚ, Pref. Pres. Indef. 2. p. plur. p. 49.

ⲱⲀⲨ, Pref. Pres. Indef. 3. p. plur. p. 49.

ⲱⲀϥ, Pref. Pres. Indef. 3. p. sing. m. p. 49.

ⲱⲟⲨ, Pref. implying worthiness. p. 79. 105.

ⲱⲦⲈⲘ, Pref. negative. p. 87, 88.

ϥ, Suff. 3. p. sing. m. p. 37, 46, 97.

ϥ, Pref. 1. Pres. 3. p. sing. m. p. 46.

ϥⲚⲀ, Pref. 1. Fut. 3. p. sing. m. p. 50.

ϥⲚⲈ, Pref. 1. Fut. 3. p. sing. m. p. 50. Bash.

ϩⲀ, *a person, master,* &c. p. 106.

ϩⲀⲚ, Indef. Article. plur. p. 12.

ϩⲈⲚ, Indef. Article. plur. p. 12.

ϩⲚ, Indef. Art. plur. p. 12.

ϫⲀ, Verb. p. 92.

ϫⲈ, Conjunction p. 99 and verb. p. 92.

ϫⲓⲚ, Participle, taking the article and infixes. p. 65.

ϫⲞⲞ, Verb. p. 92.

ϫⲠ, Forms the Ordinal numbers for hours. p. 45.

ϫⲱ, Verb. p. 92.

ϭⲓⲚ, Participle taking the Articles and infixes p. 65.

ϯ, Definit. Article. sing. f. p. 10, 11.

ϯ, Pref. 1. Pres. 1. p. sing. p. 46.

ϯ, Suff. 2. p. sing. f. p. 97.

ϯⲚⲀ, Suff. 1. Fut. 1. p. sing. p. 50.

ϯⲚⲈ, Suff. Pref. 1. Fut. 1. p. sing. p. 50.

www.ingramcontent.com/pod-product-compliance
Lightning Source LLC
Chambersburg PA
CBHW021122020726
47500CB00003B/886